Global Justice and International Economic Law

For centuries, international trade has been seen as essential to the wealth and power of nations, and defended as a system through which all could benefit. It is only recently that trade's problematic role as an engine of distributive justice has begun to be understood, due in part to globalization and the global justice debates. In this compelling new book, international legal scholar Frank J. Garcia proposes a radically new way to evaluate, construct, and manage international trade – one that is based on multiple modes of analysis and norms of economic justice as well as comparative advantage and national interest. This book examines three different ways to conceptualize the problem of trade and global justice – three "takes" on this relationship – drawn from Rawlsian liberalism, communitarianism, and consent theory. These three approaches illustrate specific issues of a general or systematic importance to the way global justice has been and should be theorized. Through these takes the book offers an alternative, pluralistic mode of arguing for global justice and highlights the unique modes of discourse we employ when engaging with global justice and their implications for how we conceptualize and argue the problem. From this analysis, Garcia suggests a new direction for trade agreements built around the possibility of truly consensual trade negotiations and the kind of international economic system they would structure.

Frank J. Garcia is a professor of law at the Boston College Law School. A Fulbright Scholar, he has lectured widely on globalization and international economic law in Europe, South America, and Asia. He has served on the executive boards of the International Economic Law and International Legal Theory Interest Groups of the American Society of International Law, and is the book review editor and an editorial board member of the *Journal of International Economic Law*. Garcia is the author of *Trade, Inequality, and Justice: Toward a Liberal Theory of Just Trade* (2003) and co-editor of *Global Justice and International Economic Law: Opportunities and Challenges* (with Chios Carmody and John Linarelli, 2012).

Global Justice and International Economic Law

Three Takes

FRANK J. GARCIA

Boston College Law School

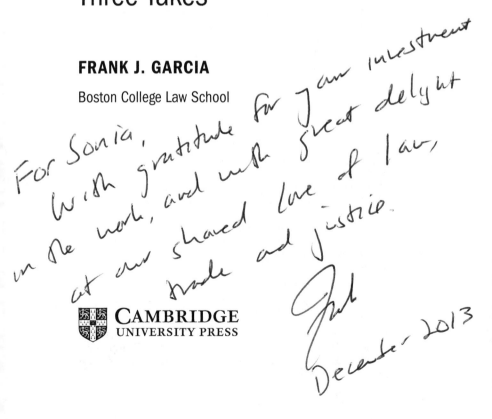

For Sonia,
With gratitude for Jam investment
in the work, and with great delight
at our shared love of law,
trade and justice.

December 2013

CAMBRIDGE
UNIVERSITY PRESS

CAMBRIDGE UNIVERSITY PRESS
Cambridge, New York, Melbourne, Madrid, Cape Town,
Singapore, São Paulo, Delhi, Mexico City

Cambridge University Press
32 Avenue of the Americas, New York, NY 10013-2473, USA

www.cambridge.org
Information on this title: www.cambridge.org/9781107031920

First published 2013

Printed in the United States of America

A catalog record for this publication is available from the British Library.

Library of Congress Cataloging in Publication data
Garcia, Frank J.
   Global justice and international economic law : three
   takes / Frank J. Garcia, Boston College Law School.
      pages   cm
   ISBN 978-1-107-03192-0 (hardback)
   1. Law and globalization   2. Distributive justice   3. Law – Economic
   aspects   4. Foreign trade regulation   I. Title.
   KZ1268.G37
   343.07–dc23   2012044093

ISBN 978-1-107-03192-0 Hardback

For Kim,

who said it could be done

But suppose the issue is not to win an argument ... but to manifest for the other another way.

Stanley Cavell,
Conditions Handsome and Unhandsome

Contents

Acknowledgments

A book like this depends on numerous conversations and on the generosity of many. I have been fortunate in my colleagues both at Boston College – Paulo Barrozo, David Deese, Vlad Perju, David Rasmussen, and Diane Ring – and beyond: Chi Carmody, Jeffrey Dunoff, John Linarelli, and Joost Pauwelyn. I want to thank in particular Sonia Rolland and Fiona Smith for their painstaking and illuminating read of the entire book in manuscript. If any errors and omissions remain, they are stubbornly mine.

I am very grateful to my editor at the Press, John Berger, for his steadfast commitment to this project, and to my anonymous readers for their comments and suggestions, which have strengthened this book.

I have also been the beneficiary of the patience and insights of the faculties and audiences at the schools kind enough to invite me to deliver portions of this work over the past few years. I'd like to thank the faculties of the University of the Andes (Colombia), Brandeis University, the University of Bremen, Cambridge University, the Massachusetts Institute of Technology, Monash University, the University of New South Wales, Oxford University, the University of Paris West Nanterre La Defense, and University College London.

Wherever I found myself in space and time, I could always count on Mark Sullivan, our International and Comparative Librarian, to find what I needed, and a small army of research assistants over the years, whose generosity, talent, and organizational skills have made this book possible. I'd like to thank in particular Dan Blanchard, Mark DeFeo, Matthew Hoisington, Joanna Kornafel, Adam Schmelzer, and Sean Wall, for whom no task was too large or too wearisome. I would also like to thank Judy Yi for the intelligent logistical support that made global work on a global project both feasible and enjoyable.

I owe a special debt of gratitude to Ms. Lindita Ciko, whose investment in and support for the project have been essential. I have been fortunate to have her as my principal research assistant for the two years during which the book really took shape, and to now count her as a collaborator and friend. Thank you, Lindita – may all professors be so blessed.

For the gift of time necessary for writing and reflection, I am grateful to Dean John Garvey, Dean Vincent Rougeau,

and the Law School Annual Fund for their support. Much of
that time was spent on Digby Neck in Nova Scotia, and the
better part of that in the company of the bottomless cup of
coffee always ready at the Petit Passage Café in East Ferry.
I'd like to thank the skipper Diane, and Brenda, Patty,
Theresa, and the rest of the crew for the coffee, hot break-
fasts, and delicious pies that fueled many a page. All books
should be written amid such hospitality and cooking.

Finally, I would like to thank my partner, Kim. For each
element of this project, and in the execution of the whole,
she has been the indispensable sounding board. She saw a
way to put these different approaches in conversation when
I could not find it. To her, with much gratitude, this book is
dedicated.

Introduction

I. Why Three Takes on Global Justice?

Global justice has become an increasingly common topic of concern and debate, and the relationship between international trade law and justice theory an increasingly accepted (yet challenging) one.[1] My goal in this book is not to document

---

[1] *See, e.g.,* Joost Pauwelyn, *Just Trade under Law: Do We Need a Theory of Justice for International Trade Relations?* 100 AM. SOC'Y INT'L L. 375 (2006) (the panel concluded "Yes"). For a recent overview of the current state of conversation between justice theory and international economic law, see *Introduction,* GLOBAL JUSTICE AND INTERNATIONAL ECONOMIC LAW: CHALLENGES AND OPPORTUNITIES (Chios Charmody, Frank J. Garcia and John Linarelli, eds., 2011) [hereinafter GLOBAL JUSTICE AND INTERNATIONAL ECONOMIC LAW].

these trends,[2] nor is it to argue for why they represent an important and welcome development.[3] Instead, I propose to step back from specific arguments and examine the different ways in which we conceptualize the problem of global justice and its relationship to trade law, and to international economic law and economic fairness more generally, in view of globalization and the diversity of normative traditions which it highlights.

My task in this book is to examine three different approaches to this problem – three "takes," if you will,[4] on

[2] Recent major works on the subject of global justice include RICHARD W. MILLER, GLOBALIZING JUSTICE: THE ETHICS OF POVERTY AND POWER (2010); GILLIAN BROCK, GLOBAL JUSTICE: A COSMOPOLITAN ACCOUNT (2009); THOMAS POGGE, WORLD POVERTY AND HUMAN RIGHTS (2008); SIMON CANEY, JUSTICE BEYOND BORDERS: A GLOBAL POLITICAL THEORY (2005); KOK-CHOR TAN, JUSTICE WITHOUT BORDERS: COSMOPOLITANISM, NATIONALISM, AND PATRIOTISM (2004); Charles Jones, *Introduction*, SYMPOSIUM: GLOBAL ETHICS, 19 CAN. J. L. & JURIS. 213 (2006); SYMPOSIUM: GLOBAL JUSTICE, 39 CORNELL INT'L L. J., 477 (2006). For an overview of the relationship between theories of justice and international economic law, see Frank J. Garcia & Lindita Ciko, *Theories of Justice and International Economic Law* in RESEARCH HANDBOOK ON GLOBAL JUSTICE AND INTERNATIONAL ECONOMIC LAW (John Linarelli, ed., 2013).

[3] Ten or fifteen years ago, however, it would have been necessary to establish both as a necessary prolegomenon to a project such as this one. *See, e.g.*, Joost Pauwelyn, *Just Trade (reviewing* FRANK J. GARCIA, TRADE, INEQUALITY AND JUSTICE), 37 GEO. WASH. INT'L L. REV. 559 (2005) (noting historic resistance of trade law to formal normative inquiry beyond trade economics).

[4] By 'take' I mean to invoke both the colloquial sense in which this can mean perspective, as in someone's 'take' on something, and the

the question of global justice – drawn from the "Western"[5] tradition of political theory: Rawlsian liberalism, communitarianism, and consent theory. There are of course many more theories of justice within Western political theory,[6] and a comprehensive approach to the ethical foundations of global justice would need to engage in a comparative study of justice in normative traditions both within and beyond the West.[7] As I will explain further in this chapter, I have

cinematic sense of 'take' as one in a series of attempts to capture a moment on film.

[5] By "Western" I mean the Greco-Roman/Judeo-Christian cultural tradition of philosophical and normative inquiry associated with Western Europe. Today, this tradition is enriched by people and currents from all parts of the world, and its ideas, institutions and systems are deeply interwoven in a global dialogue with other major cultural traditions. *See generally* ALASTAIR BONNETT, THE IDEA OF THE WEST: POLITICS, CULTURE AND HISTORY (2004). By invoking the West I do not mean to exclude anyone who finds it meaningful to participate in this tradition of inquiry, whoever and wherever they are. However, I believe that in a work that intends to be about "global" justice it is important to note that normative conversations arise within particular communities of meaning whatever their scope, and that in this book I am working within a specific such community. I will say a bit more about this in footnote seven.

[6] *See generally* A COMPANION TO CONTEMPORARY POLITICAL PHILOSOPHY 312, 312 (Robert E. Goodin, Philip Pettit & Thomas Pogge, eds., 2d ed., 2007).

[7] As Amartya Sen writes, "similar – or closely linked – ideas of justice, fairness, responsibility, duty, goodness and rightness have been pursued in many different parts of the world, which can expand the reach of arguments that have been considered in Western literature." THE IDEA OF JUSTICE xiv (2009). By working within one specific tradition in this book, I do not mean to obscure this larger

chosen these three approaches for specific reasons – not to privilege them or assert their superiority, but because they illustrate specific issues of a general or systematic importance to the way global justice has been theorized and its principles applied to international economic law and matters of economic fairness.

Specifically, I will be comparing these three approaches with respect to how they envision the relationship between international economic law and justice, and how they respond to the challenges to global justice raised by what Rawls calls "the fact of pluralism."[8] One consequence of globalization is that we are more aware than ever of the diversity in the world: a plurality of different traditions, cultures, and systems of value and belief.[9] By highlighting the relationship between justice, diversity, and international law, I hope to suggest new ways to craft a truly *global* approach to the problem of global justice and its relationship to international economic law, one that more fully takes into account the challenges and opportunities of globalization. Borrowing a phrase from Kok-chor Tan, this project can also be seen as one way to assess the current state of competition (I would prefer to say conversation, for reasons that will become clear

point. For Sen's own approach to justice in such a cross-cultural dialogue, *see id.* at xiii–xvi, 20–24, 36–39 (sampling Hindu and Muslim reflections on justice and toleration).

[8] JOHN RAWLS, POLITICAL LIBERALISM 36 (2d ed. 1996).

[9] *See, e.g.,* PAUL SCHIFF BERMAN, GLOBAL LEGAL PLURALISM: A JURISPRUDENCE OF LAW BEYOND BORDERS 3–57 (2012) (chronicling the facts of pluralism and their challenge for international law).

as we progress) among normative theories to fill the void left by the demise of Realism.[10] By Realism, I mean (and I take Tan to mean) the theory of international relations that makes two essential claims: a normative claim that states should exclusively pursue their national interest, and an empirical claim that this is in fact what states do.[11]

Realism may not in fact be quite dead yet – one has only to listen to public media discussions of international politics and statecraft to hear at least a popular version of Realism regularly invoked as a justification for state action – but it has been seriously challenged as a theory (successfully so, in my view) on both normative and empirical grounds.[12] Insofar as one can characterize the Cold War era as reflecting (and being shaped by) a Realist consensus on international relations, the interesting question now is what theory

---

[10] KOK-CHOR TAN, TOLERATION, DIVERSITY AND GLOBAL JUSTICE 1 (2000) [hereinafter TAN, TOLERATION].

[11] CANEY, *supra* note 2, at 7.

[12] Meaning, that there are persuasive reasons that states should pursue a range of goals in addition to their national interest, and considerable evidence that they in fact do. *See id.* at 136–140; Andrew Hurrell, *Another Turn of the Wheel?, in* GLOBAL BASIC RIGHTS 62 (Charles R. Beitz & Robert E. Goodin, eds., 2009). The continued prominence of Realist discourse in public commentary on global affairs may have more to do with fear and the dynamic of public opinion than with its continued normative and empirical validity as a theory of global relations. To fail to pay lip service to realist principles in public discourse on international affairs is the equivalent of being viewed as "soft on crime" in domestic affairs – no politician willingly exposes herself to the charge.

(or theories) of international relations will take its place in the post–Cold War globalizing era, particularly with respect to issues of distributive justice and international economic law.[13]

It is worth taking a moment at the outset to explain what I mean by international economic law. The scope of international economic law can be defined in a variety of ways; here, I use the term to include essentially the treaty-based rules and institutions of the Bretton Woods System as it exists today: the World Trade Organization (WTO) and international trade law, the International Monetary Fund (IMF) and international finance; and the World Bank and international development lending.[14] The recognition of international economic law as a comprehensive field consisting of what had hitherto been understood as specific, disparate treaty-based legal regimes (trade law, international finance,

---

[13] In a global market era, international economic law and international economic relations (especially economic competition) may well be taking the prominent place in international relations that arms control, ideological competition and international security issues had in the Cold War era. If so, then the global justice debate may well become the constitutive global conversation that geopolitical security was in the Cold War – but more about that later.

[14] The law of foreign investment can also be included within the scope of the term, although it will not be directly addressed here. *See generally* IGNAZ SEIDL-HOHENVELDERN, INTERNATIONAL ECONOMIC LAW 1 (2nd ed., 1992). International investment law is becoming an increasingly recognized site for the working out of global economic justice. *See* RUDOLF DOLZER & CHRISTOPHER SCHREURER, PRINCIPLES OF INTERNATIONAL INVESTMENT LAW (2008).

etc.) parallels the development of globalization studies and our increasing recognition that there is more going on within global economic relations than a mere intensification of transnational economic flows.[15] This parallelism is not an accident: as global interconnectedness develops, so does our understanding of the regulatory framework that governs and facilitates it, specifically our understanding of it *as* an integrated framework. This has specific implications for the role of justice in international economic law, which this book will to some extent address.[16]

It is also worth mentioning at the outset that I will not be examining in detail perhaps the most widely known theoretical approach to global justice, namely,

---

[15] *See* GLOBAL TRANSFORMATIONS: POLITICS, ECONOMICS AND CULTURE 149–188 (David Held et al., eds., 1998) (documenting shift in global patters of trade and trade regulation and emergence of global economic system); Frank J. Garcia, *Trade and Justice: Linking the Trade Linkage Debates*, 19 U. PA. J. INT'L ECON. L. 391 (1998); Joel P. Trachtman, *The International Economic Law Revolution*, 17 U. PA. J. INT'L ECON. L. 33 (1996).

[16] I expand upon this point at greater length in TRADE, INEQUALITY AND JUSTICE: TOWARD A LIBERAL THEORY OF JUST TRADE (2003) [hereinafter GARCIA, TRADE, INEQUALITY, AND JUSTICE]. The predominance of international trade examples throughout this book reflects the continued preeminence of trade law within economic globalization and global economic relations more generally (as well as my own professional background in trade law). However, the principles and issues discussed in this book in connection with trade law will often apply directly or with modification to international economic law more broadly; in many cases, I make the extension explicit.

cosmopolitanism.[17] Cosmopolitanism is derived from the Greek word *kosmopolitēs,* which means cosmopolite, a citizen of the world, "one who has no national attachments or prejudices."[18] Thus, the etymology of the word reveals its meaning: cosmopolitanism characterizes a family of views relying on the idea that all human beings are morally equal, and therefore constitute a single world community.[19]

For reasons I will explain further below,[20] I consider cosmopolitanism to be a problematic basis for *global* justice, despite its evident global claims and undeniable theoretical importance.[21] Therefore, in Takes One and Two, I will focus instead on alternative approaches based on other political theories which might initially (and paradoxically) seem less congenial and more problematic as a basis for global justice: Rawls's liberal theory of Justice as Fairness, which he confined to justice within domestic societies, not between

---

[17] I am indebted to Lindita Ciko for her assistance in developing the discussion of cosmopolitanism in this chapter.

[18] *See* Oxford English Dictionary Online, s.v. "cosmopolite," http://dictionary.oed.com/cgi/entry/50051143?query_type=word&queryword=cosmopolitanism&first=1&max_to_show=10&single=1&sort_type=alpha (last accessed August 25, 2010).

[19] Thomas Pogge, *Cosmopolitanism* in A COMPANION TO CONTEMPORARY POLITICAL PHILOSOPHY 312, 312 (Robert E. Goodin, Philip Pettit & Thomas Pogge, eds., 2d ed., 2007) (1993).

[20] *See infra* notes 93 to 107 and accompanying text.

[21] For a particularly elegant recent account of cosmopolitanism and global justice, *see* CANEY, *supra* note 2, from which I have learned a great deal despite my reservations about cosmopolitanism.

them[22]; and communitarian theories of justice, which also limit justice to certain social units, namely national communities.[23] The interesting question for me is what sort of global justice bricks can be made from this kind of straw. The results in Take One and Take Two are approaches to global justice that solve certain problems while creating others, thus illuminating the limits of each theory even as the theory itself seeks to throw light on the particular facets of the global justice problem it addresses.

For Take Three, I adopt an entirely different approach to the question – one that requires less in the way of traditional political theory, but instead lies closer to our lived experience of trade as an exchange of value. I begin with the ways in which both language and law[24] recognize that theft, coercion, exploitation, and trade are not the same thing,

---

[22] JOHN RAWLS, A THEORY OF JUSTICE 8 (1971) [hereinafter RAWLS, A THEORY OF JUSTICE]. For reasons I will explain, in Take One I will be internationalizing Rawls's domestic theory of justice rather than relying on his own international project as set out in THE LAW OF PEOPLES, although my approach has been quite heavily influenced by the concerns he discusses in the latter. *See infra,* notes 51, 53, 92–104 and accompanying text; JOHN RAWLS, THE LAW OF PEOPLES (1999) [hereinafter RAWLS, THE LAW OF PEOPLES].

[23] *See, e.g.,* MICHAEL WALZER, SPHERES OF JUSTICE: A DEFENSE OF PLURALISM AND EQUALITY 30 (1983) [hereinafter WALZER, SPHERES OF JUSTICE].

[24] I am working here within the English language and the Anglo-American common law tradition, though I hope in the future to extend the study to embrace at least other major European languages and the civil law tradition as well.

though value may change hands in all these cases. Using Simone Weil's ideas about consent, I try to work out exactly why that might be so, and what implications this has for trade and for the question of global justice. Take Three aims to fill some gaps identified by the other two Takes, particularly with respect to the challenge of finding a consensus basis for global legal norms in a pluralistic context, yet of course it has its own limits.

Returning to Tan's metaphor of post-Realist normative competition, I conclude that examining these three Takes side by side is not about picking a winner and discarding the others.[25] Rather, what emerges from the comparison is that there isn't (and perhaps can't be) a single path or approach to justice on a global scale in a globalizing world.[26] This is so because of the persistent reality of pluralism, central to globalization and therefore to global justice, but by no means unique to the global setting.[27] Instead, what this book suggests is that there are different kinds of reasons for justice, and each plays a necessary role in a comprehensive (but not complete or seamless) approach to global justice.

---

[25] Indeed, Amartya Sen comes out and simply says that selecting only one approach "may be a mistake." SEN, *supra* note 7, at 10.

[26] Sen writes, "there can exist several distinct reasons for justice, each of which survives critical scrutiny, but yields divergent conclusions." *Id.* at x.

[27] Sen again: "Reasonable arguments in competing directions can emanate from people with diverse experiences and traditions, but they can also come from within a given society, or for that matter, even from the very same person." *Id.*

Before turning to the substance of this endeavor, I will explain briefly in the next section what I mean by globalization, justice, and pluralism, since they form the essential background and impetus for this project.

II. Globalization, Justice and the Challenge of Pluralism

In essence, globalization today is the dramatic compression of geographic space in human social relations.[28] This compression of space is altering global social relations by interconnecting us in new and powerful ways, and it both requires and facilitates a shift in regulation away from the nation-state and toward new institutions and actors.[29] As a consequence of such changes, our decisions regarding investment, consumption, and politics, to name a few, affect one another's lives and fortunes as never before.[30] This makes it

---

[28] *See, e.g.*, GLOBAL TRANSFORMATIONS, *supra* note 15, at 15–16; ANTHONY GIDDENS, THE CONSEQUENCES OF MODERNITY 64 (1990) (discussing globalization as intensification of interdependence through spatio-temporal compression).

[29] Effective regulatory decision making increasingly involves the meta-state level, leading to a system in which states still have a pre-eminent, but not the only, role. *See, e.g.*, ANNE MARIE SLAUGHTER, A NEW WORLD ORDER (2004); MANUEL CASTELLS, THE RISE OF THE NETWORK SOCIETY (1996).

[30] Global financial crises have a way of painfully and dramatically bringing this point home. *See* MARTIN WOLF, FIXING GLOBAL FINANCE 28–57 (2008) (discussing financial crises in an era of globalization); Jeffrey E. Garten, *Lessons for the Next Financial Crisis*, 78 FOREIGN AFF. 76 (1999) (discussing the Asian Financial Crisis of the late 1990s).

necessary for us to think about new global institutions and global justice and not simply existing state and interstate institutions and domestic justice.[31]

Why do mutual effect and interconnectedness lead us to inquire about justice? That brings us to the nature of justice itself. The term "justice" essentially describes a relationship between a set of core political and social values about the distribution of benefits and burdens, and the outcomes of social processes.[32] Consider, for example, when a court delivers a ruling, a legislature passes a law, or an international conference negotiates a treaty. These are social outcomes, the products of communal deliberation through institutional mechanisms and the exercise of power, that allocate the benefits and burdens of social cooperation. There are many ways we can evaluate these outcomes, such as their effectiveness, legitimacy, or elegance. "Justice" evaluates these outcomes in terms of their consistency with the values of those affected by them.[33] Such values, when applied to the exercise of public authority, we call the principles of justice. The question of justice then, is whether affected people

---

[31] On the distinction between "global" and "international, *see* CANEY, *supra* note 2, at 2 (discussing the distinction in connection with political theory).

[32] *See* GARCIA, TRADE, INEQUALITY, AND JUSTICE, *supra* note 16, at 44–46. I am speaking here principally of distributive justice, concerning the distribution of social goods and obligations, rather than corrective justice, which addresses problems of improper gain. *Id.*

[33] *Id.*

will judge a particular institutional outcome consistent with core values about proper distributions.

The answer to this question will vary according to the people involved and their particular shared principles – that is the difference between the concept of justice and the many substantive conceptions of justice that we find in the world.[34] The exploration and elaboration of these many principles of justice and their requirements has been carried out primarily in the context of domestic societies, in which the characteristics of justice have been developed with reference to the many policy issues that arise out of domestic social interaction.

The significance of globalization lies in its transformation and extension of these social interactions and social processes beyond national boundaries.[35] When we speak of global justice we are arguing, in effect, that globalization is creating social outcomes and processes of the sort that make justice relevant at the global level and that we need to consider whether these outcomes and processes are indeed acceptable in terms of core principles.[36]

But *whose* core principles, and which ones? Put another way, is *global* justice possible, and is the very idea of

---

[34] RAWLS, A THEORY OF JUSTICE 5–6.

[35] *See* Frank J. Garcia, *Globalization, Global Community and the Possibility of Global Justice*, B.C. L. SCH. FAC. PAPERS, Paper 33 (2005), *available at* http://lsr.nellco.org/bc_lsfp/33/ [hereinafter Garcia, *Global Community*].

[36] *Id.*

it coherent? Such questions constitute a major debate among philosophers, political scientists, and globalization theorists.[37] I am not going to attempt to resolve that debate in this book, nor will I attempt to comprehensively survey the many theories of global justice in play today.[38] Instead, I will look at a central problem all these approaches encounter, a problem which in my view none of them has completely solved: how do we establish a truly *global* basis for global justice?

As I stated earlier, globalization sharpens our awareness of the richness of cultural and normative diversity in the world. However, the kind of pluralism I am referring to here is not the simple fact that the world holds an abundance of "diverse persons, nations, jurisdictions or localities," what Richardson calls "mere literal pluralities."[39] Rather, the challenge comes from the normative implications that follow from such pluralities.

First, there is the simple fact that persons, societies, cultures, nations, and religious traditions do not agree on basic questions of value. Even within avowedly liberal societies, there is great disagreement on both ends and means within

---

[37] *See* GLOBALIZATION THEORY: APPROACHES AND CONTROVERSIES (David Held & Anthony McGrew, eds., 2007) (surveying the range of globalization theory).

[38] *See supra* note 2 for such surveys.

[39] Henry S. Richardson, *Introduction*, in MORAL UNIVERSALISM AND PLURALISM 1 (Henry S. Richardson and Melissa S. Williams, eds., 2009).

a largely liberal framework.[40] This only becomes more complicated when the people (and peoples) who disagree must share an interconnected global social, environmental, economic, legal, and political space.

Second, there is the question of authority. Even this degree of normative pluralism would not necessarily pose a challenge to justice, whether domestic or global, were it not that these diverse normative traditions also make claims for authority, seeking some level of deference or allegiance from their citizens, subjects, or members, and perhaps even from noncitizens, nonsubjects and nonmembers.[41]

In the face of such pluralism, how do we put the "global" in global justice?[42] There are two basic kinds of responses: argue all the harder for the superiority of one particular claim or tradition, or recognize with John Gray that "the

[40] The irreducible nature of certain core normative disagreements is central to Rawls's later work. *See* John Rawls, *The Idea of Public Reason Revisited* 64 U. CHI. L. REV. 765, 798–805 (1997) ("There are limits, however, to reconciliation by public reason. Three main kinds of conflicts set citizens at odds: those deriving from irreconcilable comprehensive doctrines; those deriving from differences in status, class position, or occupation, or from differences in ethnicity, gender, or race; and finally, those deriving from the burdens of judgment," and "unanimity of views is not to be expected. Reasonable political conceptions of justice do not always lead to the same conclusion; nor do citizens holding the same conception always agree on particular issues.")

[41] Richardson, *supra* note 39, at 3.

[42] For this reason, Tan cites global diversity as one of the key challenges to the possibility of a global liberalism. TAN, TOLERATION, *supra* note 10, at 9.

diversity of ways of life and regimes is a mark of human freedom, not of error,"[43] and seek to make the appropriate institutional and regulatory adjustments.

In an elegant recent book on cosmopolitan global justice, Simon Caney offers perhaps the most comprehensive contemporary example of the former approach, grounding his argument for cosmopolitanism in a careful inquiry into the possibility of universal moral values, then a sustained argument for the superiority of cosmopolitan values.[44] I shall have more to say about Caney's arguments later and in ensuing chapters, but I would like to point out at this juncture that this type of argument is what Sen has in mind when he characterizes the "transcendental approach" to justice as seeking to establish reasoned agreement on a single account of the nature of a just society, which in Sen's view is just not feasible.[45] Feasible or not as a matter of theory, it is doubly difficult as a matter of global social policy, where the diversity of normative traditions is even more pronounced, and complicated by the competing claims of national and transnational normative communities.

For such reasons, I shall follow (with Sen and others) the second approach in this book, in which one's aims and methods with respect to global justice are informed, and tempered, by a positive view of normative pluralism. Making such adjustments should not be equated with a reluctance

[43] JOHN GRAY, TWO FACES OF LIBERALISM 139 (2000).
[44] CANEY, *supra* note 2, especially chapter two.
[45] SEN, *supra* note 7, at 9.

to engage substantively with other views, nor should a pluralist approach to global justice theory be equated with relativism per se, or a fashionable multiculturalism that says "I am right in my culture and you are right in yours." Certain ideas about justice may well be right or wrong, better or worse, but such distinctions do not fall neatly along the lines of specific normative traditions. Rather, it is a matter of seeking the best arguments with the broadest base toward a common goal, and there are principled ways of doing this.

Sen's own plural grounding approach is one example, about which more will be said later and in the concluding chapter.[46] Rawls's idea of public reason offers us another example. For Rawls – concerned as he is with the challenge of pluralism – the idea of public reason plays an essential role in managing such conflicts within a domestic liberal democratic society:

> [c]entral to the idea of public reason is that it neither criticizes nor attacks any comprehensive doctrine, religious or nonreligious, except insofar as that doctrine is incompatible with the essentials of public reason and a democratic polity.[47]

It is interesting to consider as one set of possible institutional and regulatory adjustments in the face of pluralism,

---

[46] As Sen writes, "Since somewhat different arguments have often been advanced in dealing with similar questions, we may miss out on possible leads in reasoning about justice if we keep our explorations regionally confined." *Id.* at xv (2009).

[47] *The Idea of Public Reason Revisited, supra* note 40, at 766.

whether the idea of public reason, suitably modified, could play a similar role in mediating the conflicts arising from global normative pluralism. Joshua Cohen and Michael Sabel suggest as much when they write:

> A transnational politics of movements and organizations – beyond the intergovernmental politics between states – now routinely contests and aims to reshape the activities of supranational rulemaking bodies. Those efforts work in part through protest, in part by representing interests to those bodies, and in part by advancing norms, values, and standards of reasonableness – that is, by suggesting potential elements of a global public reason that might serve as a common ground of argument in assessing the practices and performances in global politics.[48]

Whether or not this might indeed be possible will depend in part on the nature of our global institutions and the mechanisms we develop to organize cooperative activity across national or cultural systems of belief – I shall have more to say about this in the concluding chapter.

My principal aim at this juncture, however, is not to argue for a global public reason or any other mediating structure in particular. It is instead to firmly situate this book within this second category of responses to pluralism, insofar as

[48] Joshua Cohen and Michael Sabel, *Global Democracy?* 37 NYU J. L. & POL., 763–797 (2005); Sebastiano Maffetone, *The Fragile Fabric of Public Reason*, in THE DIALOGUE: REASON AND REASONABLNESS [*sic*] (YEARBOOK OF PHILOSOPHICAL HERMENEUTICS), 407–440 (Ricardo Dottori ed., 2005).

it seeks to make the necessary adjustments to global justice theory, as it affects international economic law, which
pluralism demands. I believe this is more consistent with
the basic project of constructing a truly *global* justice, and
not simply more powerful local arguments for justice on a
global scale. In my view, an inquiry into global justice must
assume the fact of normative pluralism, and not merely as
an imperfect starting condition, but as a permanent, and
desirable, aspect of global social life. This means looking for
ways to ground transnational normative enterprises (such
as global justice and global social regulation) on something
other than the superiority of a particular normative tradition. I believe that the alternative can lead to tyranny or
sterility.

However, this is not to say that engaging affirmatively
with pluralism solves the problem of normative conflict. One
essential consequence of this pluralism at the global level is
the problem Rawls highlights in *The Law of Peoples*: what
to do if you are a liberal state about nonliberal states, and
illiberal states,[49] as a question of just foreign relations. What
rules apply to their behavior? What rules guide your own?
The standard answer has been international law: even illiberal states are states, and hence creatures of and subject to
international law; and all states are to be guided in their
foreign relations by these rules which they hold in common.

---

[49] For definitions of nonliberal and illiberal states see infra note 82
and accompanying text.

I submit that for a globalizing world this traditional answer is inadequate, and the range and depth of the current global justice debate concerning all aspects of contemporary international relations is the best evidence of this inadequacy. In the words of Rafael Domingo, international law as traditionally constituted "is no longer capable of meeting the unique developments and needs of life in the Third Millennium."[50] International law covers a great many important procedural and substantive matters, and I don't wish to minimize for a moment the significance of this basic rule of law in international relations. However, international law by itself does not address core issues of substantive justice in any comprehensive, sustained manner.[51] Indeed, from this perspective, international law can perhaps be best understood as a system for promoting a crucial but limited degree of cooperation *in the face of* profound disagreements about justice, by simply walling off those disagreements.[52]

---

[50] THE NEW GLOBAL LAW (2012).

[51] On the "justice deficit" in international law, *see e.g.,* Thomas Pogge, *Priorities of Global Justice*, 32 METAPHILOSOPHY 6, 19–21 (2001) (criticizing the "international borrowing privilege" and "international resource privilege" which operate within the protective umbrella of traditional international law yet which allow oppressive states to indebt and strip their countries with relative impunity); Andrew Hurrell, *Global Inequality and International Institutions,* 32 METAPHILOSOPHY 34, 43–44 (2001) (cataloguing the extent to which international law reflects fundamental inequalities, and perhaps even depends upon them).

[52] *See* Andrew Hurrell, *Global Inequality and International Institutions*, 32 METAPHILOSOPHY 34, 40 (international law built

These basic issues of justice are precisely what globalization highlights, and requires us to address, but within
a pluralist framework.[53] Compartmentalizing away fundamental and complex issues such as distributive justice simply won't work as the world gets smaller and people – and
economies – more interconnected. It is particularly inadequate in the face of charges that certain actors or nations
are in fact driving global regulation toward their benefit,
at a cost to others – then such compartmentalization seems
willed ignorance at best, and exploitative at worst.[54]

It is possible, as David Held argues, that our core international law doctrine of sovereignty is evolving toward what
he calls liberal international sovereignty, thus incorporating cosmopolitan principles into the heart of international

to accommodate, not challenge, an ethic of difference and a fragmented state system). Or, if one takes a critical view, by asserting
through law one set of powerful states' views on fairness over everyone else's. *See* ANTHONY ANGHIE, IMPERIALISM, SOVEREIGNTY AND
THE MAKING OF INTERNATIONAL LAW (2007); Martti Koskenniemi,
The Politics of International Law, 4 EU. J. INT'L L. 4 (1990).

[53] To take but one example out of many, the growing problem of
inequality and its effects on globalization and on cooperative foreign relations, *see e.g.,* Nancy Brune and Geoffrey Garrett, *The
Globalization Rorschach Test: International Economic Integration,
Inequality, and the Role of Government,* ANN. REV. POL. SCI. 399–
423 (2005).

[54] *See* J. G. Ruggie, *Taking Embedded Liberalism Global: The
Corporate Connection in* TAMING GLOBALIZATION: FRONTIERS OF
GOVERNANCE 93 (D. Held & M. Koenig-Archiburgi, eds., 2003)
(globalization is being driven by powerful capital exporting developed Western states); *see also* note 51 *supra.*

legal doctrine.[55] If he is correct, this would offer a basis on which to hold even illiberal states to certain core human rights and democratic norms.[56] However, it is not clear at this point in time that as a matter of *law* we are there, or ever will be there.[57] Liberal international sovereignty may well remain the cosmopolitan dream or vision in another guise. If we ignore the real limits of consensus on this point (ignoring, in a sense, the reality of pluralism), we run the risk of imposing in an equally oppressive manner, our own conceptions of justice.

III. The Plan of This Book

So, what to do in the meantime? That is the question this book seeks to help answer, by putting three approaches to the question of global justice side by side to illuminate what they can do, what they can't do, what else needs doing, and how we might go about this. Through this comparison I also hope to make us more aware of the different ways we

---

[55] David Held, *Law of States, Law of Peoples*, 8 LEGAL THEORY 1–44 (2002).

[56] Core principles of liberal international sovereignty include self-determination, democracy and human rights as the basis of legitimate authority, rather than the mere possession of effective power over a territory and a people. *Id.*

[57] *See, e.g.,* Fred Halliday, *Global Governance: Prospects and Problems*, 4 CITIZENSHIP STUDIES (2000); Robert A. Dahl, *Can International Organizations Be Democratic? A Skeptic's View*, DEMOCRACY'S EDGES (Ian Shapiro & Casiano Hacker-Cordon, eds., 1999).

think and talk about justice, and suggest new approaches to theory and policy. In essence, this book argues that in order to create a more just global order, we need a comprehensive approach to justice, incorporating several different kinds of reasons for justice, but all sharing a basic commitment to pluralism and an engagement with globalization. In saying this, I don't intend to offer a new, more comprehensive theory of global justice – that would defeat the spirit of the enterprise. Instead, I want, through this comparative approach, to suggest a different kind of conversation about justice, one in which there is plenty of room at the table for a wide range of theoretical approaches and new regulatory strategies.

One approach would be to begin with the views on justice we develop in our own domestic societies, and begin to think about how it might work if we were to treat others the same way beyond our boundaries. As I am writing from within the tradition of Western political liberalism, I will couch this thought experiment from the perspective of liberal states.[58] Perhaps the most challenging vision of liberal justice articulated with respect to domestic society is

[58] By liberal states I mean states "with some form of representative democracy, a market economy based on private property rights, and constitutional protection of civil and political rights." Anne-Marie Slaughter, "International Law in a World of Liberal States," 6 EJIL 1, 7 (1995) (citing Michael Doyle). Although this list could be constructed different ways, one rough guide would be the membership of the Organization for Economic Cooperation and Development (OECD), the European Union (EU), and the Commonwealth. Id at 15.

that of Rawls's Justice as Fairness. Rawls goes straight at our deepest intuitions about moral equality, and their most comprehensive and problematic implications with respect to distributive justice. For this reason, I use his theory of Justice as Fairness as the basis for my account of Liberal Internationalism in Take One. As the basis for an exploration of liberal states' responses to the problems of global justice, I adopt an internationalized form of domestic Justice as Fairness, rather than Rawls's own modified approach in *The Law of Peoples*. For reasons I will explain later in this chapter, I agree with the many subsequent commentators (Pogge, Barry, and Beitz foremost among them) who view an internationalized Justice as Fairness as a more adequate theory for international justice, despite Rawls's own objections to such an extension.[59]

Following an approach to the legitimacy of transboundary state action first worked out by Lea Brilmayer,[60] Take

---

[59] By adopting this approach in Take One, I am thus (for that chapter) firmly within the camp of "those critics who are generally sympathetic to the Rawlsian framework, [whose] most common move has been to 'redo' Rawls' later views by appealing to his earlier work." BROCK, *supra* note 2 at 29. However, as I will explain below and in Take One, I differ from that general approach by limiting the reach of an internationalized Justice as Fairness to the scope for liberal justice he sets in THE LAW OF PEOPLES, namely, the foreign policy of liberal states, and not a general theory of global justice. Thus my take on Rawls is something of a hybrid of his two approaches.

[60] Her so-called vertical thesis. *See* Take One *infra*. *See generally* LEA BRILMAYER, JUSTIFYING INTERNATIONAL ACTS (1989).

One assumes a model of transboundary justice as essentially similar to domestic justice, in that it roots the legitimacy of state action in a state's constitutive political theory, regardless of whether such action crosses territorial boundaries. Liberal states must therefore consider liberal principles in their foreign policy as well as in their domestic policy, as a matter of their own legitimacy. In this model, international economic law would be subject to the same liberal normative criteria as domestic law because the same liberal states are actively asserting their power in both arenas.

The greatest advantage of Take One is that it is not contingent upon the existence of any global normative consensus on justice or upon the persuasiveness of local theories of justice across national boundaries. Instead, it confines itself to articulating what kinds of global economic policies a liberal state should pursue in order to be broadly consistent with its own normative commitments.[61] This would apply equally to situations in which the state acts unilaterally, and when it acts through an international organization by advocating for, or influencing, that institution's policies.

In terms of one of the aims of this book – to highlight the various modes of discourse through which we conceptualize

---

[61] States do not, of course, have simple or unified normative positions either domestically or regarding foreign relations, nor is consistency with normative principles a straightforward matter in domestic or international policy. Nevertheless, we can speak meaningfully about this at least in broad outline – more will be said in Take One.

justice in transnational matters – this transnational extension of Justice as Fairness reveals one core way in which we think and talk about justice, which I am going to refer to as "Justice as Integrity."[62] In this mode of discourse, we conceptualize justice as a matter of integrity to one's moral commitments, regardless of the presence or absence of shared agreement on normative principles, or other special relationships that include the objects of our actions. The substantive content of Justice as Integrity is not essential to the mode (and thus it should not be confused with an internationalized Justice as Fairness, for example, or other domestic principles of justice). The key to this conceptualization of justice is the reference to one's own standards for behavior when formulating, and evaluating, the treatment of others, whether one is a state or a person.

As the next chapter will further illustrate, Justice as Fairness extended to an international context is limited to being a theory of transboundary justice for liberal states. Therefore, Justice as Fairness in the present context is an obligation on the foreign policy of liberal states rather than a vision of global justice as *global*.[63] This would be true of

---

[62] I am not seeking to invoke Dworkin's conception of law as integrity here – at least not explicitly. *See* Allan, T. R. S., *Review: Dworkin and Dicey: The Rule of Law as Integrity*, 8 (2) O.J.L.S, 266–277 (1988). Dworkin's emphasis is on faithful interpretation – mine is on the rhetorical basis for moral obligation. See the discussion in Take One infra.

[63] *See, e.g.*, Samuel Freeman, *The Law of Peoples, Social Cooperation, Human Rights and Distributive Justice*, 23 Soc. Phil. & Pol. 29

any theory of transnational justice that operates within the Justice as Integrity framework. It is not "Global Justice as Fairness" because the basis for justice is not a social relationship shared by all affected states, such as participation by all in an underlying cooperative scheme for mutual benefit (such will be the basis for the approach in Take Two and, in a sense, Take Three). We pursue a particular policy not because we believe all agree to it or should agree, but simply because it is how we believe others are to be treated. Thus it remains a liberal state's commitment to Justice as Fairness in its foreign relations.

By forgoing the search for a global normative theory, Take One articulates a strong claim on liberal states, but it cannot reach beyond liberal states to other states, some of which are the ones pursuing the most destructive policies. Integrity is powerful, but it is limited. This mode does not offer arguments as to why illiberal states are obligated to pursue those foreign policies we in liberal states consider to be "just" or necessary, nor does it necessarily give us guidance on how to manage relations between liberal and

(2006) (Rawls's approach to transnational justice is best understood as an inquiry into the foreign policy of liberal states, rather than as an argument for global justice more generally); *but see* BROCK, *supra* note 2 at 31 (Rawls himself invites evaluation according to this broader goal, on which he is arguably less successful). It is worth noting that Freeman is characterizing the Rawls of THE LAW OF PEOPLES, whereas I am pursuing an internationalized Justice as Fairness; nevertheless, I believe the characterization is correct in both cases.

illiberal states, a problem that preoccupied Rawls at the end of his life.[64]

Moreover, this approach does not, by itself, offer a theory of global justice that applies directly to *international organizations*.[65] As a brief section on the World Bank and the IMF will illustrate, this approach *can* help liberal states determine what normative constraints and objectives apply to the positions they take and advocate for within such organizations. However, this approach does not offer an independent normative argument for binding international institutions qua institutions to principles of distributive justice. Instead, if such institutions happen to follow just policies (on this view of justice), it will only be because they are controlled by a majority of liberal states that have decided to fulfill their liberal commitments through those institutions and have found or created the politics necessary to enact this agenda, not because the institution is independently obligated to do so.

---

[64] See, e.g., RAWLS, THE LAW OF PEOPLES, *supra* note 22.

[65] A theory of justice can apply directly to states, and indirectly to international institutions, insofar as the theory influences state behavior in and through institutions, viewing institutions in this sense as agents or tools of states. *See, e.g.,* Delegation and Agency in International Organizations (Darren G. Hawkins et al., eds., 2006) (surveying issues in agency theory view of international organizations). Alternatively, a theory of justice can apply directly to international institutions as distinct legal entities with legal personality, social practices and allocative decisions of their own. *See* Andrew Hurrell, "Global Inequality and International Institutions," 32 Metaphilosophy 34 (2001). It is the former that

For these reasons, this approach can be criticized for demoting transnational justice to *merely* the foreign policy of liberal states – certainly a cosmopolitan would object on this ground (and others). Of course, as an element of their foreign policy, liberal states will always find implementation of Justice as Fairness conditioned by international political realities. However, this is not the same as saying that liberal states are free in their international relations to pursue pure *realpolitik*. Rather, it recognizes that implementing liberal justice in a nonliberal world requires strategy, compromise, and careful calculations of self-interest and sustainability.

Nevertheless, embracing the ideal of a just foreign policy does mean that, at minimum, the goal is always clear for liberal states, even when the realization is not, and that liberal states are responsible not simply for surfing the politics of the moment, but for working to create the politics necessary for justice on liberal terms. As Rawls himself trenchantly observes:

> Our answer [to the possibility of a just international order] affects us before we come to actual politics, and limits or inspires how we take part in it. Rejecting the idea of a just and well-ordered Society of Peoples as impossible will affect the quality and tone of those attitudes and will determine our politics in a significant way.[66]

concerns us here in Take One, but understanding both kinds of obligations is important for global justice theory.

[66] RAWLS, THE LAW OF PEOPLES, *supra* note 22, at 128.

In the meantime, however, as Take Two points out, the world within which liberal states (indeed all states) operate is changing, and "globalization" is the single best term to describe this change.[67] In contrast to Take One, Take Two directly engages the "global" aspect of global justice and develops an alternative approach rooted in the relationship between justice and society – in this case, the possibility of meaningful global social relations and the obligations they create.

The question of justice and its connection to under-lying social relations is a complex one, with opponents to global justice citing both theoretical and empirical obstacles. Two branches of justice theory present this challenge most acutely: the social contract tradition and the communitarian approach to justice. Both present the limiting factor to justice in terms of social relationships, though they each approach the question in very different ways and look for very differ-ent constitutive elements. Contractarians cite the absence of a social contract beyond national borders, and communitar-ians the absence of something more: the sorts of communal bonds, expressed in terms of shared traditions, practices, and understandings that go beyond social contract requirements and are the true (in their view) ingredients of justice.[68]

---

[67] *See, e.g.,* Introduction, Global Transformations 1 (David Held et al., 1999) (globalization 'an idea whose time has come' which, though in danger of becoming a cliché, does in fact capture in specific ways fundamental changes in contemporary global social relations).

[68] *See* Take Two infra for a fuller discussion of these points.

This is where globalization comes in. The core insight of Take Two is that globalization is creating the possibility for exactly those sorts of relationships, thereby opening the door to new normative possibilities.[69] As will be argued in that chapter, globalization is changing the possibilities for justice on a global level, because it is changing social relationships on a global level.

By reducing or eliminating the significance of time and space in social relations, globalization is intensifying relationships irrespective of boundaries and physical distance, and creating the sorts of knowledge and connection that arguably form the basis for even communitarian forms of justice. Rainer Forst has aptly captured this effect in a passage worth citing in full:

> [I]n the contemporary world the degree of globalized interdependence has reached a point where it is impossible not to speak of this context as one of justice: in addition to a global context of trade, there is now also a global context of production and of labor, and important actors in those spheres are to be characterized as "transnational" (especially large companies); there is a global ecological context with all the problems of scarcity of resources, pollution, and so on; there is a global context of institutions from the United Nations to the International Monetary Fund (IMF) as well as of nongovernmental institutions (Greenpeace and Amnesty International, for example); there is a global context of legal treaties and obligations,

[69] Garcia, *Global Community,* at 4.

of technological interdependence (just think of the consequences of an aggressive virus emerging in the World
Wide Web), of military co-operations as well as conflicts,
of migration within and across continents; and there is, of
course, an ever-growing global context of cultural production, consumption and communication.[70]

Members of this global web of relationships are increasingly
aware of each other's needs and circumstances, increasingly
capable of effectively addressing these needs, and increasingly contributing to these circumstances in the first place.
They find themselves increasingly engaged in a multitude
of transnational cooperative schemes for mutual benefit
within an emerging global market society,[71] and together
they look to the same organizations, especially those at the
meta-state level, to provide regulatory approaches to governing this market and addressing problems of global social
policy.

This does not mean that global community has emerged
fully formed, with the richness and force of national political communities. However, it is my contention that these
developments allow us to begin to speak in important ways
of limited degrees of community, or "spheres of justice" to

---

[70] Rainer Frost, *Towards a Critical Theory of Transnational Justice*,
32 METAPHILOSOPHY 160 (2001).

[71] Aaron James characterizes this as the shared social practice of
market reliance. *Global Economic Fairness: Internal Principals*,
in GLOBAL JUSTICE AND INTERNATIONAL ECONOMIC LAW, *supra*
note 2.

borrow Walzer's phrase, with respect to different issues, institutions, or sets of social relations within the global social space. For states, other communities, and individuals, participation in the multiple kinds of transboundary social interactions that constitute globalization creates certain transboundary relationships that may satisfy contractarian or communitarian criteria of justice. That is, one finds among global social relations certain groupings that a contractarian may recognize as collaborative schemes constituted for mutual benefit, or within which a communitarian might recognize a meaningful degree of shared traditions, practices, and understandings.

There are of course important differences between contractarian and communitarian accounts of justice and between limited transnational communities or transnational shared enterprises, as contractarians and communitarians will readily assert. However, at this juncture, it is not essential to distinguish between contractarian and communitarian accounts of these entities, if we accept that they have certain key features in common. For example, if we view the WTO as one such transnational shared enterprise with its own "constitution," we can look at the system for protection of Members' justified expectations through the Dispute Settlement Understanding (DSU) as one of the core constitutive commitments of the enterprise. Alternatively, we can look at Members' justified expectations as themselves a set of shared understandings, and the protection of such expectations as itself one of the core understandings which all Members share and which is embodied in the DSU and its practices. On either account, for WTO Members this is the "justice" most closely associated with this enterprise or peculiar to this community.[72]

What is essential to both accounts, as I will argue in Take Two, is that the relational structure of a group such as the WTO implies that some level of justice is both possible and necessary, whether on contractarian or communitarian grounds, for its members. Thus we can speak of "limited global community" as embracing that level of "community" necessary to support relations of justice, even if it is not a full-blown social contract on the domestic model or does not manifest that level of community necessary to speak of "global community" in the fullest communitarian sense.

Returning to our theme of highlighting modes of discourse about transnational justice, Take Two therefore introduces another mode, with two variants: the Relational Mode of Justice. In contrast to the Integrity Mode discussed in Take One, the Relational Mode predicates just behavior on the existence of certain kinds of relationships between

---

[72] *See* Chios Carmody, *A Theory of WTO Law*, J. INT'L ECON. L. 1 (2008). Incidentally, this norm also illustrates the internal approach to justice in international economic law, because it is an internal norm, as opposed to more traditional external approaches applying exogenous norms of political theory to institutional settings. I will say more about this in Take Three. *See also* Garcia & Ciko, *Theories of Justice and International Economic Law, supra* note 2.

actors, rather than simply as a matter of integrity to one's own principles of behavior independently of any relationship. Depending on one's account of the necessary relationships, this mode can be a Shared Enterprise Mode, predicating justice on one's participation in a cooperative scheme for mutual benefit and limiting justice to one's co-participants (the contractarian version); or a Communal Mode of justice, in which obligations of justice depend on deeper shared commitments and understandings which the literature calls "community" (the communitarian version).

In the transnational context, the principal advantage of the Relational approach of Take Two is that it tries to directly address the question of *global* justice by articulating the basis for justice in a *global social relationship*, be it a global shared enterprise or global normative community, thus directly taking on the changing and plural nature of global social reality. On this view, globalization itself is in the process of creating new and more extensive networks of shared global enterprise, or new global communities, consisting of shared understandings, practices, and traditions capable of supporting obligations of justice at a global level.

The power of this approach can also be expressed in terms borrowed from the theory of integration economics, which distinguishes between important "static" welfare effects of trade (a one-time shift in the production possibility frontier of a given economy because of trade liberalization), and the transformative "dynamic" effects of trade liberalization on an economy's rate of growth over time.[73] In contrast to Take One, which can be characterized as the "static" extension of a domestic theory of justice (Justice as Fairness) into the realm of foreign relations through a series of adaptations, Take Two is a "dynamic" extension of a domestic theory of justice (contractarian or communitarian) into global relations through an understanding of the transformation of its underlying social basis, and the far-reaching implications of this transformation for the normative scope of the theory.[74]

Because Take Two posits a transformation of social relations on a global level, it also lays the foundation for a shared global approach to fundamental norms, which can be called a global minimal ethics approach, after Messner,[75] or a global basic package approach.[76] This is similar to, but conceptually distinct from, Walzer's notion of thin morality.[77] Thin morality takes the current degree of normative overlap or consensus from existing communities (again in a static framework), and suggests quite importantly that this is the basis for some degree of global normative consensus on at

---

[73] *See* BELA BALASSA, THE THEORY OF ECONOMIC INTEGRATION (1961).

[74] The latter effect is in a sense more intimate and ongoing.

[75] Dirk Messner, *World Society – Structures and Trends,* in GLOBAL TRENDS AND GLOBAL GOVERNANCE (Paul Kennedy, Dirk Messner & Franz Nuscheler, eds., 2001).

[76] Frank J. Garcia, *Globalization and the Theory of International Law* 11, B.C. L. SCH. FAC. PAPERS, Paper 75 (2005), *available at* http://papers.ssrn.com/sol3/papers.cfm?abstract_id=742726.

[77] MICHAEL WALZER, THICK AND THIN (2006).

least the most critical issues.[78] However, the reality of globalization means that this zone of overlap is a dynamic one, and (I would argue) with a generally upward slope (if such a thing could be graphed), due to the community-building effects of global institutions and our shared responses to global challenges.

When viewed in this light, cosmopolitan accounts of global justice may prefigure what in fact could emerge through a gradual process of increasingly global communal relationships arising from, and constitutive of, globalization itself. Thus at some horizon point cosmopolitanism and communitarianism might converge.[79] At a minimum for now, these trends allow us to speak of emerging or limited communities with a global minimal ethics that applies to everyone within these communities.

[78] To some extent, Sen's project is consistent with this approach, in that it looks broadly and cross-culturally at similar arguments made for justice, with the aim that this will more readily allow us to develop the consensus necessary to attack the most critical problems we face. SEN, *supra* note 7, at xiv.

[79] *See* Frank J. Garcia, *Globalization, Global Community and the Possibility of Global Justice*, B.C. L. SCH. FAC. PAPERS, Paper 33, (2005) *available at* http://lawdigitalcommons.bc.edu/lsfp/33 This assumes, of course, that the process of global community building and global norm-creation proceeds along liberal cosmopolitan lines, which is not a foregone conclusion. My criticism of cosmopolitanism, then, is simply that it mistakes one vision of where we might be heading for where we are actually standing, even though there could well be at least one plausible line of development which indeed brings this about. I shall have more to say about this in the concluding chapter.

Intriguingly, certain emerging communities within globalization may be more deeply integrated and more fully developed from an institutional point of view than others. At the same time, they may be identified more clearly with a particular shared normative view. I am thinking here of the global economy, which is perhaps the single most inter-connected aspect of our global environment and is managed through a set of broad-based membership institutions and sets of domestic policies that share a basic commitment to economic liberalism, though as within any liberal commu-nity there is of course disagreement or controversy surround-ing the nature of liberalism itself and its implications.

In this sense, the global economy may well constitute a liberal community, capable of supporting deeper commit-ments than a global minimal ethics approach would dictate, though not yet as deep as the Justice as Fairness approach of Take One. Such a mid-level form of consensus could pos-sibly support, for example, a limited degree of distributive justice, as in the form of wealth transfers to offset the global social costs of capitalism,[80] and a shared commitment to

---

[80] Such as the Tobin Tax, for example, currently resurrected in the form of a Financial Tax and being widely considered among devel-oped market societies in the wake of the global financial crisis. *See* Ross P. Buckley, International financial System: Policy and Regulation 132–35 (2008); Phillip Inman, Finance Experts Call for 'Tobin Tax' on Foreign Exchange Trades, The Guardian, July 18, 2010, *available at* http://www.guardian.co.uk/busi-ness/2010/jul/18/tobin-tax-financial-transactions. On the issue of justice-driven transnational taxation schemes generally, see Brock, *supra* note 2 at 117–150.

individual economic freedom, even in societies that don't yet support a broad range of individual civil and political freedoms (I am thinking, for example, of China, Cuba, or Vietnam).[81] Thus participants in a global economy may be entitled to expect deeper degrees of justice and freedom than they might receive through participation in other aspects of global social life. I shall have more to say about all of this in Take Two.

The reality of varying types, and degrees, of freedom enjoyed throughout the world brings me to my third approach, based not on political theory but on a notion of consent and its relationship to trade. One of the fundamental questions raised by Rawls in *The Law of Peoples* is how far the tolerance of liberal societies must extend to nonliberal societies. Put another way, to what extent can liberal societies engage in cooperative international schemes (such as a regulated global market) with nonliberal societies before compromising their own principles? For Rawls, the answer involves a distinction between liberal and "decent" hierarchical states on the one hand, and benevolent absolutisms, burdened

---

[81] On the domestic effects of China's and Vietnam's role in the global economy though membership in the WTO and adherence to its rules, *see e.g.* Robert Winthrop, *Trade and Human Rights: Policy Linkages in Chinese Accession to the WTO* (April 2001) *available at internationalecon.com/v1.0/ch25/china/winthrop.pdf; but see* Terry Collingsworth, *The Key Human Rights Challenge: Developing Enforcement Mechanisms,* 15 HARV. HUM. RTS. J. 183 (2002); Alberto R. Coll, *Harming Human Rights in the Name of Promoting: The Case of Cuban Embargo,* 12 UCLA J. INT'L L & FOREIGN AFF. 199 (2007).

states, and outlaw states on the other.[82] For the former, full membership in the Society of Peoples is warranted, and full engagement is possible. For the latter, something less: limited foreign aid, the international rule of law, and where necessary, armed conflict and intervention.[83]

I have great respect for this careful attempt to work out the international implications of liberalism, but I submit that for a globalizing world this again is not enough. To take but one example, the global economy, it is clear that with the exception of a small handful of truly isolated states (perhaps similar to, if not identical with, the set of Rawls's outlaw states), the overwhelming majority of states (both liberal and nonliberal) are engaged to one degree or another in the global economy, which can be understood as a vast, complex and multitiered cooperative scheme for mutual benefit.[84]

---

[82] In THE LAW OF PEOPLES, Rawls distinguishes between five types of society: liberal, hierarchical or decent societies, outlaw states, states burdened by unfavorable conditions, and benevolent absolutisms. Of these, the first, liberal democracies, offer basic rights and freedoms to its citizens and adopt distributive measures; the second includes nonliberal societies that are morally acceptable because, among other things, they offer consultative channels between the people and their government; the third is a category of rogue states that adopt expansionist policies and against whom aggression can be justified; the fourth are societies that fail due to unfavorable conditions; finally, benevolent absolutisms are societies that respect basic human rights but are not democratic. *Supra* note 22, at section 8.

[83] *Id.* sections 14 and 15.

[84] Garcia, *supra* note 35, at 22.

Can it really be that justice requires liberal states to evaluate (identify? designate?) which nonliberal states are decent (in Rawlsian terms) and which are not, and isolate the latter from the global economy? That seems neither prudent nor practicable (think again of China, Cuba, or Vietnam), and yet this is precisely what liberal critics of Rawls would have us do, criticizing Rawls for extending tolerance to even "decent" nonliberal states.[85] After all, even Rawls recognized the potential benefits of inclusion and example in reforming the political cultures of nonliberal states.[86] Yet to treat economic regulation as purely technical and engagement in a cooperative scheme such as the global economy purely functional (making the difference between trading with Canada and trading with North Korea irrelevant) also seems dissatisfying to our intuitions.

In my view, this illustrates both the limits of liberal theory for a global social environment and the need for an alternative approach. It would seem that a flourishing global economy would require a basis for joint regulation that is not simply international law as currently constituted, with the limits discussed above, and which offers a principled guide to economic conduct that cuts across genuine normative differences.

This is where a consent-based approach to trade law might play a role. What if there was another avenue to

[85] *See, e.g.*, TAN, TOLERATION, *supra* note 10, at 28–45; FERNANDO TESON, A PHILOSOPHY OF INTERNATIONAL LAW 114 (1998).
[86] RAWLS, THE LAW OF PEOPLES, *supra* note 22, at 15.3.

understanding trade law that did not devolve into "liberal versus nonliberal," but began instead closer to participants' immediate experience of economic interactions? Such an approach might offer a basis for mutually agreed regulation that evades both the limits of particular normative communities (Take One) and the ambiguity of emerging global social relationships (Take Two). This will be the Take Three "experiment."

In Take Three, I look at how economic interactions themselves have certain intrinsic requirements or characteristics that both support and require what we might otherwise describe as "just" behavior. Instead of working from first principles, this approach seeks to work from experience and the language that arises from experience. I suggest in this Take that "consent" on the part of both individual and state participants in an economic transaction and its regulation is the essential characteristic that makes economic exchanges "trade," rather than theft, coercion, exploitation, or the like.

I begin by looking at some aspects of our language, concepts, and cultural experiences of trade as a human phenomenon, suggesting a preliminary definition of trade as consensual exchange. I then apply this mode to international trade agreements, using aspects of contemporary trade treaty negotiations and substantive law, in order to illustrate how this approach can identify those elements of trade agreements that represent dynamics other than trade, such as predation, exploitation, or coercion.

A fundamental aim of this approach is thus to identify aspects of trade law and trade agreements that look and act like trade, but are something else, and that damage the subject of trade because they do not reflect consensual exchanges, generating social and economic costs that impede trade's flourishing. In this way, I attempt to shed light on subtle but important forces at work in contemporary trade relations, particularly as they involve substantial inequalities in power among participating states, which undercut global justice through their effects on the rules of the game and on the possibility of true consensual exchanges.

Consent on the part of individuals in a private exchange, and consent on the part of a state to a process of economic bargaining and the resulting rules and patterns of exchange are, of course, two different things. They are related, however, in that state-based rules should recognize and protect the role of private economic consent if consent is important, and rules that states agree to without consent or with diminished consent cannot be said to construct a consensual framework for exchange, regardless of the underlying private consent or lack of it within ensuing economic exchanges. Moreover, insofar as state rules affect or restrict the range of choices and the value of options and assets for private actors, nonconsensual state-based rules can be said to impose nonconsensual economic harms on private actors.

The principal implication of this approach is that in matters of global rule making, which today means principally economic rule making through trade agreements, we should aim for actual consent and structure these negotiations to achieve and reflect such consent, rather than simply employ abstract notions of consent for theoretical purposes. Insofar as trade transactions by their very nature require consent in order to be trade and not something else, we can posit that all economic actors, and to some extent their law-makers even in nonliberal states, have an interest in at least considering the possibility of real consent, in order to increase the chances of real trade and the economic and social benefits which flow from it.[87]

Creating a framework for genuine trade, and not something else, may well be the most we can agree to in our transnational relationships with all manner of states, liberal and nonliberal alike. This would still constitute a remarkable achievement, however, as it would safeguard the conditions for a real market, and create and enlarge pockets of consent even within nonliberal states (I am thinking again of China and Vietnam), simultaneously helping make liberal states' foreign relations consistent with their domestic

---

[87] It may be that for truly illiberal states, what Rawls would call outlaw states, full membership in the global economy would not be possible. However, as will be seen in Take Three, the reason here would be fundamentally different. It is not their illiberalism per se that requires isolation, but the fact that they are "constitutionally" unsuited to trade as trade, since they are committed instead to what I would call predation, coercion, or exploitation domestically as well as internationally.

commitments to some degree (the protection of individual consent as a liberal value).

Putting this approach in the context of modes of justice discourse, this third approach represents what I am calling a Transactional Mode of justice. In this mode, justice is specific to the requirements of a particular transaction or exchange between the participants. It does not depend on the actor's own commitments (the Integrity Mode) or the existence of any enduring social relationship between the participants (the Relational Mode) other than the transaction itself. Instead, the requirements of justice (here understood as a transaction that is satisfactory to both parties) will depend on the nature of the transaction itself and its own internal requirements.[88] The particular approach in Take Three – consent – suggests that consent is the necessary element, because trade is the underlying transaction, and trade depends upon consent to be trade and not something else. A different transaction could result in different requirements – what is essential to this mode is that justice flow from the transaction itself.

This also illustrates the difference in starting point between Rawls's project and Take Three. Rawls begins by constructing a deep version of liberal justice for domestic societies, Justice as Fairness, and then attempts to work

---

[88] There is thus a close relationship between the Transactional Mode and the internal approach to thinking about trade and justice. *See* Garcia and Ciko, *supra* note 2, at 26–33.

outward in concentric circles, determining just how far liberal states can go. In contrast, this project begins from the largest possible circle, the globalized transacting planet, and attempts to work inward from there, seeing what sorts of justice and fairness conversations can make sense within that larger circle.

Nevertheless, this approach still leaves unanswered one of the larger questions (at least for liberals and liberal states) raised by Rawls's project, namely, how can cooperative engagement with all but the most illiberal, outlaw states be structured so as to influence such states toward increased respect for democracy and human rights? In other words, how can engagement contribute to the progressive realization of liberal values?

One answer suggested by Take Three, but from a different direction, involves that most liberal of institutions, the market itself. In addition to the benefits of recognizing and protecting the role of consent itself as an expression (or an embodiment) of the liberal value of individual freedom, there may be ways to organize the incentive structure of the market itself to reward freedom and discipline oppression, as a way of protecting and encouraging *trade itself.*

One possibility is to treat the social effects of illiberality (oppression, violence, and other forms of extreme social control) as economic costs associated with the production of goods (insofar as that regime is engaged in international trade), and to internalize such costs through regulation as with any other social costs of production (pollution and safety risks to employees, for example). If the social costs of oppression can become part of the final market price of the economic fruits of oppression (through a social tariff, for example), then consumers in the market will simply bypass such goods in favor of truly less expensive goods produced by other states that are both more efficient and less oppressive. That might accomplish on economic grounds some of what Rawls and others seek to accomplish on moral grounds, namely, to incentivize the move to a more liberal domestic culture.[89]

The role of consent and its implications for the idea of a social tariff are but one example of how examining a particular approach to the question of global justice, in comparison and conversation with others, can suggest new possibilities to explore.[90] In my concluding chapter I attempt to draw lessons from this type of comparative approach, in the spirit of Sen's concept of "plural grounding."

[89] Social labeling and the "Fair Trade" movement can be seen in this light to be working toward similar goals, in a manner perhaps even more consistent with a free market than a social tariff. It would be an interesting study to compare their relative effectiveness in achieving a social purpose through market incentives. *See* Frank J. Garcia and Soohyun Jun, *Trade-based Strategies for Combatting Child Labor, in* CHILD LABOR AND HUMAN RIGHTS: MAKING CHILDREN MATTER (Burns Weston, ed., 2006). (market incentives and the trade-human rights nexus).

[90] With respect to addressing the most pressing social issues we face, Sen writes: "The use of a comparative perspective, going well beyond the limited – and limiting – framework of social contract, can make a useful contribution here." SEN, *supra* note 7, at xi.

By plural grounding, Sen means the use of a number of different lines of condemnation with regard to egregious social behavior, without seeking an agreement on their relative merits:

> The underlying issue is whether we have to agree on one specific line of censure for a reasoned consensus on the diagnosis of an injustice that calls for urgent rectification. What is important to note here, as central to the idea of justice, is that we can have a strong sense of injustice on many different grounds, and yet not agree on one particular ground as being *the* dominant reason for the diagnosis of injustice.[91]

The Conclusion therefore begins with a synthetic overview of the theories covered in Takes One, Two, and Three, emphasizing their various strengths and weaknesses. The heart of the chapter, however, is the application of a plural grounding approach to the question of global justice. The key is to recognize that our discourse about justice offers a wide range of theories including the three Takes profiled here, and employs multiple rhetorical strategies – the Integrity Mode, the Relational Mode, and the Transactional Mode, among others – through which to judge a situation unjust, and motivate others to action. Taking each element of this approach step by step, I first examine how our three Takes offer distinct, reasoned diagnoses of injustice; distinctive

---

[91] *Id.* at 2.

rationales for action; and different benchmarks for assessing any improvement in the justice of a given situation.

The second half of the chapter turns to a forward-looking examination of the implications of this approach for the global justice debate itself and for our many efforts to promote global justice in the world. The plural grounding approach allows us to examine how different theories of justice contribute to the larger effort to envision and argue for a just world, but through a multiple of perspectives rather than a single, totalizing theory. This approach also highlights one of the limits of current thinking on global justice, namely, the lack of a coherent structure through which to embrace normative pluralism while advocating change. The plural grounding framework allows us to explore the extent to which there is any consensus on the elements of global justice in contemporary global justice theory, through a distillation of the three approaches examined in the book, supplemented by cosmopolitanism and other key theoretical perspectives.

The chapter concludes with a reenvisioning of international trade agreements as frameworks for enhancing global justice through the protection of consensual bargaining. This approach, based principally on Take Three but drawing on the project as a whole, assumes that if free to agree or refuse particular economic transactions, private parties will move the global economic order gradually toward a more just arrangement because they are less likely to accept unjust outcomes themselves in their bargaining.

Expressed in terms of modes of discourse, I am arguing that the Transactional Mode of justice has unique strengths and advantages in a plural context in which participation in a global market may be the single most widely shared social experience.

For this approach to work there has to be an overhaul of the international trade negotiation process. The objective here is to construct a global network of consensual treaties, promoting and protecting consensual bargains, but without depending on a prior normative consensus. In a manner reminiscent of the *jus gentium* in the Roman era, such an arrangement recognizes a pragmatic need for orderly economic relations under a rule of law, in the absence of underlying bonds of joint citizenship or other shared norms. The framework of agreements I am proposing is justifiable in an environment of normative pluralism because it does not depend on shared normative commitments beyond the mutual recognition of consensual bargaining as essential to trade itself and to the objectives of the market participants themselves. Inspired by Kant's vision of a federation of democratic republics in *Perpetual Peace* and the transitional role he assigns to trade in bringing this about, my model offers instead a network of truly "free" trade agreements, contributing to global economic well-being while the global community continues to evolve its shared norms on global justice.[92]

---

[92] IMMANUEL KANT, *Perpetual Peace: A Philosophical Sketch,* in KANT: POLITICAL WRITINGS 116, 93–130 (H.S. Reiss ed., H.B. Nisbit trans., 2nd ed., Cambridge University Press 1991) (1784).

IV. Closing Thoughts

The goal of this book is to clearly articulate the benefits, limits, and contributions of all three featured approaches, within the contours of the larger project of global justice of which they are a part and which they in turn enrich and broaden. The core argument of this book is that building global justice requires all three approaches, and others as well. Before turning to the main discussion, however, I want to conclude this introduction with a few more words as to why I do not highlight cosmopolitanism – surely a leading approach and deservedly so – or in Take One simply follow Rawls's *Law of Peoples* for the substance of Liberal Internationalism, despite my "big tent" approach in this book to the global justice conversation. I will begin with cosmopolitanism.

There are two main strands of cosmopolitanism, moral and political (also called legal or institutional).[93] Moral cosmopolitanism concerns itself with human equality across

---

[93] Thomas Pogge gives an exhaustive list of the various strands of cosmopolitanism, but for our purposes, at least, they can readily sort in one of the two categories mentioned. *See* Pogge, *supra* note 6. Pauline Kleingeld and Eric Brown agree with the two categories but also include economic cosmopolitanism in their survey of the concept. However, I forgo any discussion of it here, since economic cosmopolitanism is an idea entertained almost exclusively by economists. *See* Pauline Kleingeld and Eric Brown, *Cosmopolitanism*, THE STANFORD ENCYCLOPEDIA OF PHILOSOPHY (2006) *available at* http://plato.stanford.edu/entries/cosmopolitanism/

national political boundaries, whereas political cosmopolitanism concerns itself with the implications of moral cosmopolitanism for the nature of institutions, namely, global institutions. As I mentioned earlier in this chapter, moral cosmopolitanism seeks to ground global justice in the universal nature of human dignity, which would seem a naturally global approach.[94] Similarly, some of the most ambitious and elegant arguments for global justice at the institutional level are cosmopolitan in nature.[95] Thus, any rejection or minimization of cosmopolitanism would seem paradoxical, given that cosmopolitanism would appear to be ideally and conclusively suited to global justice.

I do not in any way object to the liberal basis of cosmopolitanism or to its engagement with human rights, and I am deeply in sympathy with its vision of a just world order built on human dignity. For all of these reasons, and consistent with the plural grounding method, cosmopolitanism has in my view an enduring, even leading role in the conversation about global justice, which this book does not seek to undercut. However, I think cosmopolitanism has one serious vulnerability that has led me to look to other, less travelled routes for the (re)conceptualizations I offer here: both the

---

[94] *See, e.g.*, CANEY, *supra* note 2, at 2–4.

[95] Most recently, for example, in the work of Simon Caney, and stretching all the way back to Kant himself (though Kant refrained from what for most political cosmopolitans is the ultimate step – world government). *See* CANEY, *supra* note 2, at 2–4; KANT, *Perpetual Peace*: *supra* note 92.

political and moral forms of cosmopolitanism can be criticized as, in different ways, implausible for the world as we find it, and by this I do not mean simply the status quo.

The characteristic form of political cosmopolitanism – arguments for a world state – has been widely rejected on normative and pragmatic grounds even by some cosmopolitans.[96] Caney argues, however, that critiques of political cosmopolitanism do not in themselves impugn the basis for moral cosmopolitanism, and I agree. However, while it is true that there are other less strong forms of political cosmopolitanism (such as ideas for a world federation of states or for the free movement of persons across national boundaries),[97] I believe the problems associated with the strong political form of cosmopolitanism are indicative of issues running through the entire approach, namely, that the global projection of liberal values at either the normative or institutional level breaks down in the face of certain key realities about how people reason morally and act politically. In order to explain what I mean, it is necessary to include the second, moral branch of cosmopolitanism.

As Gillian Brock – herself a cosmopolitan – puts it, moral cosmopolitanism "highlights the responsibilities we have *to those we do not know and with whom we are not intimate*, but whose lives *should* be of concern to us" (emphasis

---

[96] *See* CANEY, *supra* note 2, at 5.

[97] *See* KANT, *supra* note 93; Joseph Carens, *Aliens and Citizens: The Case for Open Borders, in* THE RIGHTS OF MINORITY CULTURES 331–349 (Will Kymlicka, ed., 1995).

supplied).[98] It is precisely here that communitarians criticize cosmopolitanism on the basis of its moral psychology: it fails to take into account how human beings actually form their identities and moral commitments (within specific communities), and fails to take into account the normative implications (in their view) of this process: the moral priority of local or national communities over thinner, more abstract "global" communities.[99] Quoting Brock again:

> Cosmopolitanism as a thesis about identity also denies that membership in a particular cultural community is *necessary* for an individual to flourish in the world. Contra [other] claims on the matter, cosmopolitans deny that such membership is necessary for an individual's living a fulfilling life. Belonging to a particular culture is not an essential ingredient in personal identity formation or maintenance: one can pick and choose from the full smorgasbord on offer, or reject all in favour of other options.…[100]

In contrast, communitarians argue that one's community (social, political, normative) is *essentially* tied to one's identity, integral to one's flourishing, and constitutive of the very concept of justice itself, and to whom we owe it.[101] In the communitarian view, cosmopolitans are guilty

---

[98] *See* BROCK, *supra* note 2, at 9.

[99] *See* DAVID MILLER, ON NATIONALITY 65–69 (2nd ed., 2002); WALZER, SPHERES OF JUSTICE, *supra* note 21.

[100] BROCK, *supra* note 2, at 8.

[101] This summary statement necessarily simplifies the complex views of a range of "communitarian" thinkers such as Sandel, Taylor,

of a moral projection: having developed their own identities and moral commitments largely within developed
post-industrial liberal national communities, they imagine
that their "locally derived" moral universalism is a global
normative theory, whereas it is really an increasingly common international view among Western liberals from such
communities.[102]

From this perspective, cosmopolitanism is no different
from any other universalizing ideology – in Brock's words:
"One could *see* oneself as a member of a global community
of human persons for all sorts of reasons, such as religious
commitments – Christianity is often thought of in this connection – and there is also a strong Marxist justification for
holding this position as well" (emphasis added).[103] In other
words, one imagines one's self to be part of such a community, and then attempts to reason morally from this imagined membership.

Returning to my preoccupation with how we talk about
justice, this way of thinking typifies a fourth mode of discourse about justice – which I will call the Universal Mode –
in which one conceives of justice as rooted in a principle or

Miller, Walzer, and others. *See* Take Two for a more nuanced discussion of these views.

[102] Caney argues forcefully that cosmopolitans need not be liberals
and that liberals need not be cosmopolitans. *Supra* note 2, at 5. I
agree with the latter point (and indeed will discuss Rawls – his
chief example – later and in Take One) but am not convinced by
the former (and Caney cites no examples).

[103] BROCK, *supra* note 2, at 11.

condition equally applicable to all persons (human dignity, being a child of God, etc.). In this sense, it is not an unreasonable basis at all from which to attempt to formulate our behavior toward others, and resembles in some ways what we call the act of empathy, in which we attempt to imaginatively understand another's situation and thereby form a genuine connection to it. However, as a basis for constructing a theory of global justice with claims to global adherence, it is quite another matter. Continuing the metaphor, the Universal Mode of justice can just as easily lead us into the *opposite* of empathy: if we are not careful, in this mode we can be accused of *imagining* we understand another's situation, and then acting as if we have in fact understood it, and holding others to the principles we believe they have, or ought to have.

By asserting this view, I do not mean to categorically dismiss cosmopolitanism or write a blank check to nationalism or parochialism. Indeed, the Universal Mode of justice discourse that cosmopolitanism typifies is one of the most powerful modes of discourse we have – one need only think of the tremendous sacrifices people have been moved to make on the basis of a universalist vision, to recognize its power. This is precisely where the paradox lies, however. Universalist visions are powerful motivators to *individuals* who have acquired this dream within specific communities that hold and nurture such beliefs, and they have often (and very sadly) been deployed in conflict against other equally fervently held universalist visions – one need only think of the horrors of "religious" wars to recognize this too well. Great (and small) injustices are daily justified by recourse to incompatible universalist claims.

Put in more technical terms, I am suggesting that communitarians and other critics of cosmopolitanism may have gotten something right with respect to moral psychology, and at a minimum have gotten something right about moral anthropology. Brock writes that "the pervasive influence of national, ethnic, or religious identity in people's lives" is equally as noteworthy to an observer of global affairs as the pervasive presence of suffering on a massive scale.[104] The majority of people understand themselves with reference to specific communities and for this reason place the welfare of these communities ahead of other groups of people.

Caney attempts to downgrade communitarian critiques on this basis as objections to "cultural cosmopolitanism," which he considers to be a superficial and distinguishable form of cosmopolitanism.[105] However, I think Caney misses the mark here – depending on one's view, the critique I and others are making either goes deeper than this (if one accepts Caney's view of cultural cosmopolitanism as superficial), or is more powerful than Caney acknowledges, if one views objections to cultural cosmopolitanism as really getting to

---

[104] Id., at 4.

[105] CANEY, supra note 2, at 6. By cultural cosmopolitanism, Caney means (following Waldron and others) the view that a good life is one that draws upon and is open to different cultures and traditions.

the heart of the enduring role of one's culture in the formation of normative obligations and life meanings.[106]

For these reasons, I do not consider cosmopolitanism particularly well-suited to serve as the basis for a truly global
approach to justice in a multi-ethnic, pluralistic world of different religious, philosophical, legal, and cultural traditions
and communities.[107] I believe cosmopolitanism can be more
accurately characterized as a liberal ideal of global justice,
with considerable meaning and rhetorical or symbolic power
within liberal communities, but without a strong or exclusive claim to universal validity; it is more a vision than a
path at this point.

This does not mean that cosmopolitanism has no place in
global justice theory – quite the contrary. Cosmopolitanism
has played and continues to play a very important role in
our thinking about global justice (my own included), and
consistent with the plural grounding approach it has a vital
role to play in the movement toward global justice, as I will

[106] Cosmopolitans such as Tan have attempted to integrate the thrust
of the communitarian challenge by acknowledging its role in fore-
grounding the importance of nationality and citizenship in giving
worth and meaning to one's goals and ends, thus supplementing
and rendering more complex an essentially liberal view of justice.
TAN, TOLERATION, *supra* note 10, at 13–16. This suggests the possibility of a fruitful synthesis, but of course from the cosmopolitan
side.

[107] *But see* CANEY, *supra* note 2, at 4 (reciting evidence of cross-cultural
consensus on cosmopolitan tenets); AMARTYA SEN, DEVELOPMENT
AS FREEDOM, 242–44 (1999) (values underlying human rights and
democracy have widespread cross-cultural basis).

explain in the Conclusion. It may well be that at some future points the lines will all converge and the globe will be so deeply interconnected at a symbolic level that its community will support cosmopolitanism in the deep sense – but more about this later. Whatever the future may bring, in my view cosmopolitanism does not now play a *trumping* role in the global justice debate, and shouldn't, for the reasons I have explained here.

Turning to Rawls, despite my great respect for and sympathy with his basic project as expressed in *The Law of Peoples*, I believe it is similarly and fundamentally limited. *The Law of Peoples* is centrally about the problem of pluralism, and in that sense Rawls's analysis informs and supports this present project. However, when it comes to international law and the applicable principles of justice in a transnational context, Rawls stops short. Thus the relationship between this book and Rawls's own work is a complex one: while this project is heavily influenced in its basic inquiry by the spirit of *The Law of Peoples*, I reject its approach to global justice at the most fundamental level for being "liberalism-outward" rather than "global-inward," as I mentioned earlier in connection with Take One. I am also critical of its approach to international law for being insufficiently future-oriented (as I will explain), and its specific approach to distributive justice as inadequate for the technical reasons I set out here and in Take One.[108]

[108] This ambivalence is characteristic of the larger conversation within the field of global justice theory concerning Rawls's later

In *The Law of Peoples*, Rawls aims to extend the liberal idea of tolerance to serve as the basis for principles governing the peaceful relations among "well-ordered" peoples.[109] By "well-ordered" Rawls does not just mean liberal peoples – he acknowledges the diversity that exists in the world and that it would not be reasonable to expect all peoples to endorse liberalism:

> Just as a citizen in a liberal society must respect other persons' comprehensive religious, philosophical, and moral doctrines provided they are pursued in accordance with a reasonable political conception of justice, so a liberal society must respect other societies organized by comprehensive doctrines, provided their political and social institutions meet certain conditions that lead the society to adhere to a reasonable law of peoples.[110]

In so doing, Rawls attempts to recognize and incorporate at a constitutive level the fundamental implications of pluralism for his project, which is one of the reasons he believes

---

work. *See* BROCK, *supra* note 2, at 19 (THE LAW OF PEOPLES is enormously influential yet controversial within the global justice debate).

[109] By so characterizing his goal, I am gesturing toward those critics who fault Rawls for being more concerned in that book with peaceful and stable international relations, rather than *just* international relations, without fully agreeing with such critics. *See* BROCK, *supra* note 2, at 31.

[110] RAWLS, THE LAW OF PEOPLES, *supra* note 22, at 43.

his model is a "realistic" Utopia.[111] In Tan's words, "Rawls wants his global toleration to be, as in the domestic case, a liberal ideal and not one based on a compromise of liberal principles in order to accommodate global diversity."[112] In my view, this commitment is one of Rawls's most important and enduring contributions to the development of global liberalism and global justice theory.[113]

In order to generate his theory, Rawls adopts a two-stage methodology. In the first step, Rawls treads familiar ground by deriving through an Original Position heuristic the appropriate principles for the domestic justice of liberal peoples, mirroring his work in *A Theory of Justice*. However, when it comes to the second Original Position in which representatives of all the world's peoples are to choose principles for their mutual interrelations, Rawls does not engage in a thorough reconstruction of international principles of justice based on a process of reflective equilibrium, as he does for domestic principles of justice in *A Theory of Justice*.

---

[111] *Id.* at 13.

[112] TAN, TOLERATION, *supra* note 10, at 24. To do otherwise with respect to the numerous "decent" nonliberal societies of the world would, Rawls fears, "frustrate their vitality by coercively insisting that all societies be liberal." THE LAW OF PEOPLES, *supra* note 22, at 62.

[113] His approach, however, is not without critics even within liberalism. *See* BROCK, *supra* note 2, at 28–29 (surveying criticisms of Rawls's approach to toleration).

Instead, Rawls simply assumes as a starting point the existing content of international law, summarized in eight principles drawn in fact from Brierly's *Law of Nations*:

1. Peoples are free and equal and their freedoms are to be respected by other peoples,

2. Peoples are equal and parties to their own agreements,

3. Peoples have the right to self-defense, though no right to instigate war,

4. Peoples are to observe the duty of nonintervention,

5. People are to observe treaties,

6. Peoples are to observe justice in war,

7. Peoples are to honor human rights, and

8. Peoples have a duty of assistance toward other peoples unable to acquire just or decent institutions due to unfavorable economic or social conditions.[114]

Most important, Rawls casts his project as the development of a justification for these received principles:

> I consider the merits of only the eight principles of the Law of Peoples listed [earlier]. These familiar and largely traditional principles I take from the history and usages of international law practice. The parties are not given a menu of alternative principles and ideals from which to

---

[114] THE LAW OF PEOPLES, *supra* note 22, at 37 (citing J.L. BRIERLY, THE LAW OF NATIONS: AN INTRODUCTION TO THE INTERNATIONAL LAW OF PEACE [Sir Humphrey Waldock, ed., Oxford University Press, 6th ed., 1978] [1966]).

select, as they are in *Political Liberalism*, or in *A Theory of Justice*.[115]

This method bears a superficial resemblance to his "rational reconstruction" in *A Theory of Justice* of our moral intuition on liberty and equality, but the resemblance is only superficial.

Rawls does rather categorically "contend that the eight principles of the Law of Peoples are superior to any others," but he does not evaluate this claim or argue for this superiority with reference to prior moral principles, nor does he even set out why these principles reflect our moral intuitions on the subject.[116] By taking this route, Rawls limits the reach of his project, failing to distinguish between the domain of a plausible account of current widely recognized norms of international law, and the domain of our present and evolving intuitions regarding transnational moral obligations and the problems of global justice in a globalizing world. The two might be identical, but such identity cannot be assumed. It is quite possible, indeed likely, that international justice would in fact go beyond the basic principles of international law Brierly distilled decades ago (indeed as will be seen in Take Two even Walzer and Miller would recognize this), but we are left to consider this possibility without the benefit of Rawls's insight.

[115] RAWLS, THE LAW OF PEOPLES, *supra* note 22, at 41.
[116] *Id.*

The contrast is perhaps sharpest with respect to the Difference Principle, a cornerstone of Justice as Fairness in *A Theory of Justice*, but rejected in *The Law of Peoples*. When he argues for the Difference Principle in *A Theory of Justice*, Rawls deploys sophisticated arguments at many levels to advocate for a principle of justice which, although it might well reflect existing moral intuitions, clearly went beyond the state of contemporary political theory at the time, not to mention contemporary law and policy, in its redistributive implications.[117] However, when it comes to a similar stage in the argument in *The Law of Peoples*, Rawls states that the representatives in the second Original Position "simply reflect on the advantages of these principles of equality among peoples and see no reason to depart from them or to propose alternatives."[118]

While this may describe Rawls's own view, the strenuous objections of Pogge, Beitz, Barry, Richards, and others from the theory's first publication would suggest that such hypothetical representatives might not in fact be so sanguine about the status quo.[119] The extent of criticism Rawls has

---

[117] *See generally* Thomas Pogge, *Rawls on International Justice (book review)*, 51 PHIL. Q. 246 (2001); Frank Garcia, *Book Review*: THE LAW OF PEOPLES, 23 HOUSTON. J. INT'L L. 659 (2001).

[118] RAWLS, THE LAW OF PEOPLES, *supra* note 22, at 41.

[119] With her characteristic understatement, Brock notes that Rawls's insistence on this point despite widespread opposition from cosmopolitans and others was "a disappointment." BROCK, *supra* note 2 at 20. Others have been less circumspect. *See, e.g.*, THOMAS POGGE, REALIZING RAWLS 246 (1989) ("I am at a loss to explain

received and continues to receive by rejecting the Difference Principle in his vision of international justice is at least evidence of significant disagreement over the content of such international moral intuitions.[120] In my view, Rawls's liberal justification of existing international law doctrines, while important and useful, is inadequate as an indicator of how international law is evolving and where globalization might be suggesting that international law needs to go, particularly with regard to the specific issues of global distributive justice.

Charting the possible paths for international law to move toward global justice in a manner that embraces both pluralism and globalization is, in my view, the single most important challenge for international legal theory today. For these reasons and despite the fundamental ongoing importance of the cosmopolitan tradition and *The Law of Peoples* to the creation and development of the contemporary global justice debate, I am interested in evaluating alternative or supplementary approaches to the question of global justice, which in my view more fully respond to the reality

Rawls' quick endorsement of a bygone status quo"). *But see* Leif Wenar, *Why Rawls Is not a Cosmopolitan Egalitarian, in* RAWLS' LAW OF PEOPLES: A REALISTIC UTOPIA? 95 (Rex Martin & David A. Reidy, eds., 2006) (mounting a defense of Rawls based on the latter's work on political liberalism, not Justice as Fairness).

[120] For an excellent summary and evaluation of the critical debate surrounding THE LAW OF PEOPLES, *see* BROCK, *supra* note 2, at 36–40; *see also* RAWLS' LAW OF PEOPLES: A REALISTIC UTOPIA? (Rex Martin & David A. Reidy, eds., 2006).

of pluralism and the progressive possibilities for law which globalization opens.

Each of the three approaches examined in this book – liberal internationalism, global communitarianism, and consent-based trade theory – offers a different way of addressing this central problem of normative pluralism. Each "Take" assumes a different conception of the relationship between international trade law and justice, represents a different mode of justice discourse, and makes different demands on international economic law with respect to the promotion of global justice. Both Cosmopolitanism and the Law of Peoples are other "Takes" that have been the subject of other books and could perfectly well have been part of this one – in that sense, there are many "Takes" on global justice and there should be. By setting these three specific approaches side by side here and highlighting their strengths and weaknesses, I hope to suggest some new directions for the trade and justice inquiry, which might capitalize on the strengths of all three Takes while avoiding some of the pitfalls.

1

Take One

International Justice, or Global Justice as the Foreign Policy of Liberal States

If proponents of global justice from within the tradition of Western liberalism want to take seriously the reality of normative pluralism in the pursuit of global justice, one approach is to deliberately stop short of trying to develop global norms, and instead work toward justice in and through the foreign policy of liberal states.[1] This approach does not attempt to look for or establish a shared normative basis for justice among states or peoples,[2] instead, it

---

[1] This would, of course, be *liberal* justice. While this strategy could equally well work with any theory of justice, liberal or not, I am confining my discussion here to a liberal approach, for the reasons mentioned in the Introduction.

[2] Rawls concedes as much when he writes in THE LAW OF PEOPLES (1999) that this is not about establishing liberalism as a shared conception of justice, because that defeats the very principle of liberalism. John Rawls, *The Law of Peoples*, CRITICAL INQUIRY 37, 39 (1993).

simply asks the following question: what are the foreign policy obligations of liberal states by virtue of their liberalism? Put another way, are liberal states obligated to pursue a liberal vision of global justice in their international relations by virtue of the fact that they are liberal? And if so, what might that look like?

In the traditional reading of international political theory, states are free to pursue pragmatism and realism in their interstate relations, regardless of their domestic political values.[3] They can embrace constitutional democracy at home, and *realpolitik* abroad. Underlying this view is the assumption that foreign relations take place in a sort of value-free zone.[4] There may be such a thing as domestic justice, but there is no global justice: among states, there are only politics and power, and to some extent, law.[5]

---

[3] *See generally* MARTI KOSKENNIEMI, FROM APOLOGY TO UTOPIA: THE STRUCTURE OF INTERNATIONAL LEGAL ARGUMENT (2006) (states are destined to vacillate between these two poles); Ernst-Ulrich Petersmann, *Constitutionalism and International Organizations*, 17 NW. J. INT'L L. & BUS. 398 (1997) (discussing the "Lockean dilemma" in liberal constitutionalism). This view may be changing. *But see* David Held, *Law of States, Law of Peoples*, 8 LEGAL THEORY 1–44 (2002).

[4] KOSKENNIEMI, *supra* note 3. This view goes all the way back to Hobbes, if not earlier: absent the requisite global institutions and rule of law, there is no basis for global normative obligations. *See, e.g.*, CHARLES R. BEITZ, POLITICAL THEORY AND INTERNATIONAL RELATIONS 3 (2nd ed., 1999) [hereinafter BEITZ, POLITICAL THEORY].

[5] *See, e.g.*, RAYMOND GEUSS, PHILOSOPHY AND REAL POLITICS (2011) (offering a realist approach to political philosophy as an alternative

One way to challenge this view is to adopt a cosmopolitan approach and assert that there are overarching principles of human dignity that apply even in international relations, regardless of national boundaries and differences in normative traditions, and which have strong redistributive implications.[6] As discussed in the Introduction, a cosmopolitan approach to global justice appears to solve the "global" part, but at the price of assuming a normative consensus or asserting a normative superiority that is problematic in a diverse global context. Another avenue is through a human rights approach to global justice, which reflects cosmopolitanism's claim to universalism to some extent through human rights' status as positive international law. However, in matters of global economic justice, international human rights law is widely considered to be inadequate.[7]

to an ideal theory of rights); STANLEY HOFFMANN, *Ethics and International Affairs*, in DUTIES BEYOND BORDERS 1, 1–43 (1981) (sketching out the limits of moral choice in international relations from the viewpoint of a "Liberal Realist").

[6] For Rawls's view on cosmopolitanism *see, e.g.,* Leif Wenar, *Why Rawls Is not a Cosmopolitan Egalitarian,* in RAWLS' LAW OF PEOPLES: A REALISTIC UTOPIA (R. Martin and D. Reidy, eds., 2006); *but see* Simon Caney, *Survey Article: Cosmopolitanism and the Law of Peoples*, 10 J. POL. PHIL. 95 (2002).

[7] The enforceability and relatively widespread recognition enjoyed by core human rights concerning life and the integrity of the person drop off significantly the further one gets from this core and the closer to economic justice and any redistributive implications. This, too, may be changing however. See KATHERINE G. YOUNG, CONSTITUTING ECONOMIC AND SOCIAL RIGHTS (2012).

Instead, this Liberal Internationalism approach – "Take One" on the question of global justice – embodies a more limited objective, namely, contributing to global justice by holding liberal states accountable abroad to their political principles at home. We can call this a "static" approach, in that it assumes the status quo – states and global international relations as we find them today – and simply seeks to extend states' obligations outward. How does one do this?

A. The Model

1. *Analyzing Liberal State Obligations*
The international work of legal theorist Lea Brilmayer offers us one place to begin. In *Justifying International Acts*, she begins with this question: how are international acts by states justified? Her answer is the so-called vertical thesis: treat the justification of international acts as a question of the legitimacy of state action.[8] For Brilmayer, governmental action extending across international borders is governmental action nonetheless and must be justified normatively in the same manner as domestic action by reference to some form of political theory, or it will lack legitimacy as a state policy. Thus, the authority for transboundary state action is ultimately derived from its justification in domestic political theory.[9]

---

[8] LEA BRILMAYER, JUSTIFYING INTERNATIONAL ACTS 2 (1989).
[9] *Id.* at 22.

Such justification is "vertical," in that it is drawn "upward" from the political norms regulating the underlying relationship between the individual and the relevant political institution.[10] This is in contrast to the traditional "horizontal" approach to the justification of state behavior, which analyzes the ethics of international relations by reference to the norms applicable to co-equal state actors. In other words, in the vertical account, justification comes out of the political morality governing the state's relationship with its own citizens, rather than out of any notion of the morality of a state's relationship to other states.[11]

Brilmayer's theory is a powerful argument for the view that states act within a coherent moral universe, in which the legitimacy of *all* their actions, both domestic and international, derives from their observance of the same set of core political principles. The justification of a state's international acts "must be analyzed by reference to the constituting political theory that grants it authority to act domestically." This is the essence of the Justice as Integrity Mode of discourse, about which more will be said later.[12] Thus, for the

---

[10] *Id.* at 2.

[11] BRILMAYER, *supra* note 8, at 29. In this way, Brilmayer's theory is part of a general shift away from a "society of states" model of international law. *See* Frank J. Garcia, *Globalization and the Theory of International Law*, 11 INT'L LEGAL THEORY 9, 10–12 (2005) [hereinafter Garcia, *Theory of International Law*]. However, as I will further discuss in the conclusion to this chapter, Take One can nevertheless be seen as reinforcing this outmoded view.

[12] *See infra* notes 112 – 116 and accompanying text.

governments of liberal states, this entails that they act as liberal states in their dealings abroad, in the same way their citizens expect them to act as liberal states domestically. Such an understanding could offer liberal states one answer to the charge of legal, political, or cultural imperialism insofar as they seek to enact liberal principles through their unilateral or institutional acts, namely, that they seek merely to act consistently with their own principles. This is one implication of a "Justice as Integrity" mode of discourse.

This leads to the next question: if liberal states must act as liberal states abroad, what does a liberal foreign policy look like? With respect to global justice in particular, what does a liberal foreign policy entail in the area of economic relations and economic justice? According to the vertical thesis, one must begin by reference to the state's domestic liberalism, which for present purposes means its principles of economic justice.

In order to work out one possible model for what a liberal state's foreign policy might look like with respect to economic justice, I will employ Rawls's famous theory of "Justice as Fairness."[13] I have opted for this theory, despite its problematic relationship to the question of justice across borders,[14] for two principal reasons. First, for reasons I have argued elsewhere, I find it to be the most powerful liberal

---

[13] RAWLS, A THEORY OF JUSTICE 3 (2nd rev. ed., 1999) hereinafter, RAWLS, A THEORY OF JUSTICE

[14] As discussed in the Introduction, Rawls does not extend his theory to matters of international justice, and in THE LAW OF PEOPLES he

approach to the central problem of inequality as it affects economic justice, in that it most fully grapples with the liberal dilemma of moral equality and natural inequality.[15] Other liberal theories of justice such as utilitarianism and libertarianism founder in one way or another on this central problem. Second, as discussed in the Introduction, I am not convinced by Rawls's own reasons for refusing to extend his theory to problems of transboundary justice[16]; instead, I find the logic of his argument for domestic justice convincing, regardless of national boundaries.[17]

In the discussion that follows, I will assume familiarity with the outlines of Rawls's basic theory and offer only a summary of its essential features.[18] I will focus the majority of the discussion on noting a few specific issues of significance

is critical of those who do. Instead he opts for a more limited "duty of assistance" on matters of economic justice, which has opened him to considerable criticism. *See* Frank J. Garcia, *The Law of Peoples*, 23 Hous. J. Int'l L. 659 (2001) (book review).

[15] See Frank J. Garcia, Trade, Inequality, and Justice: Toward a Liberal Theory of Just Trade, 110–118 (2003) [hereinafter Garcia, Trade, Inequality, and Justice].

[16] *Id.* at 124–128. This has been a common and constant criticism since The Law of Peoples first came out. *See, e.g.*, Thomas Pogge, *Rawls on International Justice*, 51 The Philosophical Quarterly, 246, 252 (2001).

[17] All the more so if one takes a Brilmayer approach, in which it is precisely the domestic liberalism of a state that furnishes the starting point for its transboundary liberalism. *See* Brilmayer, *supra* note 8, at 22.

[18] I am referring here to the canonical account of his theory of Justice as Fairness in A Theory of Justice.

that arise in the extension of his basic theory to transboundary justice and international trade law, though not of course in a manner that would satisfy Rawls himself.[19]

Rawls is concerned with inequalities that arise in the distribution of social primary goods, such as wealth, status, rights, privileges, and opportunities. Inequalities in the natural distribution of natural primary goods, such as size, strength, brain capacity, and basic health, deeply affect people's life chances but are not themselves the subject of justice because they are arbitrary natural facts; rather, it is how a society responds to such inequalities that forms the basic subject of justice.[20] The fundamental problem of distributive justice is that inequalities in natural primary goods often lead, through the operation of social institutions, to inequalities in the social distribution of social primary goods.[21] In other words, people are morally equal yet socially unequal, often for reasons having to do with these arbitrary natural factors. Rawls's core liberal commitment is that such consequent inequalities in social primary goods are not deserved, since they are deeply influenced by these arbitrary, underlying natural inequalities.

[19] For a fuller discussion of these points, *see* Frank J. Garcia, *Developing a Normative Critique of International Trade Law: Special & Differential Treatment* 5–22 (2010) University of Bremen TranState Working Paper No. 66, 2007, http://www.sfb597.uni-bremen.de/pages/pubApBeschreibung.php?SPRACHE=en&ID=76 [hereinafter Garcia, *Normative Critique*].

[20] *See, e.g.*, RAWLS, A THEORY OF JUSTICE, *supra* note 13, at 100–108.

[21] *Id.* at 72.

Rawls argues that as a result, the basic structure of society must be arranged "so that these contingencies work for the good of the least fortunate."[22] The distribution of natural talents is to be considered a common asset, and society is to be structured so that this asset works for the good of the least well-off. Through his celebrated account of the "Original Position" as a hypothetical problem involving the choice of first principles, Rawls develops this view into the theory of Justice as Fairness. A particularly important element of his theory for our purpose is the "Difference Principle," which states that inequalities in the distribution of social primary goods are justifiable only to the extent they benefit the least advantaged.[23]

Satisfying this criterion could entail a variety of social measures, ranging from altering the structure of public incentives to reward actions that benefit the least advantaged, such as the charitable gifts deduction found in income tax codes, to the outright redistribution of private wealth through progressive tax and welfare legislation. Rawls contends that a society so organized would meet the Kantian imperative of mutual respect: to treat each other as ends and not as means to an end.[24]

So far, this is domestic Rawls – the starting point for determining the foreign policy implications of liberalism. The next step toward Liberal Internationalism involves

[22] *Id.* at 102.
[23] *Id.* at 75.
[24] *Id.* at 179.

adapting the theory for use in an international context, involving, in this case, international economic law. This is the key step in operationalizing a domestic theory of justice into coherent principles to guide a state's foreign policy, within the static framework of Take One. Doing so requires an examination of the basic assumptions of the theory in its domestic context, and evaluating the extent to which those assumptions can be carried over into the international context, or if they need modification in view of the unique social reality of the transboundary environment. We then need to analyze whether the same arguments in favor of the domestic theory can be advanced in favor of its transnational extension.

As stated, the core normative assumption underlying a Rawlsian account of inequality is that differences in natural endowments are undeserved. In Rawls's terms, they are "arbitrary from a moral point of view."[25] Translating this to the international setting, it is important to recognize that inequality works at two levels: on individuals, as in the domestic context, and between states (here considered as territorially associated groups of persons).[26] However, the distinction may be more a matter of emphasis, as states and individuals are both affected in similar ways by the same inequality issues, with negative effect for persons in both cases. Setting aside the cases of migration and conquest,

---

[25] *Id.* at 72.

[26] *See* Garcia, *Normative Critique, supra* note 19, at 7–10.

states and the people born into them must, in general, accept the extent of resources to be found within their territories.[27] Such national boundaries and the resource endowments they encompass have a profound distributional impact on individuals' life prospects.[28] These natural inequalities at both the individual and state levels, the arbitrariness of their distribution, and their profound social consequences, form the subject of justice in a transboundary setting.[29]

[27] The arbitrariness of international borders and the particular resource "bundles" they circumscribe is becoming a key issue in global social policy today. *See generally* FREE MOVEMENT: ETHICAL ISSUES IN THE TRANSNATIONAL MIGRATION OF PEOPLE AND OF MONEY (Brian Barry and Robert E. Goodin, eds., 1992). However, modern forms of overseas economic "expansion" through lease and contract may well be blurring these boundaries, leading to new forms of transboundary national economic resource extraction in a post- (or neo-?) colonial globalizing economy. I am thinking here of the appropriation of large areas of agricultural land in Africa by Korea, Saudi Arabia, and China, among others. *See* John Vidal, *Ethiopia at Centre of Global Farmland Rush*, THE GUARDIAN, March 20, 2011, http://www.guardian.co.uk/world/2011/mar/21/et hiopia-centre-global-farmland-rush; see *also* Javier Perez, Myriam Gistelinck, and Dima Karbala, *Sleeping Lions: International Investment Treaties, State-Investor Disputes and Access to Food, Land and Water,* Oxfam Discussion Paper (May 2011) http://www. oxfam.org/sites/www.oxfam.org/files/dp-sleeping-lions-260511-en. pdf. I am indebted to Fiona Smith for pointing this out.
[28] *See, e.g.*, Thomas W. Pogge, *An Egalitarian Law of Peoples*, 23 PHIL. & PUB. AFF. 195, 198 (1994) (asserting borders have tremendous distributive impact).
[29] Rawls would not agree, as he considers material inequalities primarily the subject of domestic justice. *See* RAWLS, THE LAW OF PEOPLES, *supra* note 2; however, for the reasons I argue elsewhere,

A cosmopolitan approach would proceed on the basis of the inequality effects on individuals, treating inequality between states as either a second-order phenomenon or a complicating factor with respect to addressing the justice of an individual's life circumstances.[30] Instead, the approach taken here focuses primarily on inequality between states, as we are situating global justice primarily in the obligations liberal states owe other states and their citizens – this is the essence of Take One.[31]

For liberal states, the next step is to determine the extent to which their domestic principles of justice must also guide them, and the transnational social institutions they influence, when responding to inequality problems or making distributive allocations that will impact transboundary social inequalities.[32] Put in Rawlsian terms, we must

Rawls's position on the exclusively domestic nature of material inequality is problematic. *See* GARCIA, TRADE, INEQUALITY, AND JUSTICE, *supra* note 15, at 124–128. *But see* Mathias Risse, *How Does the Global Order Harm the Poor?* 33 PHIL. & PUB. AFF. 349 (2005) (offering a defense of Rawls's position in THE LAW OF PEOPLES that domestic institutions are the chief determinant of material inequality).

[30] *See* Caney, *Cosmopolitanism and the Law of Peoples, supra* note 6 (reflecting this approach in his critique of Rawls's treatment of the rights of people of decent societies).

[31] It is also more consistent with Rawls's own approach. *See* 6–8, *supra*; *See, e.g.*, David Boucher, *Uniting What Right Permits with What Interest Prescribes: Rawls Law of Peoples in Context, in* RAWLS' LAW OF PEOPLES, *supra* note 6, at 19–37.

[32] Garcia, *Normative Critique, supra* note 19, at 13.

determine the relationship between the principles of Justice as Fairness developed in a domestic setting, and the issues of transboundary distributive justice.

The heart of the argument is that the principles of justice developed domestically in Justice as Fairness apply in their essential features to transboundary problems of distributive justice.[33] To put the matter in more technical terms, the argument is that Rawls's hypothetical "representatives" in the Original Position would choose the same principles of Justice as Fairness for transboundary issues as they do for domestic issues, because the choice problem is the same.[34]

---

[33] *See* GARCIA, TRADE, INEQUALITY, AND JUSTICE, *supra* note 15, at 131–136. There are of course many complex issues involved in transposing domestic liberalism into a transnational setting, which I have discussed elsewhere and will not recapitulate here. See *Id*. My point is simply that the basic logic of the argument continues to hold at the new level.

[34] Thus simplified, I have glossed over several interesting technical issues. For example, critics and proponents of a Rawlsian approach to international justice have argued whether a second, "international" Original Position is required, which is the approach Rawls takes; or whether the principles chosen in the "domestic" Original Position would, by extension and without further choice, apply to transboundary state action. *See* GARCIA, TRADE, INEQUALITY, AND JUSTICE, *supra* note 15, at 131–133. In TRADE, INEQUALITY AND JUSTICE I opted for a second Original Position as most consistent with Rawls's own (limited) approach to international justice, for reasons germane to my argument there. *Id*. at 132. For the purposes of this chapter and in line with Brilmayer's vertical thesis, it makes more sense to speak in terms of a single Original Position, as the principles of justice chosen there will apply equally to domestic and foreign policy choices.

Under circumstances in which people do not know their particular social and economic position in the world, including what state they will be born into and what resources that state commands, they would choose principles of justice that would maximize the social distribution to the least advantaged individual or state, because they may turn out to be that person or be born into that state.[35]

This has profound implications for the foreign policy of liberal states: they must pursue distributive justice in foreign relations as they do through their domestic institutions. Put another way, liberal states must engage in transboundary acts and policies that satisfy the Difference Principle, as an element of a just foreign policy. They must do so in order to act consistently with their core domestic principles of justice, because the logic of these principles applies with equal force in the transboundary setting.

To state the position this way is not to suggest that the principles of Justice as Fairness can be applied *identically* or *easily* in a transboundary setting. In particular,

---

[35] This is the position taken by the leading proponents of a Rawlsian theory of international distributive justice. *See, e.g.*, BRIAN BARRY, THE LIBERAL THEORY OF JUSTICE 131 (1973) ("I can see no reason why within Rawls' theory the representatives of different countries should not, meeting under the conditions specified, agree on some sort of international maximin"); BEITZ, POLITICAL THEORY, *supra* note 4, at 138 (logic of original position would by analogy lead to choice of a global resource redistribution principle); POGGE, *supra* note 16, at 245 (parties in original position would favor a global economic order sensitive to distributional concerns).

it is not to suggest that a liberal justice approach by itself solves the twin problems of liberal international politics, namely, determining what strategies are necessary to enact principled measures internationally, and what modifications or compromises to such commitments are necessary (and acceptable) in view of the political realities of a fragmented, nonliberal international society.[36] These are formidable problems, but their difficulty does not detract from the transformative significance of accepting ab initio that liberal states *have* liberal foreign policy commitments, however realized or realizable.

2. *Implementing Liberal State Obligations in International Economic Law*

Having established the relevance of Justice as Fairness to international distributive issues as well as domestic ones, the analysis now turns to an examination of the rules and institutions of contemporary international economic law. It is through such rules and institutions that liberal states most deeply affect distributive relationships on a global level, both unilaterally and in concert with other states. The task, then, is to see how these principles apply to liberal states' actions through international economic law.

---

[36] The latter issue was of particular interest to Rawls later in his life, as evidenced by his concern in THE LAW OF PEOPLES with the question of liberal states' duties in the face of hierarchical and illiberal states.

It is impossible to carry out or even thoroughly summarize such an analysis within the confines of this chapter; however I will summarize positions that I and others have argued elsewhere in order to illustrate the reach, and limits, of this approach to justice. I will look first at international trade law, focusing on the subset of rules for developing countries, then at international economic law more broadly, focusing on the conditionality practices of the World Bank and IMF with respect to international development and crisis lending. Through these three examples, I hope to illustrate how an internationalized Justice as Fairness can be the basis for a robust, detailed critique of existing law and can suggest specific reforms in law and institutional practice that liberal states should pursue as a matter of their liberal foreign policy commitments. This is possible, in part, because Justice as Fairness yields a clear, normative benchmark for regulatory policy: are the rules designed so that the social process of allocation they structure works to the benefit of the least advantaged?

a. Liberal Justice and International Trade Law. Once the basic principles of justice have been identified, the next step according to Rawls is "to choose a constitution and a legislature to enact laws, and so on, all in accordance with the principles of justice initially agreed upon."[37] In other words, we create institutions through which to manage

---

[37] RAWLS, *supra* note 13, at 13.

interdependence and cooperation, and distribute the benefits and burdens of such cooperation.

The fact of economic interdependence among the world's societies through the global economy is one element in establishing the possibility of international distributive obligations.[38] In the case of international trade, we also already have the equivalent of a constitution and a legislature, albeit imperfect ones, in the form of international trade law and the GATT/WTO (General Agreement on Tariffs and Trade/World Trade Organization) system.[39] The WTO serves as a forum in which to negotiate new rules, as an agency to oversee the system and facilitate members' cooperation and information exchange, and as a dispute settlement mechanism to adjudicate disputes about the rules and supervise enforcement, which occurs horizontally between members.[40]

As the international trade regulatory system has grown in scope and institutional capacity with the creation and

[38] For example, in his study of the concept of fairness in international law, Thomas Franck concludes that the requisite level of community has emerged at the international level to sustain a fairness analysis. *See* THOMAS FRANCK, FAIRNESS IN INTERNATIONAL LAW 12–13 (1995). I shall have more to say about this in Take Two.

[39] On the constitutional and law-making function of trade institutions, and their shortcomings in this regard, *see* Ernst-Ulrich Petersmann, *Constitutionalism and International Organizations*, 17 Nw. J. INT'L L. & BUS. 398 (1997).

[40] *See e.g.*, Thomas Cottier, *The Legitimacy of WTO Law* (NCCR Trade, Working Paper No. 2008/19, 2008).

growth of the WTO, so too the gains from such social cooperation increase, as do the institutional capabilities for allocative decision making and enforcement of resulting norms.
The need to allocate such benefits raises precisely the same
sorts of issues that are raised in domestic society when such
benefits stand to be allocated.[41] Of course, as a delibera-
tive body composed of state-members, each with their own
domestic principles of justice, the "legislative" task to be
performed through the WTO will be more complex, as will
the process of translating domestic principles of justice into
cooperative action through law and policy. These are the
sorts of issues that make a distributive analysis of international institutions qua institutions – a task outside the scope
of Liberal Internationalism – so necessary.[42] In the present

[41] In a similar sense, Pogge argues that the emergence of a single
global institutional scheme involving both international law and
territorial states, has made all human rights violations "at least
potentially everyone's concern." Thomas Pogge, *Cosmopolitanism
and Sovereignty*, 103 ETHICS, 48, 51 (1992). *But see* Samuel
Freeman, *Distributive Justice and The Law of Peoples, in* RAWLS'
LAW OF PEOPLES: A REALISTIC UTOPIA? 243, 247 (Rex Martin and
David Reidy, eds., 2006) (characterizing these institutions as "secondary" in nature and not a global basic structure).

[42] *See* Frank J. Garcia, *Evaluating IMF Crisis Prevention as a Matter
of Global Justice*, 14 ILSA J. INT'L & COMP. L. 467 (2007–2008);
Andrew G. Brown and Robert M. Stern, *Fairness in the WTO
Trading System* (IPC Working Paper Series No. 109, 2010). An
institutional distributive analysis certainly complements Take
One, but the focus would be on distributive obligations on these
institutions by virtue of their functions, rather than on the distributive obligations of their controlling states, which do or do not
honor these obligations in how they manage these institutions.

context, I believe the phenomenon of translating principles of justice into law and policy through a political process is similar enough at both the domestic Rawlsian level and this transnational context for the extension to hold.[43]

Looking at this regulatory system from a liberal perspective offers some important insights into the requirements of global justice through a Take One approach. One key conclusion is that justice requires liberal states to support free trade, but that free trade alone is not enough for a just global economic order. The core normative commitment of contemporary trade law is to the principle of free trade: that international economic relations are to be free, or as free as possible, from governmental restrictions in the form of tariff and nontariff barriers, and nondiscriminatory with respect to country of origin (the most-favored-nation rule) and domestic origin (the national treatment rule).[44] The starting point, therefore, in the elaboration of a liberal theory of trade policy is to examine whether, from a normative point of view, this commitment to free trade is justifiable.[45]

[43] It might be that such a process, sifting as it will among different states' conceptions of justice and arriving through politics at a consensus or compromise policy, is in fact an essential element in developing shared global understandings about justice or the sort of "thin" morality Walzer writes about, but that is more properly the concern of Take Two. *See infra* Take Two and Conclusion.

[44] For a clear and concise overview, *see* MICHAEL J. TREBILCOCK & ROBERT HOWSE, THE REGULATION OF INTERNATIONAL TRADE 20–38 (3d ed., 2005).

[45] The discussion that follows is drawn from Garcia, *Normative Critique*, *supra* note 19, at 13–15.

One can deduce from the principles of Justice as Fairness that a well-ordered society requires free trade as a policy.[46] First, we can argue from Rawls's first principle of justice, the Principle of Equal Liberty,[47] that the freedom to make economic decisions as purchaser and consumer would be best protected by a system in which all had equal liberty with respect to such decisions, without interference from government-imposed restrictions and distortions.[48] Tariff and nontariff barriers interfere with such liberty because the market effects of such public interventions distort purchasing and producing decisions.

Free trade can therefore be expressed as a basic commitment to protect such freedom on the part of producers and consumers, by reducing or eliminating such interference. To this extent, a Rawlsian view of just trade is consistent with other liberal theories, such as libertarianism.[49] In Rawlsian terms, with respect to international economic activity, free trade guarantees "an equal right to the most

[46] For an alternative approach justifying free trade as an actual principle of justice chosen in a Rawlsian original position, *see* Ethan B. Kapstein, *Distributive Justice and International Trade*, 13 ETHICS & INT'L AFF. 175, 175–182 (1999).

[47] "[E]ach person is to have an equal right to the most extensive basic liberty compatible with a similar liberty for others." RAWLS, A THEORY OF JUSTICE, *supra* note 13, at 60.

[48] This is consistent with the requirements of Rawls's first principle of justice, which while focused more on political liberties, embraces rights to private property and freedom from unlawful interference.

[49] GARCIA, TRADE, INEQUALITY, AND JUSTICE, 105–106.

extensive basic liberty compatible with a similar liberty for others."[50] Most-favored-nation status and national treatment function as corollary doctrines guaranteeing that such liberty is equal with respect to producers and consumers in all countries.[51]

But adherence to the full extent of the principles of Justice as Fairness also requires evaluation of free trade in distributive terms. Rawls's second principle of justice, the Difference Principle, requires that inequalities in the distribution of social primary goods be justified by their contribution to the well-being of the least advantaged. This implies for trade policy that free trade is not enough. The reason for this is the problem of inequality and its effects on trade relations.

Rawls understood that given a world of natural inequality with respect to attributes such as intelligence, strength, and speed, a pure system of open competition for social goods would not result in a pattern of distribution consistent with our moral equality.[52] Similarly, the natural inequality in the global distribution of natural resources leads, through a complex variety of domestic and international private and public actions and institutions, to social inequalities in wealth, privileges, rights, and opportunities among states and, by extension, their citizens.[53]

[50] See RAWLS, A THEORY OF JUSTICE, *supra* note 13, at 60–61.

[51] Kapstein, *supra* note 46, at 188–189.

[52] See RAWLS, A THEORY OF JUSTICE, *supra* note 13, at 10–14

[53] Garcia, *Normative Critique, supra* note 19, at 20.

Using comparative economic size as a marker for such inequalities, empirical studies suggest that the size of an economy does matter, and that these inequalities are not, on the whole, working for the benefit of the least advantaged – it is actually quite the reverse.[54] Smaller economies are the most vulnerable to adverse changes to their trade patterns in the global economy, and to adverse changes in the pattern of economic regulation in the international economic law system, therefore, they face the most obstacles to economic development and effective competition.

In light of these facts, applying Justice as Fairness to international trade leads to a very basic question that liberal states must address in their international economic relations: given the fact of inequality and its adverse effects on the least advantaged (the smallest economies and the people living in them), how can the international economic system be restructured to ensure that such inequalities work to the benefit of the least advantaged?

Framing the question in this way is one of the core benefits of the Take One approach, and answering this question would naturally lead to a comprehensive review of the structure and operation of trade law from top to bottom, both its substantive rules and its negotiation and decision-making procedures, with this metric in mind. One could in fact understand much of contemporary trade law scholarship around topics such as development, fairness, and legitimacy

[54] *Id.*

as explicitly or implicitly carrying out just such a review.[55] Here, I want to look only at a particular subset of trade rules, known as Special and Differential Treatment (S&D), to both evaluate their role in this larger project of justification and illustrate the application of this theory and approach to justice in economic law matters.[56]

At the core of S&D is the practice of asymmetric trade liberalization, involving the terms on which states allow access to their markets and expect access in return. S&D attempts to secure the benefits of social inequality in developed countries, in the form of the wealth and resources of their markets, for the least advantaged states, through preferential market access which is granted unilaterally under a multilaterally approved exception to GATT/WTO rules.[57]

---

[55] *See, e.g.,* Sonia E. Rolland, Development at the WTO (2012); Bernard Hoekman, *Operationalizing the Concept of Policy Space in the WTO: Beyond Special and Differential Treatment*, 8 J. Int'l Econ. L. 405 (2005).

[56] *See* Garcia, Trade, Inequality, and Justice, *supra* note 15, at 155–162. S&D has been criticized as ineffective or worse. *See* Jeffery L. Dunoff, *Dysfunction, Diversion and the Debate over Preferences: (How) Do Preferential Trade Policies Work?* in Developing Countries in the WTO Legal System 45 (Chantal Thomas and Joel R. Trachtman, eds., 2009). Nevertheless, it represents the sole systematic effort within trade law to address the problem of inequality on a structural level.

[57] *Differential and More Favourable Treatment, Reciprocity and Fuller Participation of Developing Countries*, L/4903 (November 28, 1979), GATT B.I.S.D. (26th Supp.) at 203 (1980) (establishing the Enabling Clause); *Generalized System of Preferences,* L/3545 (June 25, 1971) GATT B.I.S.D. (18th Supp.) at 24 (1972) (adopting

That is, states with larger economies allow access into their wealthier markets to states with smaller economies, on terms that are both preferential and nonreciprocal. These terms are preferential in that access is on better terms than those received by other larger economies; they are nonreciprocal in that the larger economies granting the concessions do not expect equivalent concessions from smaller economies in return.

It is this asymmetry that enables S&D to play a key role in justifying inequalities in the international allocation of social goods.[58] By opening their markets to exports from smaller economies on a preferential basis, large economies in effect place the consumption power of their larger, richer consumer market at the service of the smaller economies, which can increase their exports and thereby strengthen their economic base.[59] Thus, preferential market access for developing countries allows the inequalities that manifest themselves in the form of wealthy consumer markets in certain states to work to the benefit of the least advantaged,

the first GSP waiver). *See, e.g.,* Donald H. Regan, *What Are Trade Agreements For? – Two Conflicting Stories Told by Economists, With a Lesson for Lawyers,* 9 J. INT'L ECON. L. 951 (2006).

[58] Market access is managed through the two principal components of S&D: market access preferences and market protection mechanisms. In this chapter, I will focus on the market access branch of S&D. For an evaluation of market protection mechanisms, as well as the wealth transfer aspects of S&D, *see* GARCIA, TRADE, INEQUALITY, AND JUSTICE, *supra* note 15, at 67–86.

[59] Garcia, *Normative Critique, supra* note 19, at 23.

thereby meeting the central criteria for liberal distributive justice.

In the form of S&D, the international economic law system thus already incorporates laws, policies, and social norms that can function as redistributive mechanisms and that, in normative terms, can therefore serve as the basis for liberal states discharging their duty to work toward a just international trade law. Liberal Internationalism would therefore require liberal states (quite often also the states with these larger, richer domestic markets) to establish, maintain, and reform such policies unilaterally and through their managing role in multilateral institutions such as the WTO.[60] This is the cornerstone of the theory of Justice as Fairness, as applied through Take One to international trade rules in the context of economic inequality.

Having determined this basic obligation, the stage is now set for a detailed normative analysis and review of existing unilateral trade preferences and multilateral trade laws for their consistency with this mandate. This is the logical next step that this kind of normative analysis makes possible, and although such a review is not the subject of this book, the outlines of such an analysis will be sketched here. While S&D as currently embodied in unilateral preference programs plays an important role in justifying inequalities, a Rawlsian analysis also reveals how much work still needs to be done to craft international trade rules

[60] *Id.*

that truly satisfy the core requirement of a liberal theory of justice; namely, that social inequalities work to the benefit of the least advantaged. In case after case, the details of the rules and how they operate actually subvert the normative purpose and basic framework of such rules, working to the benefit of the most advantaged states instead of the least advantaged.[61] Thus Take One illuminates both the duties of liberal states in this regard, and their persistent failures.

Taking the U.S. GSP (Generalized System of Preferences) program as an example, it is structured as a discretionary, unilateral program and not a binding obligation on the part of the United States, as is the case with most GSP benefit programs. Instrumentally, extending trade preferences through unilateral programs is questionable on several grounds. To begin with, this format renders them inherently unstable because as programs they are subject to periodic renewal, and within each program the beneficiaries must continually requalify for the preferences. These uncertainties create problems for business and investment planners on both sides of the preference. The uncertainty surrounding both periodic qualification decisions and decisions concerning continuation of the program has also – understandably – led to criticism from beneficiary countries that they remain in dependent relationships subject to the whim of the granting state.[62]

[61] *See* GARCIA, TRADE, INEQUALITY, AND JUSTICE, *supra* note 15, at 147–192.
[62] *Id.* at 156–167.

When looked at from the perspective of the Difference Principle, the unilateralism of existing trade preference programs is even more inappropriate. If a state has an obligation to justify its own social advantages, and the mechanism it chooses is to place the strength of its consumer market at the service of the least advantaged states through preferences, then it is difficult to justify the decision that such an obligation should be effectuated through an optional mechanism in the sole discretion of the advantaged state. The structure of the policy is not consistent with its underlying normative purpose.

Moreover, these deviations from the normative benchmark are not the sort that can be justified by political circumstances, that is, they do not reflect necessary compromises to secure essential policies; rather, they represent self-serving modifications under the guise of other-focused programs.[63] To take one example, the rules governing which goods are eligible for trade preferences (central to the benefits of S&D) establish criteria that have more to do with the domestic industries and foreign policy goals of the granting state than they do the economic needs of the beneficiary state. In U.S. GSP practice, actual availability of the preferences at any given time is subject to a wide variety of conditions imposed by the granting state, such as the disavowal of communism, cooperation with regional anti-narcotics efforts, and the offer of assurances by the beneficiary that

[63] *Id.*

it will provide the United States "equitable and reasonable access to the markets and basic commodity resources" of the beneficiary.[64]

Such conditions are normatively unjustifiable and have nothing to do with necessary accommodations of these policies to facts on the ground. Instead, the nature of these conditions suggests that the policy actually protects and advances the foreign policy agenda of the granting state rather than ensuring the benefits of inequality flow to the least advantaged, turning their normative justification on its head. To condition preferences on the basis of a failure to meet such conditions is to directly subvert the principle of justice, which should on this approach inform the trade policy of liberal states.

This brief analysis of the structure of S&D under WTO law illustrates some of the advantages of approaching justice as a foreign policy obligation of liberal states, and some of the weaknesses inherent in Take One. Individual states often have significant, indeed tremendous, economic impact on the circumstances of other states and people, and formulating the justice obligations applicable to such states' trade policies and foreign economic relations can harness

---

[64] *E.g.*, DESIGNATION OF BENEFICIARY DEVELOPING COUNTRIES, 19 U.S.C. § 2462 (c)(4) (2011). For such reasons, Argentina is no longer a GSP beneficiary due to the Azurix arbitration award dispute – Argentinian courts did not enforce the award and the investor petitioned the president under Sec 301 of the Trade Act of 1974.

powerful economic dynamics for good, as with the principles behind S&D. Moreover, the fact that domestic justice
theory is (comparatively) well understood allows us a rich
base of theory to draw on in evaluating transnational laws
and policies according to familiar justice metrics such as
the Difference Principle. However, the unilateralism of this
approach is too close to the kind of political unilateralism,
and latent *realpolitik*, that render ostensibly justice-oriented
policies so often mere exercises in instrumental calculation
and self-serving political agendas.

I will say more about this in conclusion, but first I want
to turn to other aspects of international economic relations
and examine the issues that arise when states work through
multilateral institutions outside the trading system, to illustrate how the analysis works in other areas of international
economic law.

b. Liberal States and the Bretton Woods Institutions. The basic
analysis set out here in Take One is not limited to trade
law or to unilateral state action such as preferences but can
be applied to any aspect of international economic law in
which states act either unilaterally or through international
institutions to influence distributive outcomes. For example,
one can also apply Justice as Fairness to the work of the
Bretton Woods institutions – the International Monetary
Fund and the World Bank – in order to determine what
responsibilities liberal states might have within such

institutions to influence their policies so as to benefit the least advantaged.[65]

The World Bank consists of several interrelated institutions and affiliates which collectively I will refer to as the "Bank." The Bank carries out its core lending functions through two institutions, the oldest of which is the International Bank for Reconstruction and Development (IBRD). Created in 1945 to help finance the reconstruction of Europe after World War II, its mission quickly broadened into supporting development investment on a global scale through what is often considered the Bank's core activity, development lending at preferential (but near-commercial) rates. The second lending institution, the International Development Association (IDA), was created in 1960 to focus on assisting the World Bank's poorest clients through concessional (zero-interest) lending and outright grants; it shares the same office, staff, and project evaluation standards as the IBRD.[66]

The International Monetary Fund (the Fund) was created to bring stability to the exchange rate system and,

---

[65] The discussion which follows draws from my chapter on *Justice, the Bretton Woods Institutions and the Problem of Inequality, in* THE FUTURE OF INTERNATIONAL ECONOMIC LAW 23 (William J. Davey and John Jackson, eds., 2008).

[66] BAHRAM GHAZI, THE IMF, THE WORLD BANK GROUP AND THE QUESTION OF HUMAN RIGHTS 24–26 (2005). However, the two institutions differ in important ways when it comes to their source of funds. The IBRD finances its lending activities primarily through sales of bonds on the international capital market, whereas the IDA is funded primarily through donations from member states.

in general, to facilitate cooperation on international monetary matters in the wake of the Great Depression. The exchange rate aspects of its operation changed significantly in the 1970s when first the United States and then other states abandoned the so-called Bretton Woods system of gold-pegged exchange rates. Today, the core of its operations involves monitoring and intervening in the global distribution of currencies states need to satisfy external financial obligations.[67] The Fund engages in short- and medium-term lending in response to balance-of-payments difficulties (with accompanying Fund "conditions" involving domestic policy reforms), although the Fund also continues to monitor and investigate member states' exchange rate policies, and work to encourage members to remove any exchange controls.[68] The Fund carries out this lending through a variety of distinct lending programs or "facilities," each with different terms and conditions suited to different categories of borrowers in different types of needs.[69]

---

[67] The Fund has also tried to reinvent itself as a crisis lender or crisis preventer with respect to macroeconomic problems not directly related to balance-of-payments problems (such as the current global financial crisis), with limited success. *See* Garcia, *Evaluating IMF Crisis Prevention as a Matter of Global Justice, supra* note 42; Jonathan T. Fried & James A. Haley, *Crisis Prevention: The International Agenda* (2007) (unpublished manuscript, on file with the author).

[68] S. Hagan, *IMF General Counsel*, Proceedings of the 93rd Annual Meeting, ASIL (March 24–27, 1999).

[69] The IMF's activities are funded from both member states' quota subscriptions, and from the IMF's own line of credit with banks and governments. Ghazi, *supra* note 66.

Despite their central importance to the global economy, the work of these two institutions is significantly under-theorized from a normative point of view.[70] Further research is needed along two dimensions: theorizing the distributive justice obligations applying to the Bank and Fund directly, as allocative institutions; and analyzing the distributive aspects of Bank and Fund operations in order to determine the distributive obligations of states-members acting through the Bank and Fund. I am here concerned with the latter, specifically using Justice as Fairness to develop normative guidelines for liberal states as they discharge their governance role within the Bank and the Fund with respect to specific policy choices and operational decisions.[71] This requires, first, that we characterize the work of both institutions with respect to their distributive roles in transnational economic relations.[72]

---

[70] *See, e.g.,* Sanjay G. Reddy, *Just International Monetary Arrangements, in* GLOBAL INSTITUTIONS AND RESPONSIBILITIES 218, 218 (Christian Barry & Thomas W. Pogge, eds., 2005) ("[D]espite the acknowledged centrality of monetary arrangements in modern economies, they have received surprisingly little attention from philosophers concerned with distributive justice, whether in the national or the global context"); Ghazi, *supra* note 66.

[71] Much of the analysis of Bank and Fund structure and operation would be germane for both, but here the task is to focus on the obligations of the managing liberal states, not the institutions themselves. For preliminary moves toward the latter, *see* Frank Garcia, *Global Justice and the Bretton Woods Institutions*, 10 J. INT'L ECON. L 481 (2007) [hereafter Garcia, *Global Justice and the Bretton Woods Institutions*].

[72] It is difficult to properly evaluate the morality of a state's foreign policy without a clear understanding of the moral framework

The core operational commitment of both the Bank and the Fund, and therefore the appropriate policy nexus in which to apply Justice as Fairness, is lending – development lending in the case of the Bank, and financial crisis/balance of payments lending in the case of the Fund. Therefore, developing a theory of liberal state obligations with respect to international development and currency lending when such states act through multilateral institutions will involve analyzing the lending activities, terms and policies of the Bank and the Fund with reference to liberal distributive justice criteria.

The key in both cases is to recognize the allocative role of these institutions. Both the Bank and the Fund are social institutions created and managed by states, through which states (at least the governing states) manage the allocation of primary social goods: development capital and the terms of access to such capital through the Bank; and currency reserves and the terms of access to such reserves through the Fund. Through both institutions, states are managing social resources that are not the unique provenance of any one state, even a wealthy state.[73]

of the institutions through which it acts. *See* Nancy Kokaz, *Theorizing International Fairness*, *in* GLOBAL INSTITUTIONS AND RESPONSIBILITIES 65, 71–72 (Christian Barry & Thomas W. Pogge, eds., 2005).

[73] This characterization emphasizes these institutions' derivative, functional nature as state instrumentalities, as befits the Take One focus on state-level obligations. An institutional justice analysis would emphasize the allocative decision making of the institutions

To take the work of the Bank as an example, development capital is a socially produced resource. A country's supply of development capital reflects a complex blend of natural and social factors. It reflects the country's natural resource endowment and the complex blend of its history, its domestic policies, and its international economic and political relations, all of which affect the capacity of the system to generate surplus capital for development and the amounts of such capital. Moreover, under natural conditions, states will be in a condition of dynamic instability with respect to the supply of development capital: at a given point they will either have too much, too little, or just enough. Few if any states can safely assume they can be entirely self-sufficient in the matter of development capital.

All of the foregoing leads to a rational policy choice for states: it is useful to create an international market for development capital. Through such a market, development capital can be made available, in the form of investment capital and lending capital from private banks, at rates set by the market. Such a market serves the self-interests of borrowers and lenders alike. Lending states put their surplus capital to work, generating interest and future economic opportunities for themselves, as well as contributing to stability in foreign relations through support for other states' development

themselves as a basis for their own independent obligations to do justice. *See generally* Andrew Hurrell, *Global Inequality and International Institutions*, 32 METAPHILOSOPHY 34 (2001) (discussing allocative role of such institutions).

aspirations. Borrowing states have access to levels of development capital they could not develop domestically.

However, because of the facts of inequality, just as reciprocal market access would not in all cases benefit the least advantaged states with respect to international trade, so too in the case of development capital a private market alone would not be equally beneficial to all states. Due to the same kinds of natural and social inequalities that affect a state's capacity to generate development capital, not all states can afford to borrow sufficient development capital to meet their needs on commercial terms in the private market. For this sort of reason, states created the Bank, which draws its capital from the same sources (in the case of the IBRD through bond sales to the private market), but is institutionally oriented to meet the specific development lending needs of less wealthy states and can lend on other than commercial terms.[74]

As with the Bank, the Fund is a social institution, through which states raise and allocate a primary social good (also a form of wealth): global currency reserves and the terms of access to such reserves. Globally valuable currencies that states need to satisfy their external obligations are an exhaustible social resource.[75] As with market size

[74] For example, the conditions set out in Article 3 section 4 of the IBRD Articles of Agreement reflect the particular needs and available credit resources of states.

[75] *Accord* Rosa Maria Lastra, *The International Monetary Fund in Historical Perspective*, 3 J. INT'L ECON. L.507, 516 (2000) (Fund

in the case of trade and capital supply in the case of development, the socioeconomic factors that influence both the market's determination of which currencies are "hard" and which are "soft" and the type of currency in which a country's external debts will be denominated, reflect a complex blend of natural and social inequalities. These include the arbitrary distribution of natural resources and good or bad luck, and contingent social factors such as sound or unsound policy choices, historic patterns of economic development, or exploitation or oppression, all of which culminate in which states are the borrowers, and which states are the lenders.

The fact that certain currencies are globally in demand and others are not necessarily creates inequalities in the distribution of such currencies, essentially rooted in the fact that currencies are national in nature. Those states whose currencies are preferred have a built-in advantage in the supply of that currency[76] and a capacity to self-generate (to

resources are finite hence their use is subject to oversight). While it is true that countries whose currencies are hard could in theory print more money, it is in the very nature of hard currency countries that they not pursue such policies or risk the tradability of their currency. Therefore, hard currency is in essence exhaustible even for hard currency countries.

[76] The fact that in today's floating exchange rate environment most currencies are freely convertible does not itself alter the preference on the part of international firms and central banks for those currencies considered "hard" when seeking reserve currencies or the settlement of trade debts. Thus, the demand for such currencies continues, and with it the genesis of balance-of-payments problems, and the advantage which those jurisdictions have in supplying their own demand for it.

a point), whereas those states whose currencies are not preferred are always at risk of scarcity and cannot create this resource endogenously.[77] More fundamentally, however, differences in the demand for certain currencies reflect underlying inequalities that tend to make certain states the lenders and their firms the exporters, and others the borrowers and importers. These inequalities include natural resource distribution, luck, and domestic policy choices, as well as broader contingent historic factors such as the colonial legacy of the global economic system, all of which contribute to inequalities in the demand for certain currencies and their supply.

The core function of the Bank and the Fund with respect to such resources is to manage their allocation among client states through their lending decisions and policies. This intimately involves states managing the Bank and the Fund in distributive justice concerns, since these lending decisions and policies reflect the decisions, policies, objectives, and leadership of the managing states. Liberal Internationalism means that states managing the Bank and the Fund must therefore ask themselves by what principles and rules these social goods are allocated and for whose benefit, as a function of their own normative commitments.

With trade law, we looked at the function of market access for exports; here, in view of the Bank's and Fund's roles as

---

[77] I am setting aside for the moment the issue of whether by making better policy choices they could harden their currency. This would not in any case deal with natural inequalities or historical contingencies.

lenders, we focus on client access to development capital and currency reserves.[78] As an initial matter, each state's access to development capital and reserve currencies is a function of national treasuries and central banks, supplemented by commercial banks, private capital, and currency markets at national and global levels. However, a state's supply of both resources reflects natural inequalities that are morally arbitrary, compounded by social inequalities. For this reason, the key normative implication of extending Justice as Fairness to such resource lending is that states do not in a significant sense *deserve* their relative supply of development capital and currency reserves.[79] This means that

[78] Hockett suggests a further theoretical link between justice and lending, or as he puts it between justice theory and finance theory, on an insurance model, namely, that both involve risk allocation under conditions of uncertainty. *See* Robert Hockett, *From "Mission Creep" to Gestalt Switch: Justice, Finance, the IFIs, and Globalization's Intended Beneficiaries*, 37 GEO. WASH. INT'L L. REV. 167, 179–181 (2005).

[79] I recognize this is a strong argument, and I refer skeptical readers to my fuller discussion in Garcia, *Global Justice and the Bretton Woods Institutions*, *supra* note 71. I also recognize that in making this argument, I must also face the problem of how to account for the fact that good social policy choices contribute to an abundance of development capital and a globally valued currency, or in other words the problem of ambition-sensitivity transposed into institutional distributive theory. *See* GARCIA, TRADE, INEQUALITY, AND JUSTICE, *supra* note 15, at 61. Hockett, for example, suggests in this regard that global distributive justice by BWIs should focus on what he calls "ethically exogenous" benefits and burdens only. *See* Hockett, *supra* note 78, at 193.

states cannot be presumptively entitled to (or consigned to) their own particular supply of development capital and hard currencies, and that resulting inequalities in the distribution of development capital and hard currencies must be justified.

This has significant implications for how liberal states should structure the Bank's and Fund's roles as development and crisis lenders. The Bank and Fund exist to make capital and currencies available to states that for one reason or another cannot meet their needs through their own economic activities, with their own public finances, or through the private lending and currency markets.[80] Therefore, for the Bank the question is whether the terms on which the Bank lends and manages development capital benefit the least advantaged. With respect to the Fund, this means evaluating whether its currency lending and intervention policies benefit the least advantaged.

Taking the Fund as an example (an illustration that, *mutatis mutandis*, applies equally to the Bank), the currency reserves that the Fund manages and the terms of access to these reserves through its various facilities are themselves a social resource. By making reserve currencies available on near-commercial terms to the economies of states without adequate indigenous supplies of such currencies, the

---

[80] *See* Hockett, *supra* note 78, at 193 (existing necessity of both markets, and justice, to the possibility for international financial institutions to deliver on their social promise).

Fund is conferring a benefit on less advantaged states.[81] However, whenever there is a general economic crisis or a country-specific crisis, it is much harder for certain states to generate or borrow such currencies. Moreover, the demand for such currencies exceeds currency-poor states' ability to pay commercial rates, so if the only access to reserve currencies was through private banks at commercial rates, economic opportunities would go unrealized.[82]

This brings us to the issue of the *terms* on which the Fund makes hard currency available. The Fund offers two basic types of facilities: "regular" or non-concessional facilities, which are not in fact loans but purchase and repurchase agreements[83]; and concessional facilities, which are truly currency loans to developing countries.[84] In other words, the terms on which the Fund makes its currencies available through regular facilities (preferential rates), and the terms on which the Fund makes its currencies available through

---

[81] JOHN W. HEAD, THE FUTURE OF THE GLOBAL ECONOMIC ORGANIZATIONS: AN EVALUATION OF CRITICISMS LEVELED AT IMF, THE MULTILATERAL DEVELOPMENT BANKS, AND THE WTO, 95–96 (2005).

[82] Exporting states would lose sales, importing states would lose much-needed goods and services, and less advantaged states would be tempted to employ currency controls, devaluations, and other tools destabilizing the international monetary system to the detriment of all.

[83] *See* HEAD, supra note 82, at 24 (describing operation of SBA and EFF purchase/repurchase obligations).

[84] *See* Rosa Maria Lastra, *The International Monetary Fund in Historical Perspective, supra* note 75.

concessional facilities (concessional rates) are themselves a further socially produced, and socially allocated, resource.

In this sense, the Fund's regular facilities lending is similar to the principle of free trade in the WTO and to the Bank's preferential lending through the IBRD – helping to equalize opportunities to access currencies in a manner consistent with the basic requirements of Justice as Fairness. However, just as with trade it was the case that a system of purely free trade was not enough due to the facts of inequality, so too the global lending system would be inadequate if it consisted of pure private market currency and lending transactions, or even a blended system of private bank commercial currency transactions and Fund preferential lending, or private commercial lending and preferential lending through the IBRD. Because developing countries have limited domestically generated supplies of capital and reserve currencies and limited resources to borrow such resources at or near market rates, they cannot get enough through these avenues to satisfy their development needs, meaning that the overall inequality in capital and currency supplies will not work to their advantage.

Continuing the analogy to free trade, private market and preferential lending are therefore necessary, but not sufficient, for international justice. It is not enough that capital and currencies be made available even at below-commercial terms. The Difference Principle asks that such resources be made available under such terms and in such a manner that it benefits the *least* advantaged.

Put in terms of the Difference Principle, this suggests for the Fund that to be consistent with liberal principles as applied to currency lending, states managing the Fund must ensure that access to hard currencies benefit the least advantaged by offering concessional access to development capital. The Fund's concessional facilities consist of the Poverty Reduction and Growth Facilities (PRGFs), which replaced the earlier Structural Adjustment Program(s) (SAPs) and Enhanced SAPs, and charge only 0.5% interest per year.[85] These PRGFs are, in the balance-of-payments lending context, the structural analogue to the WTO's Special and Differential Treatment policies in trade: concessional access to reserve currencies as a tool for justifying inequality. They represent that specific aspect of the Fund's activity that most directly addresses the inequality in the distribution of hard currencies from the perspective of the least advantaged. The liberal states managing the Fund must therefore see to it that this most valuable social good – concessional access to hard currencies – is in fact structured so as to benefit the least advantaged.

With respect to the Bank's role in development capital lending, the same argument means that to justify inequalities in the distribution of development capital, liberal states must ensure that access to development capital is structured so as to benefit the least advantaged. In this respect, it is significant that the Bank's activities are divided between

---

[85] *Id.* at 519–20.

the IBRD and the IDA, as it is the IDA's programs that have the most potential for justifying inequalities in development capital.

The IDA's specific mission is to make development capital available to the least advantaged states on deeply preferential terms, involving concessional lending and outright grants. IDA credits are typically repaid on a very long term (35–40 years), with a 10-year grace period on any principal repayment.[86] Complementing IDA lending is the initiative for Heavily Indebted Poor Countries, or HIPC, which consists of outright loan forgiveness for the most heavily indebted countries as their IDA credits become due.[87]

IDA grants and credits, therefore, constitute a particular social resource allocated by states exclusively through the Bank: concessionary access to development capital. Moreover, HIPC loan forgiveness itself is a social resource as well.[88] In distributive terms, liberal states must see to

---

[86] GHAZI, *supra* note 66, at 26.

[87] *(HIPC) The Enhanced Heavily Indebted Poor Countries Initiative*, WORLDBANK.ORG, http://web.worldbank.org/WBSITE/EXTERNAL/TOPICS/EXTDEBTDEPT/0,,contentMDK:20260411~menuPK:64166739~pagePK:64166689~piPK:64166646~theSitePK:469043,00.html (last updated March 13, 2012) (Bank initiative providing debt relief to the world's poorest nations).

[88] The creation of HIPC is part of an overall trend in Bank lending toward poverty reduction. Since the 1960s the Bank has shifted its resources more toward poverty reduction and the poorest countries (Ghazi estimates from 37% of total average commitments before 1968 to 61.3% in 1989–90). However, as Ghazi points out, during that time and since, inequality has increased as a function

it that these very limited and valuable social resources are themselves allocated in a manner that benefits the least advantaged. In this sense, in the lending context, the IDA's policies and programs are the structural analogue to the WTO's Special and Differential Treatment policies reviewed in the trade justice analysis earlier – concessional access to capital as a tool for justifying inequality.

Having determined the basic obligations applying to liberal states when directing Bank and Fund lending, the stage is now set for a detailed normative analysis and review of existing lending practices for their consistency with this mandate. A thorough evaluation of the justice of Bank and Fund operations, and therefore a thorough evaluation of liberal state obligations in the area of international monetary policy, would require taking these general principles and deepening the analysis through a program-by-program evaluation of Bank and Fund operations: are they in fact structured to benefit the least advantaged, and do they in fact operate this way? And if not, what kinds of positions and reforms must liberal states therefore adopt and advocate? This is the logical next step that this kind of normative analysis makes possible for economic law more broadly, and while such a review is outside the scope of this book, I will illustrate this approach with an example.[89]

of globalization, so the policies are certainly not enough and may not be working. GHAZI, *supra* note 66, at 76.

[89] *See* Garcia, *Justice, the Bretton Woods Institutions and the Problem of Inequality, supra* note 71.

In this chapter, as with S&D in my discussion of trade, I am going to focus on one aspect of international lending activity: involvement by the Bank and the Fund in the domestic policies of borrowing states, or conditionality.[90] Consistent with their prudential obligations, the Bank and the Fund have a role in evaluating the degree to which the domestic social policies of borrowing states are themselves part of the capital shortage or fiscal crisis bringing them to these institutions and the degree to which such policies risk squandering Bank and Fund assets, which are exhaustible social resources.[91]

Despite this demonstrably prudential role, conditionality has been one of the most controversial aspects of both Bank and Fund operations. The conditions the Fund imposes, for example, as a cost of its intervention have a tremendous impact on the domestic policies and development strategies of recipient countries.[92] Such conditions can include reforms to such sensitive domestic policies as wage

[90] Other promising areas include the Fund's mission and priorities, its system for allocating special drawing rights (SDRs), its decision-making structure, and its system for choosing and evaluating projects. *See* Garcia, *Evaluating IMF Crisis Prevention as a Matter of Global Justice, supra* note 42; *see generally* HEAD, *supra* note 82 (summarizing critiques).

[91] This is the "coercive" aspect of Fund operations. GHAZI, *supra* note 66; Hockett, *supra* note 78, at 195.

[92] *See generally* Ngaire Woods, *Order, Globalization and World Politics*, in INEQUALITY, GLOBALIZATION AND WORLD POLITICS 8, 30–33 (Andrew Hurrell and Ngaire Woods, eds., 1999) (surveying impact of IMF).

rates and public expenditures.[93] Criticism is largely due to two factors: the leverage the Fund has by virtue of its role to insist on domestic policy reforms,[94] and the controversy surrounding the soundness and ideological basis of the Fund's approach to domestic policy.[95]

Although both the Bank and the Fund have begun to acknowledge shortcomings in their conditionality programs,[96] Justice as Fairness requires that liberal states go further than a mere recognition of problems in the implementation of Bank and Fund policies – they must work to re-cast Bank and Fund policies such as conditionality according to the basic benchmark of Justice as Fairness: they must ensure that Bank and Fund involvement in the domestic policy of borrowers operates to the benefit of the least advantaged.

Taking the Bank as an example, candidates for the Bank's program for Heavily Indebted Poor Countries have

---

[93] *See generally* GHAZI, *supra* note 66, at 16–17.

[94] *But see* HEAD, *supra* note 82, at 75 (downplaying the leverage aspects of conditionality in view of borrowing countries' formal right to say no).

[95] I am referring here to the Fund's ideological approach, which has been called "unrepentant neoliberalism." Bob Deacon, *Social Policy in a Global Context*, in INEQUALITY, GLOBALIZATION AND WORLD POLITICS, *supra* note 93; *see generally* Joseph E. Stiglitz, GLOBALIZATION AND ITS DISCONTENTS (2003). *But see* HEAD, *supra* note 82, at 61–63, 69–75 (summarizing and rejecting the ideology, or what he calls the "bad medicine" critique).

[96] *See* HEAD, *supra* note 82, at 72–73 (discussing 2002 reforms to Fund conditionality policies).

to be eligible for concessional assistance from the Bank and Fund, face an unsustainable debt burden beyond available debt relief mechanisms, and have established a record of reform and policies which the Bank and Fund judge as "sound."[97] All this may seem justifiable on first glance, but a justice perspective means that one needs to look carefully at whether these conditions in fact operate in a manner consistent with the obligations of liberal states managing Bank policy. Justice as Fairness requires us to inquire into what goes into a determination that a HIPC candidate's economic policies are "sound." What conditions are imposed on participants? Do these conditions bear a demonstrable relationship to the overall policy and normative goal of debt relief and benefit to the least advantaged? Or are there disguised preferences built in to conditionality that favor other Bank constituencies?

On this issue, it is significant that civil society critics have argued that the structure and disbursement of HIPC lending in fact disproportionately benefit multinational enterprises and the wealthy elites within HICP borrowing countries, thus furthering "the globalization agenda of the donor governments of the industrialized North."[98] This raises the possibility that with respect to its actual operation, HIPC may not be fulfilling the requirements of either the Bank's mission or of international distributive

---

[97] GHAZI, *supra* note 66, at 73.
[98] *Id.* (citing report by CorpWatch).

justice – the program is not in fact operating in a manner that meets our core normative criteria: benefiting the least advantaged. Instead, it may be further benefiting the already advantaged.

The Fund has been similarly criticized for failing to adequately take into account the redistributive effects of its policies, especially conditionality.[99] When a Fund member needs to draw on the Fund for hard currencies in excess of its own reserve account, such draws are subject to conditions negotiated between the Fund and the drawing country, which often include sensitive domestic issues such as wage rates, levels of public expenditures, budget deficits, and export levels.[100] Similar conditions are also imposed on Bank client states as a function of a borrower's participation in the Bank's HIPC program, through the link between HIPC and participation in the Fund's PRGF.[101]

It is true that the Fund has begun to publicly note the distributive impact of its policies[102] and to develop new

[99] *See, e.g.,* HEAD, *supra* note 82, at 81–84 (summarizing and largely endorsing the distributive critique of Fund policies). Hockett, for example, argues that BWIs need to take a stronger public position on the normative justification of social insurance programs. Hockett, *supra* note 78, at 198.

[100] *See generally* GHAZI, *supra* note 66, at 16–17.

[101] Charles Abugre, *SAPping the Poor: Structural Adjustment – the Forgotten Issue* (1999), *available at* www.wdm.org.uk/resources/reports/debt/sappingthepoor01061999.pdf (citing link between HIPC participation and PRGF).

[102] Hockett, *supra* note 78, at 223.

approaches to conditionality. For example, the Fund now guides its concessional lending through Poverty Strategy Reduction Papers, ostensibly designed in consultation with borrowing states, and supplemented since 2001 by the social impact analysis (SIA) program, through which the Fund attempts to assess the consequences of its conditionality policies on the well-being of different social groups, with a special focus on the vulnerable and the poor.[103]

While these laudable reforms seemingly address several of the most prominent critiques of Fund conditionality, criticisms of Fund efforts in this area continue.[104] In the words of one commentator largely sympathetic to the Fund, "the IMF still does not give enough attention to issues of distributional and social justice."[105] In particular, with respect to the subject of this chapter, these reforms do not specifically address the most critical issue highlighted by the Difference Principle, namely, that conditionality policies be specifically tailored to benefit the least advantaged. The Fund's "social impact analysis" program does seem designed to at least assess impact on the least advantaged, but it is intended more to mitigate adverse effects than to make the benefit

[103] Int'l Monetary Fund [IMF], *Annual Report of the Executive Board for the Financial Year Ended April 30, 2006,* Appendix 11, (2006), http://www.imf.org/extemal/pubs/ft/ar.2006/eng/index.htm, (last visited March 22, 2008).

[104] See e.g. GHAZI, *supra* note 66, at 72; Abugre, *supra* note 102; *but see* HEAD, *supra* note 82, at 82 (equity criticisms understate Fund efforts in this area).

[105] *See* HEAD, *supra* note 82, at 83.

of the least advantaged a policy priority.[106] Instead, following the Difference Principle, liberal states need to redirect the thrust of Fund activity toward using its "enforcement" powers[107] to pursue conditionality policies more specifically tied to the benefit of the least advantaged.[108]

Returning to our larger theoretical task in this chapter, this brief analysis illustrates how Liberal Internationalism requires the states that set Bank and Fund policy, which are ostensibly liberal states, to more explicitly acknowledge the redistributive impact of these institutions, and use the

[106] Moreover, the Fund's response to finding threats to the least advantaged include policies that have not worked particularly well even in wealthy societies, such as cash subsidies, price controls on essential commodities, and job retraining.

[107] Daniel Bradlow, *The World Bank, the IMF and Human Rights*, 6 TRANSNAT'L L. & CONTEMP. PROB. 47, 72 (1996). Bradlow suggests that the Fund use its "implementation powers" through surveillance and technical assistance to collect information and offer expertise supporting such policies.

[108] Outgoing IMF Managing Director Michel Camdessus offered a broad vision for "social conditionality" shortly after leaving office in 2001. Michel Camdessus, *The IMF at the Beginning of the Twenty First Century: Can We Establish a Humanized Globalization?* 7 GLOBAL GOVERNANCE 363, 374–377 (2001). *See also*, e.g., Namita Wahi, *Human Rights Accountability of the IMF and the World Bank: A Critique of Existing Mechanisms and Articulation of a Theory of Horizontal Accountability*, 12 U.C. DAVIS J. INT'L L. & POL'Y 331 (2006) (critical of conditionality from a human rights perspective); Ofer Eldar, *Reform of IMF Conditionality: A Proposal for Self-imposed Conditionality*, 8 J. INT'L ECON. L. 509 (2005) (proposing that conditionality be entirely borrower-driven, with Fund approval).

tools that justice theory offers as a vehicle to more accurately fulfill their relevant normative commitments in this area. If justice means ensuring that inequalities in the international distribution of social goods work to the benefit of the least advantaged, then liberal states must ensure, among other things, that the Bank and Fund delve far enough into domestic social policy, and with appropriate criteria, to reach and affect those structures that actually determine whether capital and currency inequalities, and state interventions through multilateral institutions will or will not work to the benefit of the least advantaged.

B. Contributions and Limits of This Model

To recapitulate, in the past section I have outlined one "take" on the question of global justice and international economic law; namely, to approach justice as a matter of the foreign policy obligations of a liberal state with respect to transboundary questions of economic justice. Following Brilmayer's vertical thesis, this approach has assumed a model of transboundary justice as essentially similar to domestic justice, in that it roots the legitimacy of state action in a state's constitutive political theory, regardless of whether such action crosses territorial boundaries. In this model, international economic law is subject to the same normative criteria as domestic law because the same liberal states are actively asserting their power in both arenas.

The greatest advantage of this approach is that it is not contingent upon the existence of any global normative consensus on justice or upon the persuasiveness of local theories of justice across national boundaries. Instead, it confines itself to articulating what kinds of global economic policies a liberal state should pursue in order to be consistent with its own normative commitments. This would apply equally to situations in which a state acts unilaterally, and when it acts through an international organization by advocating, or setting, that institution's policies. In the latter case, such policies would not necessarily be liberal, or fully liberal, given the compromise nature of institutional governance. However, such an outcome is an inherent risk in this Take, since an institution's ultimate policies will represent the views of other managing states, its own staff, institutional politics, and compromise.[109]

This approach offers interested parties seeking global justice a route toward advocacy directed at the state policy level and an immediately available set of normative and rhetorical tools with which to address the many problems of global distributive justice, at least insofar as liberal states are actively involved through their own policies or through the organizations they influence. Reformers do not need to initially win any

[109] This will be the case particularly where there is no institutional model of justice in place, only individual states contending for control. In this sense, a liberal internationalist approach and an institutional analysis of the distributive obligations of IOs qua IOs complement each other.

controversial theoretical battles or design new global institutions. Instead, they need only point out the global distributive ramifications of current political, legal, and institutional commitments, within the context of a state's overall liberal tradition. This approach also encourages greater coherence in liberal states between domestic and international policies, which has its own functional benefits.[110]

Independent of any instrumental benefits, the notion of coherence points us toward the underlying mode of discourse informing Take One's approach to transnational justice, which I characterize as Justice as Integrity. As I discussed in the Introduction, one of the aims of this book is to look at certain common discursive modes or analytic tropes concerning justice and to see how these operate "beneath" the various substantive conceptions of justice, and influence the ways in which we conceptualize (and disagree about) justice in transnational matters independent of the merits of substantive arguments.[111] Moreover, the "takes" and "modes" are

[110] *See* Michael Javid, *Increasing the Coherence of Global Economic Policy-Making – Suggestions for Improving the Governance Structure of the International Economic Law Regime* (Spring 2009) (unpublished manuscript, on file with the author) (discussing the benefits of policy coherence). Such increased "vertical" coherence may be purchased at a cost of some degree of "horizontal" coherence between states without an overarching shared commitment to a view of justice, but that again is a cost of this model.

[111] *See* Introduction *supra* at 7–15. *See also*, Richard Little, *Hedley Bull's The Anarchical Society, in* THE BALANCE OF POWER IN INTERNATIONAL RELATIONS: METAPHORS, MYTHS AND MODELS 128–166 (2007).

not interchangeable: many different takes (or substantive conceptions of justice) may share a single rhetorical strategy or mode. For example, the "society of states" approach to international justice and the communitarian approach to domestic justice (and transnational justice as we shall see in the next chapter) could not be more different substantively, but both share the Relational Mode of discourse: both locate the possibility of justice in the relationships among the actors, states in a society of states model on the one hand, and individual members of a national political community on the other.

By calling this mode "Justice as Integrity," I am not seeking to invoke Dworkin's notion of law as integrity.[112] In Dworkin's theory of law, integrity functions as an interpretive principle – judges seek the interpretation of law most consistent with past legal practice. Here, integrity functions as a way of characterizing the locus or source of one's moral obligation: in one's own principles rather than in the presence or absence of a specific kind of relationship or agreement. The *nature* of one's obligation and the *manner* of discharge may vary according to the relationships involved, but the obligation exists as a function of one's own commitments, not because of the nature of the relationship. The essential characteristic of Justice as Integrity is the move to ground just behavior in consistency with one's own principles of how one is to behave, and not in any specific normative principles

[112] RONALD DWORKIN, LAW'S EMPIRE (1987).

agreed by all those affected as appropriate to the situation (the Shared Enterprise version of the Relational Mode), or in the presence or absence of any special degree of social relationship that might give rise to obligations that would otherwise not exist (the Communal version of the Relational Mode).

A transnationalized Justice as Fairness illustrates the Justice as Integrity Mode, because it links a liberal state's foreign policy back toward that state's own normative commitments. The focus is not on what other states (or persons) should or should not do, what principles they value, or whether one is in a particular kind of relationship with others. These are *contingent* factors affecting one's implementation decisions, not *constitutive* factors determining one's obligations. Specific relationships are not irrelevant to Justice as Integrity – we may owe additional duties to our spouse or countrymen, for example,[113] but in Justice as Integrity our focus is on how *we* think a spouse or fellow national should be treated, not on whether they happen to agree with us or not.

In an international context, this means that when we speak in the mode of Justice as Integrity we talk about what kinds of duties liberal states have in their foreign relations, regardless of whether other states agree with them on

---

[113] On that subject, *see, e.g.,* Robert E. Goodin, *What Is so Special About Our Fellow Countrymen?* 98 ETHICS 663 (1998); David Miller, *The Ethical Significance of Nationality*, 98 ETHICS 647 (1998).

normative principles. This is precisely the problem Rawls wrestles with most usefully in *The Law of Peoples* – how do we take into account the differing values of other states, while maintaining the integrity of our own?[114] In that account, Rawls concludes that the principles which other states hold to, does influence the way in which a liberal state treats them – but the basis for a liberal state's obligation to act *as a liberal state* lies in its own commitment to liberalism and not in the presence or absence of agreement or relationship with the other.

Justice as Integrity as a mode of discourse should not be confused with the specific account of an internationalized Justice as Fairness that I set forth in Take One – the latter is a substantive theory of justice and only one example of the Integrity Mode I am describing here. The substantive content of Justice as Fairness is not essential to the Integrity Mode – it is only one way that liberal states might reason toward their obligations through an Integrity Mode of discourse.

In an Integrity model, we ultimately ground our behavior toward others on the principles we hold – "this is who I am" – and not simply or exclusively on the degree of relationship or agreement present with the other – " this is who you are" or "this is what we both value." Nonliberal and illiberal states would of course hold different values and undertake

---

[114] *See supra* Introduction; *see* RAWLS, THE LAW OF PEOPLES, *supra* note 6.

different commitments, and if they based their commitments to others on the basis of these values then all subsequent positions would reflect the Integrity Mode of justice discourse. The values others hold – including other states – and any relationships we share – or not – with them may well be relevant to our ultimate behavior, but not to the basic presence or absence of moral constraints on our behavior. What is key to the Integrity way of conceptualizing justice is the reference to one's own commitments when formulating, and evaluating, one's treatment of others.

We can see one of the advantages of an Integrity Mode of justice in the fact that Take One also offers liberal states a familiar basis on which to evaluate their own transboundary actions, because it resembles the kind of evaluation already carried out for domestic policies.[115] As Thomas Nagel has written, when compared to global justice theory, "domestic political theory is very well understood."[116] Precisely because it operates within the conceptual and rhetorical universe of traditional domestic political theory, this approach is particularly well suited to offer concrete normative benchmarks for evaluating international law and policy. Thus, in both the trade and lending contexts, applying Justice as Fairness

---

[115] For example, Rawlsian analyses of domestic tax policy abound. *See, e.g.*, James Repetti, *Democracy and Opportunity: A New Paradigm in Tax Equity*, 61 VAND. L. REV. 1129 (2008); Linda Sugin, *Theories of Distributive Justice and Limitations on Taxation: What Rawls Demands from Tax Systems*, 72 FORDHAM L. REV. 1991 (2004).

[116] Thomas Nagel, *The Problem of Global Justice*, 33 PHIL & PUB. AFF. 114, 113–147 (2005).

suggested specific and workable normative principles to guide liberal states as they work through the WTO, IMF or World Bank to address issues of economic fairness from a liberal perspective.

As I also sought to illustrate through abbreviated analyses of S&D with respect to trade law, and conditionality with respect to international development and currency lending, Justice as Fairness can also be the basis for a robust, detailed critique of the success or failure of specific liberal policies as enacted through existing law, and can suggest specific reforms in law and institutional practice. This is possible, in part, because Justice as Fairness yields a clear, normative benchmark for regulatory policy: are the rules designed so that the social process of allocation they structure actually work to the benefit of the least advantaged? Other substantive conceptions besides Justice as Fairness would yield other liberal benchmarks, but in general one can expect they would be similarly workable, because they are drawn from the deep reserve of domestic experience with policy formulation and policy reform. In fact, I would venture to suggest that ease of applicability (not to be confused with ease of policy implementation) is a hallmark of normative criteria emerging from an Integrity approach to justice discourse.

However, as is often the case, the limits of this approach flow directly from its strengths. By forgoing the search for a global normative theory, Take One articulates a strong claim on liberal states, but it cannot reach beyond liberal states to other states, some of which are those pursuing the most destructive policies. Integrity is powerful, but it is limited. This model does not offer arguments as to why nonliberal states are obligated to pursue those foreign policies we in liberal states consider as "just" or necessary.

In this respect, Take One is bound to disappoint cosmopolitans, the majority of whom are deeply engaged in working out the normative implications of their views for others. But I believe this also illustrates the effect of underlying modes of discourse on our agreements and disagreements about justice. One can speak of cosmopolitanism in the mode of Justice as Integrity – as what *I* owe to *others* – and it is quite compatible in spirit with Take One – both can be seen as efforts to work out liberal obligations *to others* on an international plane. The complications arise when cosmopolitanism shifts to another mode – let's call it Justice as Discipline – in which the conversation is about obligations *on others* – what *others* are to do as a result of *our* view of what justice demands in a given situation. It is at this juncture that Take One (and Justice as Integrity) part company from cosmopolitanism (and Justice as Discipline), by explicitly eschewing this outward-focused rhetoric. However, the disagreement between Cosmopolitanism and Liberal Internationalism may have more to do with the incompatibility of the two underlying modes of discourse – Integrity versus Discipline – than with any deep substantive differences in their liberalism.[117]

[117] I will have more to say about this in the Conclusion.

By characterizing this limited reach as a critique of Take One, I do not mean to suggest that a transnational approach to justice *should* impose its principles on others – that would be completely contrary to the global pluralism I spoke of in the introduction – nor do I wish to minimize the significance of persuading even liberal states to consistently follow a liberal theory of justice internationally – that by itself would be transformative. After all, liberalism is the normative tradition of many of the most wealthy and powerful states, which are primarily Western or Western-style liberal democracies, and the impact of a commitment to global justice on the part of these states is potentially quite substantial.[118] However, the limitations of this approach are real, and built-in at the theoretical level. From this perspective, the Millennium Development Goals illustrate the advantages and disadvantages of a Take-One style approach to transnational justice: posit certain aspirational economic fairness goals but leave it to individual states – and their individual traditions of justice and politics – to justify this commitment and act (or not) on it. We can see for ourselves the results.

Moreover, this approach can be seen as reinforcing two problematic aspects of international relations: the "society of states" model and the "liberal hegemony" problem. The dominant contemporary account of the social basis of international law has been the "society of states" model.[119] In

---

[118] JOHN RAWLS, POLITICAL LIBERALISM, XXIV (1995).

[119] *See generally* SIMON CANEY, JUSTICE BEYOND BORDERS: A GLOBAL POLITICAL THEORY 10–12 (2005); BEITZ, POLITICAL THEORY, *supra*

this view, to the extent that international law constructs an ordered social space (a claim contested since Hobbes if not before), it is a social space in which states are the subjects. In terms of the modes of discourse discussed here, this older "society of states' account of international morality is within the Relational Mode of discourse (discussed further in Take Two) – but the necessary relationship is between states and *states* (as opposed to the communitarian or contractarian versions in which the relationship is among persons). International law exists to order this community in which states are the members, and within this community states owe moral duties (to the extent they have them) to other states.

This view of international law as regulating a society of states has two important normative implications, both flowing from the core analogy of states to persons underlying the model. First, it asserts a strong view of state autonomy: like persons in domestic society, states in international society are viewed as autonomous sources of moral ends, immune from external interference.[120] Second, there is no principle of distributive justice to which states are subject; they are presumed to be entitled to the resources they control.[121]

note 4, at 67–123 (1979) (overview of the society of states model of international relations, superseding earlier Realist paradigm).

[120] Beitz, *supra* note 4, at 65–66.

[121] Beitz has analogized this to 19th -century liberalism at the international level: "a belief in the liberty of individual agents, with an indifference to the distributive outcomes of their economic interaction." *Id*.

Taken together, this approach can be called the "morality of states" model of international justice.[122] Pressure on this model began in earnest in the mid-20th century, through human rights, international economic law, and the emergence of international civil society, all of which render the "society of states" model increasingly deficient both empirically and normatively.[123]

Now, Take One does ground transboundary liberalism in a state's own domestic political theory governing its relations with its own citizens (Brilmayer's vertical thesis), and it does yield an approach that supports distributive obligations on states (liberal states) grounded in their own domestic legitimacy. However, the approach in Take One could be seen as undercutting this move away from the society of states model, insofar as it characterizes global justice as a matter of how states treat other states. Within the Relational Mode of justice discourse, it could be seen as reinforcing the impression that it is the relationship between states that matters, even though this Take is in fact based on a less public relationship between a state and its own citizens. One could argue that locating justice at that level goes against the normative thrust of the human

---

[122] *Id.*

[123] *See, e.g.,* THOMAS RISSE ET AL., THE POWER OF HUMAN RIGHTS: INTERNATIONAL NORMS AND DOMESTIC CHANGE (1999); Dianne Otto, *Nongovernmental Organizations in the United Nations System: The Emerging Role of International Civil Society,* 18 HUM. RTS. Q. 197 (1996); CHARLES R. BEITZ, THE IDEA OF HUMAN RIGHTS (2009).

rights movement, namely, that states owe certain obligations to human beings as human beings, without the need for any mediating domestic theory.

Such implicit statism highlights, by contrast, a key contribution of the cosmopolitan approach to global justice: namely, that individuals have moral as well as legal standing in international relations. Despite the limits of cosmopolitanism discussed above and in the introduction, it is clear that international society has moved beyond merely a society of states, and largely thanks to the human rights movement has encompassed individuals as subjects of international law.[124] In this sense, Take One can be seen as a partial solution at best to the global justice dilemma that imposes its own costs, including minimizing individual normative and legal status for increased binding force on states.

Second, by situating justice within the realm of unilateral state action and state influence over multilateral institutional policy, Take One reinforces the problematic link between power and ideology in international relations. The key in Take One to the relationship between global justice and multilateral institutions lies in the political positions states are willing to adopt and advocate in their governance of these institutions. This happens to bode well for liberal states and the potential impact of their adopting a liberal foreign policy, since in political terms the Bretton Woods

---

[124] *See* Garcia, *Theory of International Law*, 11 INT'L LEGAL THEORY 9, at 10–12 (2005).

institutions (BWIs) are controlled by states that consider themselves part of the liberal political tradition. Moreover, the BWIs are themselves creatures of international law and the postwar liberal internationalist period, all of which grew out of the same tradition that gave us political liberalism, namely, that of Western European states.[125]

The foregoing confluence may well be an advantage for liberalism, in that it further reinforces the compliance pull, if you will, of liberal theories of justice in this arena, and also illustrates the importance of understanding the normative framework within which institutions and their cultures operate.[126] This is particularly important for the global justice movement, since if one develops arguments for justice in the language of liberalism, it is harder for such states to ignore them either unilaterally or in their institutional practices.

However, the very preponderance of global economic power held by the United States and European states (as a group the most prominent liberal states), coupled with their history of colonialist and neo-colonialist activity, sets the stage for a critique of any activity toward "justice" on their part as yet another ideology in which "liberal" states

---

[125] On the intertwined roots of political liberalism, liberal internationalism, international law, and the modern state system, *see* Deacon, *supra* note 101, at 223 (acknowledging liberal internationalist roots of IMF); Anne-Marie Slaughter, *International Law in a World of Liberal States*, 6 EJIL 1, 503, 510.

[126] *See supra* note 72.

cloak their traditional international pursuit of power and influence.[127] Put another way, the concentration of economic and political power within liberal states does at least raise the spectre of such states masking coercive, self-serving politics in liberal ideology. Nonliberal states that are the targets of unilateral state action or, as client states, subject to multilateral institutional rules, may have reason to resent the power that allows liberal states to carry out or enact their policies, however "liberal" they seem to us or to the acting states. At best, this raises the issue of cultural relativism and respect for other normative traditions.[128] At its worst, it leads to a corrosive skepticism about liberalism in international relations as a kind of "liberal triumphalism" or cloak for self-interest.[129]

Finally, as I have suggested throughout, this approach does not by itself offer a theory of global justice that applies

[127] See JENS BARTELSON, VISIONS OF WORLD COMMUNITY 1–2 (2009) (noting paradox of "barely concealed claims to imperial power" in universalistic claims).

[128] The fact that we are talking about international justice also raises the problem of cultural relativism, since both participating states and client states of the BWIs come from other traditions besides liberalism. Some could object that should liberal states exercise their liberalism through such institutions, they are forcing a particular system or set of values. Even though I am concerned here with the obligations of liberal states, unilaterally and through institutions, and *not* in arguments for why other states should be liberal, I do recognize the risk. See Caney, *supra* note 6 (discussing the problem of multiculturalism).

[129] See BARTELSON, *supra* note 129; Anne-Marie Slaughter, *supra* note 127, at 4.

to international organizations directly. As the abbreviated analysis of the Bank and the Fund illustrates, this approach can help liberal states determine what normative constraints and objectives may apply to the positions they take and advocate through their activities within such organizations. However, this approach does not offer an independent normative argument for why international institutions qua institutions are obligated to pursue principles of distributive justice. Instead, if such institutions happen to follow just policies, it will only be because they are controlled by a majority of liberal states that have decided to fulfill their liberal commitments and have created the politics necessary to enact this agenda, not because the institution is independently obligated to do so.

This shortcoming may be symptomatic of a larger fault with contemporary political theory about global justice: a failure to closely engage with institutions.[130] Charles Beitz pioneered one early approach to addressing this gap, also drawn from Rawls's domestic work.[131] Beitz attempts to base the relationship between political theory and international economic law on the functional characteristics of international institutions as social institutions. The primary impetus toward justice, according to Rawls, is that social cooperation gives rise to certain benefits and burdens, which need to be allocated. For that cooperative social scheme to be just, those

---

[130] *See* Christian Barry & Thomas W. Pogge, *Introduction* to GLOBAL INSTITUTIONS AND RESPONSIBILITIES, *supra* note 70, at 1–2.

[131] BEITZ, *supra* note 4, at 131.

benefits and burdens should be allocated according to some relevant idea of what is "right." In Beitz's words, "the requirements of justice apply to institutions and practices (whether or not they are genuinely cooperative) in which social activity produces relative or absolute benefits or burdens that would not exist if the social activity did not take place."[132]

One can characterize such an approach as part of the Relational family of rhetorical strategies, in that it focuses on the relationship that the institution has to those affected by its decisions (reflecting the contractarian "Shared Enterprise" version of this mode). As such, the key issue is of course whether in fact the analysis correctly characterizes these relationships. Barry, for example, objects to the extension of Justice as Fairness to international society on the basis of such economic relations, questioning whether such relations are in fact sufficiently reciprocal and dependent.[133] This is the sort of theoretical obstacle that led Beitz and others to back away from this approach, and which the Take One "statist" approach is designed to avoid, but at the cost of institutional applicability.[134]

---

[132] *Id.*

[133] *See* Brian Barry, *Humanity and Justice in Global Perspective, in* NOMOS XXIV 219, at 232–234 (J. Roland Pennock & John W. Chapman, eds., 1982). It is for this reason that Beitz subsequently backed away from this approach, while maintaining that such functions at a minimum made justice relevant, if not binding, on such institutions. *See, e.g.,* Charles R. Beitz, *Cosmopolitanism and Global Justice,* 9 J. ETHICS 11 (2005).

[134] It is precisely the sort of obstacle, however, that Take Two runs into.

The absence of a liberal theory of international institutional justice is particularly important when one considers the standard realist objection that liberal states cannot, given the state of global politics, pursue liberal positions in international relations while at the same time protecting their national self-interest and political survival. As Kant points out, this is really not an objection to the difficulties or risks involved in pursuing political morality; it is an objection to political morality itself. As he writes in *Perpetual Peace*, moral obligations readily admit of discretion and prudence with regard to the means and timing of their accomplishment. To argue that it is simply not possible given human nature and circumstances to fulfill ethical obligations in international politics is really arguing against ethics itself, which most realists are not willing to do, at least explicitly.[135]

If a theory of global justice were to offer a basis for binding international institutions themselves to certain principles of justice, this would offer a way around the *realpolitik* argument against global justice, by offering a basis on which all states, liberal and nonliberal, would be obligated to pursue global justice when they act through institutions, given the nature of the institutions themselves. Liberal Internationalism cannot by its nature offer such an argument – we shall see the extent to which such an argument

[135] IMMANUEL KANT, *Perpetual Peace: A Philosophical Sketch*, in KANT: POLITICAL WRITINGS 116, 123 (H.S. Reiss ed., H.B. Nisbit trans., 2nd ed., 1991) (1784).

may be possible by taking a different route in Takes Two and Three.

For all of these reasons, I would characterize the approach in Take One as international justice, not global justice. As a theory of liberal state obligation, it can play an important role in the pursuit of global justice, but standing alone, there is nothing truly *global* about it.[136] I believe this would be true of any theory of transnational justice that operates within the Justice as Integrity framework. It is not "Global Justice as Fairness," because the basis for justice is not a global social relationship shared by all affected states, such as participation by all in an underlying cooperative scheme for mutual benefit.[137] It remains a liberal state's commitment to Justice as Fairness in its foreign relations. This is of course no small thing – if the world consisted solely of actors operating with integrity according to their individual substantive conceptions of justice, the world as a whole would very likely be a more just place. However, it is worth considering whether we would have arrived at *global* justice.

---

[136] However, following Brilmayer, Tan suggests that in the case of a hegemon like the United States, international justice can merge into global justice, as the hegemon's capacity to project global *political* power subjects it to the same criteria we would apply to a world state. KOK-CHOR TAN, TOLERATION, DIVERSITY AND GLOBAL JUSTICE 8 (2000).

[137] This will be the basis of the approaches discussed in Take Two.

2

Take Two

Globalization and the Possibility of a Global Community of Justice

Having worked through one "Take" on global justice, it is worth reviewing where we stand. Take One offers an approach to global justice which presupposes that global social relations have not changed in any significant way. In fact, as we saw in the concluding section, it reinforces a traditional view of global social relations as being principally the province of states – the "society of states" model. In essence, this limits justice to international justice, or justice between states and – through states – for their citizens.

There are undoubtedly advantages to this approach to justice on a transnational level, as we saw in that chapter. For example, confining our argument to liberal obligations on liberal states allows us to take a strong, well-understood normative base (the domestic obligations of liberalism on liberal states) and extend it to cover transboundary distributive issues in a manner that such states would find fairly compelling. Since such an extension is not without its own difficulties, successfully establishing that liberal states are so bound in their foreign relations would be no small accomplishment in itself. However, the limits of this approach are in its reach – even if successful, such an approach can only by definition apply directly to a small (but growing) number of states (liberal states), and only secondarily to global institutions through the votes and policy influence of those states. Nevertheless, as Sen reminds us, each serious theory of justice has important work to do, and this is no exception. This is worth emphasizing at the risk of redundancy, since a pluralist approach is not the conventional way to work through a variety of theoretical accounts of justice.

That being said, what about a truly *global* theory of justice – is that possible? If we are not going to proceed on the basis of a universalist account of political morality, as cosmopolitanism does (which raises the difficulties discussed in the Introduction, yet nevertheless plays an important role in the conversation), and if we are not yet willing to abandon traditional forms of political theory entirely (as Take Three will explore), then what are our options?

One possibility explored in the literature is to take a rights-based approach, and attempt to base global justice on the foundation of human rights law.[1] There are certainly

[1] For a general overview *see, e.g.,* CAROL C. GOULD, GLOBALIZING DEMOCRACY AND HUMAN RIGHTS (2004). *See also* JOHN MANDLE,

advantages to working within a framework of agreed-upon positive law, and indeed this is yet another important 'Take' on global justice. However, human rights law is a problematic basis for global justice. To take just one issue, it is widely recognized that the human rights system is most effective (though far from perfect) in the area of civil and political rights, where a strong element of domestic enforcement by states exists (at least in some regions) to back up these international norms.[2] The system does *not* work particularly well when the subject turns to economic rights, and it is precisely the subjects covered by economic and social rights – health, material well-being, education, economic opportunity and employment, for example – that are the proper subject of global distributive justice. Economic and social rights may well play an important role in galvanizing public advocacy and public opinion and organizing some degree of state action, but they will not take us as far as we need to go in the matter of distributive justice – they are not as enforceable in

GLOBAL JUSTICE: AN INTRODUCTION (2006); FUYUKI KURASAWA, THE WORK OF GLOBAL JUSTICE (2007).

[2] *See, e.g.,* Thomas Nagel, *The Problem of Global Justice*, 33 PHIL. & PUB. AFF. 113 (2005); David Miller, *National Responsibility and Global Justice*, 11 CRIT. REV. INT'L SOC. & POL. PHIL. 383 (2008); Emilie M. Hafner-Burton, Research Note: *Sticks and Stones: Naming and Shaming the Human Rights Enforcement Problem*, 62 INT'L ORG. 689 (2008); Terry Collingsworth, *The Key Human Rights Challenge: Developing Enforcement Mechanisms*, 15 HARV. HUM. RTS. J. 183 (2002).

this domain as they are in civil and political domains,[3] they may be *derivative* of certain socioeconomic conditions rather than *transformative* of them,[4] and they do not adequately encompass the range of vital interests at stake in economic and social life.[5]

An alternative approach, and the subject of this chapter, is to take seriously the "global" aspect of global justice. By this I mean that we take an approach to global justice with two distinctive elements. First, we acknowledge that, contrary to the approach in Take One and its reliance on a "society of states" model, global social relations are in fact undergoing profound changes through the process of globalization. And

[3] *See, e.g.,* Terry Collingsworth, *The Key Human Rights Challenge: Developing Enforcement Mechanisms*, 15 HARV. HUM. RTS. J. 183 (2002) (enforcement, always a difficult issue, is even more problematic outside of core life, liberty, and bodily integrity rights); but see KATHERINE G. YOUNG, CONSTITUTING ECONOMIC AND SOCIAL RIGHTS (2012) (new and dynamic processes are emerging to promote more effective means of enforcing economic and social rights).

[4] *See* Andrew Moravcsik, *Explaining International Human Rights Regimes: Liberal Theory and Western Europe*, 1 EUR. J. INT'L REL., 157 (1995) (effective human rights protection may *depend upon* certain political and socioeconomic conditions (developed liberal states) rather than be particularly adept at *forcing changes* in political and socioeconomic conditions).

[5] Sen and Nussbaum's Capabilities Approach offers an influential exploration of those areas of human life perhaps imperfectly covered by traditional economic and social rights. *See* Amartya Sen, *Human Rights and Capabilities*, 6 J. HUM. DEV. 151 (2005); *see generally* MARTHA C. NUSSBAUM AND AMARTYA SEN, THE QUALITY OF LIFE (1993).

second, we consider and seek to capitalize on whatever normative possibilities are created by the ways in which globalization is changing social relationships.

This requires an inquiry into the connection between social relationships and norms of justice, and the possibility that new and more intensive forms of social relatedness are emerging on the global level. However, before I turn to that question, I want at this juncture to note two important aspects of this inquiry. First, I want to reinforce and clarify the distinction I made in the Introduction between this approach and cosmopolitanism, since the latter is also a "global" approach. I am interested here in looking at the possible normative implications of changing global social relations, and not the possible global validity or applicability of essentially liberal norms. Obviously if global social relations are in fact changing – and were we all to become members of a liberal community of some kind on a global scale in the bargain – then cosmopolitanism might have new purchase as the normative consensus of this newly emerging global order. While I will turn to this possibility briefly at the end of the chapter, I want to clarify that were this to be the case, it might have less to do with reasons of cosmopolitan theory (the success of a universally valid argument) and more with empirical and political reasons (changing global social relations and the growing adoption of liberal political values). And, in particular, I want to emphasize that I am not beginning with the assumption that such a convergence is coming or will come to pass.

Second, I want to note that an inquiry into possibilities of community-type relationships at a global level, even if it is partly an empirical investigation, raises sensitive ideological concerns for many around the world. It has often been said, particularly by non-Western scholars, that "theories of world community are nothing but ideologies of empire, cunningly crafted to justify the global spread of Western values."[6] Any inquiry into the possibility of global community must be mindful of this concern.

Returning to my main line of inquiry, then, the question of a truly global justice requires us to consider the relationship between justice and society – in this case the possibility of global society.[7] Can we really speak of global justice independent of the question of whether there is a global society?[8] Cosmopolitanism tries to do so, but through universalizing philosophical argumentation rather than social analysis. Liberal internationalism tries to do so by focusing on the foreign policy commitments of avowedly liberal states, but as Take One demonstrated, this approach also has its limits. Moreover, in particular, we must go a step further and ask whether obligations of justice depend on

---

[6] JENS BARTELSON, VISIONS OF WORLD COMMUNITY 2 (2009).

[7] Here, of course, I am speaking of social relations among individuals and groups of individuals, not a global "society of states." *See* Frank J. Garcia, *Globalization and the Theory of International Law,* 11 INT'L L. THEORY 9, 10–12 (2005).

[8] David R. Mapel & Terry Nardin, *Introduction* to INTERNATIONAL SOCIETY 3, 3–4 (David R. Mapel & Terry Nardin, eds., 1998).

the prior existence of a certain, specific *kind* of global social relationship, namely, *community*.[9]

The question of justice and its relationship to social relations is a complex one, with opponents to global justice citing both theoretical and empirical obstacles. Two branches of justice theory present this challenge most acutely: the social contract tradition and the communitarian approach to justice. As both are within the Relational Mode of justice discourse (as discussed in the Introduction), both present the limiting factor to justice in terms of the presence or absence of certain key social relationships. Contractarians cite the absence of a social contract beyond national borders. Communitarians cite the absence of something more: the sorts of communal bonds, expressed in terms of shared traditions, practices and understandings, that go beyond social contract requirements and are in their view the necessary ingredients of justice.

Thomas Nagel has characterized these two approaches as sharing a common conception of justice, which he calls a "political conception."[10] By this he means a conception of justice that does not flow from a comprehensive prior system of morality, but rather is rooted in social relations and social institutions – in Rawls's famous phrase, justice as

---

[9] *See* Frank J. Garcia, *Globalization, Global Community and the Possibility of Global Justice*, B.C. L. SCH. FAC. PAPERS, Paper 33 (2005), *available at* http://lsr.nellco.org/bc_lsfp/33/ [hereinafter Garcia, *Global Community*].

[10] Thomas Nagel, *The Problem of Global Justice, supra* note 2.

"the first virtue of social institutions."[11] On this view, "sovereign states are not merely instruments for realizing the pre-institutional value of justice among human beings. Instead, their existence is precisely what gives the value of justice its application, by putting the fellow citizens of a sovereign state into a relation that they do not have with the rest of humanity, an institutional relation which must then be evaluated by the special standards of fairness and equality that fill out the content of justice."[12]

Accordingly, the political conception of justice offers a specific kind of challenge to the possibility of global justice; namely, that global justice requires a kind of global relationship – Nagel calls it sovereignty, others call it society or community – that we simply do not have, and maybe cannot have at the level of global interaction. But that is where globalization comes in. In my view, globalization is creating the possibility for exactly those sorts of relationships, thereby opening the door to new normative possibilities. As I will discuss later in this chapter, by reducing or eliminating the role of time and space in social relations, globalization is intensifying relationships irrespective of boundaries and physical distance and creating the sorts of knowledge and connection that form the basis for even communitarian forms of justice.

---

[11] JOHN RAWLS, A THEORY OF JUSTICE 3 (1971) [hereinafter RAWLS, A THEORY OF JUSTICE].

[12] Thomas Nagel, *The Problem of Global Justice, supra* note 2. Emphasis added.

In order to develop this "Take" on global justice, I will
first outline the nature of the objections to global justice
posed by those who link justice to necessary social relations.
To do so, I propose disaggregating the political conception of
justice into its contractarian and communitarian branches,
and proceed with the latter. As communitarianism is the
more stringent of the two challengers,[13] I will confine myself
within the limits of this chapter only to consideration of the
communitarian form of this argument.[14] I will then argue
that even if one concedes the necessity of such relationships
as a precondition for justice, globalization is altering global
social relations in such a way that global justice is becoming
possible even on these stricter lines.

In contrast to the static approach of Take One, the core
of this approach is dynamic: it begins with a domestic theory, shows how the underlying social facts it assumes have
changed, and then demonstrates how those changes trans-
form the scope and application of its principles. I will therefore close the chapter with a suggestion of what sort of global
justice this approach might support.

[13] By requiring community, and not merely society, communitarians
go beyond the criteria established by social contract theory; therefore, if one can meet the stringent standards of the communitarians, by implication, one has gone a long way toward meeting the
standards of the contractualists as well.

[14] For the other branch of the argument, *see* John Linarelli, *What Do
We Owe Each Other in the Global Economic Order? Constructivist
and Contractualist Accounts*, 15 FLA. ST. J. TRANSNAT'L L. & POL'Y
181 (2006) (offering an overview of contractualist approaches to
global economic justice issues).

A. The Model

1. *Communitarian Accounts of Justice*

Essentially, communitarians maintain that justice is a property of certain groups. Taking Michael Walzer's work as an example, the communitarian position is that global justice is not possible because on a global level we lack the sort of social relations that make justice possible in domestic society.[15]

According to Walzer, distributive justice is relative to social meanings. Only in domestic societies do we find the shared practices, traditions, and understandings which define what justice is, and which help create the social solidarity and sense of common purpose necessary to support the sacrifices and obligations of justice. In Walzer's words, justice "is rooted in the distinct understandings of places, honors, jobs, things of all sorts that constitute a shared way of life."[16] Unless these kinds of social relationships exist, there is no possibility of justice. Finding out what justice consists of requires a historical analysis of a society's shared life, not an a priori argument or a rational reconstruction of their beliefs.

Given that for Walzer it is a society's shared life that determines justice, and not the other way around, justice requires a prior community. On this view, distributive

---

[15] MICHAEL WALZER, SPHERES OF JUSTICE: A DEFENSE OF PLURALISM AND EQUALITY (1983) [hereinafter WALZER, SPHERES OF JUSTICE].
[16] *See Id.* at 314.

justice "presupposes a bounded world within which distribution can take place: a group of people committed to divid-
ing, exchanging, and sharing social goods, first of all among
themselves."[17] All relevant distributive decisions take place
according to these shared traditions, practices, and understandings of justice. In such a community, justice is determined by the members' shared understandings, not coercive
of them – otherwise, justice would be tyranny.

Given the nature of justice and the requisite degree of
social relationship, there are necessary limits to the scope
of justice. It is only within particular kinds of communities – national political communities – that you can determine what justice consists of, and who owes justice to whom.
First, it is only within national communities that you can
determine which people are to have their needs considered and reach the necessary consensus over what counts
as "need," since these are social and not determined facts.[18]
Second, justice requires a shared understanding of social
goods.[19] According to Walzer, Miller, and others, only political communities have such shared understandings, and the
preeminent example is the nation-state.

These shared understandings are not only necessary for
us to know what justice is, they are necessary to make justice *work*. Miller argues that these shared understandings

---

[17] *Id.* at 31.
[18] David Miller, *The Ethical Significance of Nationality*, 98 ETHICS
647, 661 (1988).
[19] WALZER, *supra* note 15, at 313.

of the national community are the necessary basis for solidarity, which is essential to support the individual sacrifices that justice demands.[20] In a similar sense, Walzer argues that a shared notion of the common good is necessary for the sacrifices of justice, since almost by definition justice will be invoked when someone has failed, or perceives himself as having failed, to secure his individual self-interest.

For these reasons, and given the many fundamental roles that the nation plays in the identity and flourishing of its members, these members are justified in preferring compatriots over non-compatriots in many sorts of distributions, including economic benefits. It is only within nations that justice makes sense, and it is only within nations that justice is necessary.

2. Probing the Communitarian Account of Justice

We can see in the preceding account that the communitarian argument against the possibility of global justice has two components, both working within a Relational Mode of justice. The first is an argument about the nature of justice, drawing on an analysis of how justice works in national political communities. The second argument denies that such relationships exist to a meaningful degree on a transnational level. I will address both elements in turn.

---

[20] DAVID MILLER, ON NATIONALITY, 90–96 (1997); *see* CHARLES JONES, GLOBAL JUSTICE: DEFENDING COSMOPOLITANISM, 157–158 (1999).

With respect to the claim about justice, we need to first ask whether the communitarian conception of justice is in fact consistent with the nature of domestic political communities as we find them in the world. Miller, for example, characterizes the core understandings constitutive of community in the following way: that each member belongs with the others, that the association is neither transitory nor instrumental, but rooted in a long shared history of living together that (one expects) will continue into the future; and there is a shared sense of loyalty adequate to justify sacrificing individual interests for the group.[21]

Do contemporary political communities actually embody the kinds of shared understandings, traditions, and practices that communitarians posit as essential to the obligations of justice? In other words, are complex modern political communities such as the United States and the European Union accurately described by criteria such as Miller's? Or are these descriptions of an ideal political community a rhetorical model perhaps but certainly not a prerequisite to actual justice? This is essential to the global justice debate, since it is hardly fair to expect global social relations to meet a set of standards that even acknowledged national political communities do not meet at the domestic level.

For example, we need to consider the extent to which these "shared" understandings are actually shared within

---

[21] MILLER, *supra* note 20.

political communities. Advocates of communitarian justice must account for the reality within communities of disagreement over social understandings, the evolution of new understandings, and the problem of false consciousness.[22] All three call into question the empirical reality of consensus over norms, and therefore the credibility of linking community to justice.

When responding to the fact of social conflict, particularly conflict over what are purportedly "shared" understandings, communitarians shift the level of analysis to a secondary set of practices and understandings, a system for managing conflicts over understandings and their application. For example, Walzer suggests that disagreement over the meaning of social goods – where a given social understanding is controversial – triggers a sort of "second order" set of understandings concerning how disputes are to be expressed, managed and adjudicated, and even mechanisms for "alternative distributions."[23] In addressing a similar problem concerning the relation between nationality and ethnicity in an ethnically plural nation-state, Miller creates a similar distinction, between public and private culture. Noting that nationality as a fact is often created out of disparate ethnic groups and even forced upon minority ethnic groups with prior existing identities of their own, Miller

---

[22] *See* Joshua Cohen, "Review: *Spheres of Justice*," 83 J. PHIL 457, (1986) (addressing issues in communitarian theory).

[23] *Id.* at 313.

posits a bifurcation of national culture, between a shared public culture and differing private cultures.[24]

This point about the disagreement over shared understandings also focuses our attention on the difficult problem of how we would determine in fact if communitarian communities actually exist at all, or whether a given set of social relations rises to the level of community. After all, if you disagree over the meaning and scope of these kinds of basic understandings, how shared are they? How can one tell if one is a member, or if there is a shared understanding at all? As suggested, one answer communitarians give is to change the level of analysis to "understandings about understandings," or "shared public cultures," which might help resolve the problem but also casts the community's identity in a different light. When pushed, it seems communitarians are actually linking justice to a kind of shared institutional culture rather than a true community of shared primary beliefs. The latter view would limit "community" and therefore justice to a handful of homogeneous traditional societies, leaving the majority of contemporary nation-states free of both community and justice, which is clearly not the case.

If this is so, then we are forced to ask ourselves what in fact we are looking for when we seek to find communitarian communities in the real world, and how we will recognize

[24] Miller, *The Ethical Significance of Nationality, supra* note 18, at 657–658.

them when we find them (as opposed to merely societies or associations). If we can't assume that an absence of consensus over primary rules, or the existence of conflicting private cultures, disprove the existence of political community as Walzer or Miller define it, then what will? How real are these communities? Here we have a knotty problem, one that relates essentially to the question of association versus community. Perhaps a more accurate description of what we find in the world is many kinds of societies, some of which have a stronger sense of shared national identity than others, but all of which are functioning with some kind or degree of principles of justice. From a communitarian point of view, how can this be so?

Perhaps what communitarians are identifying when they speak of the common good is really a commitment to the second-order set of understandings about disputes, the rules about rules, the public culture that both Walzer and Miller point to as the communal response to social conflict. If this is so, then what we are talking about when we discuss community at the national level, what we are seeking to find when we look out the window, is something more like governance: shared social institutions for conflict management, decision making over resource allocation, and the administration of justice, standing astride a range of smaller normative communities.

Understood this way, it is certainly much easier to determine whether a set of individuals is involved in a community of justice: do they share institutions for managing their disputes as part of a shared public culture, an understanding about how such things are done? Such a joint investment may depend for its success on some degree of a shared sense of the common good and may itself foster such a sense of the common good, but that is in a way epiphenomenal. Look for the institutions, and you will find whatever sense of the common good there is, and not the other way around – and I would suspect that the richer the sense of the common good, the more effective the institution.

In any event, this move to a second or public set of shared understandings about justice is important for the question of global justice, as will be elaborated later, because it suggests a location for understandings about global justice independent of primary understandings or nationality-based commitments, which are understandably plural and divergent in the world as we find it, and would by analogy be in the role of Miller's private cultures but on a global scale – divergent, but not inconsistent with a shared public culture. If we understand Walzer and Miller to say that shared understandings of justice in fact involve agreements over the priority of public over private culture in certain cases, or agreements about the institutional management of conflicting claims, then we can look for global justice, and the a priori community for global justice, by looking at the meta-state or public culture level for shared understandings concerning conflicting global claims. In other words, global community as far as justice is concerned, may look less like a single global community in the national sense of shared identity, culture, and history (to the degree even those are commonly shared in a modern, complex nation-state), and more like a global set of shared understandings about claims and conflicts, or a global public culture.[25] We may find more of a consensus over this public culture and these secondary understandings, than a simple survey of the diverse range of primary understandings and private cultures would suggest.[26]

However, to further develop this possibility, we need to confront more directly the second, empirical side of the communitarian position, namely, whether social relations at the global level resemble those which they assert are required for justice. Here I am not so much questioning the coherence or plausibility of the communitarian account of justice, as I am checking it against contemporary global social realities.

3. *Globalization and Communities of Justice*

As I discussed, communitarianism does not categorically foreclose the possibility of global justice: if a global community exists, then we are free to proceed to determine its justice. However, communitarians would argue, we don't have a global society, let alone a global community: we evidently

---

[25] This might resemble, for example, what Sebastiano Maffetone calls the creation of a global public reason. Sebastiano Maffetone, *The Fragile Fabric of Public Reason*, in REASON AND REASONABLENESS (THE DIALOGUE) 407 (Ricardo Dottori, ed., 2005).

[26] This starts to look more like the liberal commitment to institutions for managing social conflicts among people with differing visions of the good, and suggests more common ground with communitarians than may at first be apparent. *See infra* part IV, Chapter 2.

don't live in a single world state or society in the traditional sense, and one finds a bewildering diversity of primary understandings and private cultures in the world.

In terms of principled social relations between such communities, this leaves us with only one option: we can come up with some ground rules for how we cooperate, or not, with different societies, but that is not justice.[27] It is coexistence, a modus vivendi – an accommodation to the facts. Such forms of cooperation do not, in the communitarian view, rise to the level of community:

[A]lthough in the contemporary world there are clearly forms of interaction and cooperation occurring at the global level – the international economy provides the most obvious example, but there are also many forms of political cooperation, ranging from defense treaties through to environmental protection agreements – *these are not sufficient to constitute a global community.* They do not by themselves

---

[27] Miller recently tries to make room for what he calls "global justice" within his communitarian framework, but distinguishes it strongly from the justice we enjoy in domestic society, which he calls "social justice." NATIONAL RESPONSIBILITY AND GLOBAL JUSTICE 12–17 (2007). We are still obligated to prefer compatriots to non-compatriots in many distributive contexts, owing the latter only a duty to refrain from rights violations, and a limited contextual duty to secure the basic rights of people we are clearly responsible for as a nation. *Id.* at 44–50. This is more akin to simply recognizing existing human rights obligations and is not, I submit, a theory of global justice, resembling instead Walzer's "thin" approach I will discuss below. *See infra* notes 101–102 and accompanying text.

create either a shared sense of identity or a common ethos. And above all there is no common institutional structure that would justify us in describing unequal outcomes as forms of unequal treatment.[28]

To begin with, one can legitimately question whether communitarians are in fact correct to characterize the global social environment as lacking in the elements that they identify as necessary preconditions for the applicability of justice. Moreover, and the preceding quote from Miller illustrates this, one can fault their view of community as inherently static – they say "nothing about the criteria that would help us decide when we had reached a point of institutional change when something morally significant was happening. What might 'sufficient to constitute a global community' mean?"[29]

This is where globalization comes in. As I mentioned in the Introduction, globalization involves the dramatic compression of time and space through the new technologies of communication. This compression is intensifying social relations irrespective of territorial boundaries and indeed, of territory itself. Through globalization, we are interconnected irrespective of time and space to a degree never before seen in human history. This phenomenon has a whole range of

[28] David Miller, *Justice and Global Inequality, in* INEQUALITY, GLOBALIZATION, AND WORLD POLITICS 190 (Andrew Hurrell and Ngaire Woods, eds., 1999) (emphasis added).
[29] Andrew Hurrell, *Global Inequality and International Institutions*, 32 METAPHILOSOPHY 34, 39 (2001).

social, economic, political, legal, and cultural effects, widely cataloged and widely (and justly) debated.[30]

Among these effects, some cosmopolitans see in globalization evidence of an emerging global *society,* involving global social cooperation and an emerging normative priority for the individual through human rights.[31] They point to the fact that international law today consists of many regimes that can be characterized as associations for mutual self-interest.[32] However, for communitarians this is not enough, since they pose an even more stringent test: what about global *community?*

It is my contention that among its many often-contradictory consequences, globalization itself is changing the nature of this argument over global justice and social relations. In essence, globalization is creating, facilitating, and contributing to the sorts of relationships that communitarians and others cite as necessary for justice, but at a new, transboundary level. I am not suggesting that, at this point in our history, global social relations form the sort of full-blown political community that communitarians find in domestic social relations.[33] In my view,

---

[30] *See, e.g.,* DAVID HELD ET AL., THE GLOBAL TRANSFORMATIONS READER: AN INTRODUCTION TO THE GLOBALIZATION DEBATE (2nd ed., 2003).

[31] *See, e.g.,* Anthony McGrew, *A Global Society? in* MODERNITY AND ITS FUTURES 467–503 (1992).

[32] Leading examples include the WTO and Bretton Woods institutions and, regionally, the European Union.

[33] Conceding for the moment that such communities exist at the national level, which is debatable, as I have argued earlier.

however, globalization is creating a third alternative, something between the nation-state and a global community, consisting of "pockets" of community or "limited" degrees of community.

If we disaggregate the notion of community, we can see that globalization is creating certain *elements* of community at the global level, such as knowledge of interconnectedness and the circumstances of the other; and creating community in certain *areas* of global social relations, such as humanitarian relief and economic relations, by establishing that degree of social bond necessary to support justice, in fact *requiring* it. Moreover, we see in emerging international regimes the sorts of understandings about understandings, or second-order understandings, which as I have argued may in fact be the most essential element of what communitarians call a political community. This means that global society, taken as a whole, may not rise in all cases to the level of community that communitarians posit, but has *enough* elements of community, and contains enough *pockets* of community, to support an inquiry into justice in at least in some areas of global social relations.

To illustrate this, I will examine in greater detail three particular aspects of globalization – the globalization of knowledge, the globalization of regulation, and the effects of globalization on time, history, and narrative – in which these changes are salient. But as a threshold matter, it is important to understand how globalization is making justice relevant at a basic social level before we look at whether it is getting us into deeper forms of community. For a first pass at this, I will utilize Rawls's concept of the circumstances of justice, and apply it to globalization.

a. Globalization and the Circumstances of Justice. Rawls discusses the social foundation of justice through an inquiry into what he calls "the circumstances of justice."[34] The circumstances of justice are those conditions of our human situation that make cooperation both possible and necessary. Where they obtain, and where they in fact lead to cooperation, justice is relevant. Although Rawls is not a communitarian, his account of justice does presuppose a necessary degree and kind of social relationship, and therefore his device is useful in this context. Even though for communitarians such relations are necessary but not sufficient, this approach does give us a way into the analysis.

Rawls divides the circumstances of justice into two categories. The first category, involving objective circumstances, includes three: a moderate scarcity of resources, a shared geographical territory, and a capacity to help or harm each other. In other words, there is not enough to go around for everything we want to do; we are all going to be looking for these resources in the same places; and we have the capacity to defeat one another's goals, or work together to achieve many of them.

---

[34] JOHN RAWLS, A THEORY OF JUSTICE, 126–130 et seq. following Hume (1999).

The second, subjective, set of circumstances consists of two: people are mutually disinterested, and they have conflicting claims. In other words, we are not generally altruistic – we want what we want; and to get it, we often go after what another has.

Because of these five circumstances, we are led to cooperate as the rational means toward achieving our individual ends. This, in essence, is society, which Rawls defines as a cooperative venture for mutual advantage.[35] The principles guiding the distribution of the fruits of this venture are principles of justice. Change or eliminate the circumstances of justice, and you alter the need for, or basis of, social cooperation, perhaps eliminating the need for justice itself.

Applying these circumstances to the question of global justice and global social relations, the argument in essence is that globalization is bringing about the same circumstances of justice at the global level that Rawls described at the domestic level. To begin with, there is of course the same basic scarcity of resources at the global level. Through globalization, people are increasingly competing for these resources on a global scale in a shared territory: our planet. That they are mutually disinterested and assert conflicting claims over these resources does not need to be argued.

i. The Capacity to Help. Because of globalization, in particular its technical and economic revolutions, we increasingly find

---

[35] *Id.* at 4.

that we have a capacity to effectively respond to the needs and concerns of others beyond our boundaries in ways we hitherto could not, through the transnational mobilization of information, power, public opinion, and financial or other resources. Commentators have suggested that earlier in our history, talk of global justice was premature, in the sense that our capacity to redistribute resources across the globe was weak.[36] Globalization and its technological revolutions create the technical ability to affect global resource distribution, making the question of its justice now quite relevant.[37] For example, global nongovernmental networks facilitate the mobilization of capital,[38] labor,[39] and policy expertise[40] in response to human need and pressing global social issues, largely independent of state action and thus largely independent of our traditional mechanisms for evaluating their justice and political legitimacy.

[36] *See, e.g.,* JONES, GLOBAL JUSTICE, *supra* note 20, at 9.

[37] *Id.* at 10.

[38] ANUPAM CHANDER, *Diaspora Bonds*, 76 NYU L. REV. 1005, 160–1074 (2001) (citing the role of diaspora communities in mobilizing capital for homeland governments).

[39] Transnational NGOs such as Habitat for Humanity mobilize volunteer labor for cross-border projects in human environment restoration. Arjun Appadurai, *Patriotism and Its Futures, in* MODERNITY AT LARGE: CULTURAL DIMENSIONS OF GLOBALIZATION 158, 167 (1996).

[40] Wolfgang Reinicke, *The Other World Wide Web: Global Public Policy Networks*, 117 FOREIGN POL'Y 44 (1999–2000) (global public policy networks experimenting with new ways to gather and distribute knowledge across borders).

By creating a real capacity to respond to another's needs and concerns, globalization contributes to an important element of the rationale for both society and justice – in Rawls's terms, the capacity to help.[41] For communitarians, this is a critical element in the creation of global solidarity as well. But is such solidarity emerging? In order to answer this question, we need to develop a few more elements of the puzzle.

ii. The Capacity to Harm. Because of globalization, we increasingly find that our state's policies, and our own political and consumer choices, are influencing the life prospects of others in direct and dramatic ways. The globalization of markets means that in many cases we are directly profiting from the economic and social conditions in other parts of the world, through outsourced services, low wages, multinational production processes, mutual fund and pension plan investment returns, and other strategies. The very fabric of global society – its division of territory and jurisdiction into political entities called states – is a social arrangement we are collectively responsible for.[42] Thus,

[41] Even David Miller, a communitarian critic of global justice, acknowledges that the "prosaic observation that the rich countries now have the technical capacity to transfer large quantities of resources to the poorer countries" makes a prima facie case that such transfers have become morally obligatory. David Miller, *The Limits of Cosmopolitan Justice, in* INTERNATIONAL SOCIETY 164 (David R. Mapel and Terry Nardin, eds., 1999).

[42] Jon Mandle, *Globalization and Justice*, 570 ANNALS AM. ACAD. POL. & SOC. SCI. 126,129–130 (2000).

completing Rawls's basic conditions, we have the capacity to harm each other as well.

This capacity to harm each other on a global scale is also an important element in creating a sense of solidarity, understood as a sense of responsibility for one other. Through the interaction of our global economic interdependence, global nongovernmental organizations (NGOs), and the globalization of media, we are faced with the distant effects of local decisions about production and investment, and we are aware of the socioeconomic provenance of our products. We are forced to take seriously the possibility that we are contributing to the socioeconomic circumstances of others, a basic criterion of community.[43] Our responsibility over the effects, even attenuated, of our own conduct at the global level, is a rationale for global justice that, it has been suggested, transcends the entire cosmopolitan-communitarian divide.[44]

Together, these global circumstances of justice, especially our capacity to both help and harm each other, make justice both possible and necessary at the global level. Moreover, in their contribution to the creation of solidarity, understood as a sense of fellow-responsibility, they lay the foundation for global community. However, a communitarian would object

---

[43] This is also a basic element of justice in the social contract tradition: obligations apply when one has accepted the benefits of the social arrangement, or taken advantage of the opportunities it offers to further one's interests.

[44] Mandle, *Globalization and Justice, supra* note 41, at 29; Richard Miller, *Globalizing Civic Duties* (unpublished manuscript) (on file with author).

that the circumstances of justice may well lay the foundation for social cooperation, but that community is more than
this, in all the ways we have discussed. I will, therefore,
turn directly to two further aspects of globalization that
bring us even closer to meeting the criteria communitarians
lay down for obligations of justice.

b. A Global Community of Knowledge. One of the salient features of
contemporary globalization is its effect on information flows.
As a result of the global telecommunications revolution, the
Internet, and the development of both global media and
the capability to organize social concern at a global level
(through networks of NGOs, for example), globalization is
creating what commentators have referred to as a global
community of knowledge.[45] Through globalization we know a
great deal, immediately and intimately, about the suffering
of people in other parts of the world, more so now than at any
time in the past.[46] Moreover, this flow of information is not
simply about global harms to "poor Others." Globalization
(particularly in its global terror and global finance aspects)
is also contributing among citizens of wealthy, developed

[45] *See, e.g.,* Dirk Messner, *World Society Structures and Trends,* in
GLOBAL TRENDS AND GLOBAL GOVERNANCE (Kennedy et al., eds.,
2002).

[46] HELD, *supra* note 29, at 58 (asserting that the globalization and
telecommunications revolution brings people into other social realities they otherwise would not know).

nations to a shared sense of vulnerability to "remote" forces.[47]

One specific type of shared knowledge important to globalization is the growing recognition of the risks we share as human beings on this planet and of our shared interest in addressing those risks. In this sense, globalization is "de-territorializing" risk, creating what has been called a "community of risk."[48] The literature is remarkably consistent in its listing of common risks facing all human beings: war and security challenges; climate change and environmental degradation; economic crises and increased economic competition and dislocation; infectious disease and global pandemics; natural disasters; and rapid population growth, to name a few.[49] Moreover, the desire for security,

---

[47] Paul Schiff Berman, *From International Law to Law and Globalization*, 43 COLUM. J. TRANSNAT'L L. 485, 516 (2005) ("We [meaning the United States] also may feel the growing significance of 'remote' forces on our lives, whether those forces are multinational corporations, global terrorist organizations, world capital markets or distant bureaucracies such as the European Union"). *See also* Raj Bhala, *The Doha Round as a Failed Instrument in Counter-Terrorism*, ST. THOMAS L. REV 9, 5 (Fall 2011); Robert J. Delahunty, *Terrorism and Trade: A Reply to Prof. Bhala,* ST. THOMAS L. REV 9, 161 (Fall 2011); Frank J. Garcia, Doha, Security and Justice: A Reply to Prof. Bhala, ST. THOMAS L. REV. 9, 194 (Fall 2011).

[48] Messner, GLOBAL TRENDS, *supra* note 44, at 490.

[49] *Id.* President Obama alluded to this in his September 23, 2009, remarks to the United Nations General Assembly, in which he said the self-interests of states have never been more aligned than they are today. President Barack Obama, First Speech to the United

environmental health, and sustainable development, for example, are not unique to any one specific culture.[50]

Taken together, these various types of knowledge satisfy a basic requirement for community – that we have the effective capacity to know one another's needs, concerns, and preferences.[51] This knowledge forms the basis for the social determination of "need" and "whose needs count," as well as the basis for Walzer's shared understandings. This goes beyond the global circumstances of justice argument I suggested earlier: we not only have the capacity to help or harm each other at a global scale, but we *know* that we do, and we know what such help or harm looks like.

This kind of knowledge has also played an important role in the communitarian argument for limiting justice to certain political and territorial units (the nation-state). Traditionally, we have been hampered by time and space in our ability to develop both the "extensity" and intensity of knowledge of each other that is necessary for justice to

Nations General Assembly (September 23, 2009), *available at* http://www.cnn.com/2009/POLITICS/09/23/obama.transcript/index.html.

[50] *See* Bruno Simma & Andreas L. Paulus, *The "International Community": Facing the Challenge of Globalization*, 9 Eur. J. Int'l L. 266, 272 (1998) (listing bases for a dialogue on a minimal set of common values).

[51] *See* David Miller, *The Ethical Significance of Nationality*, 98 Ethics 647, 653 (1988) (citing Benedict Anderson, Imagined Communities: Reflections on the Origin and Spread of Nationalism [1991]) (noting the importance of media in allowing dispersed bodies of people to think of themselves as belonging to a single community).

work.[52] In this way, globalization is fundamentally altering the game board in terms of community, by reducing or eliminating the spatial and temporal barriers to our knowledge of one another's needs, preferences, and situations, making it possible to recognize, develop, and exercise effective responsibility for one another's well-being.

In this way, such knowledge about each other is also the basis for creating solidarity, that leap of the moral imagination that says that your concerns are my concerns. However, the mere fact that we are increasingly aware of one another's situation and increasingly capable of responding to one another's situation across vast distances of time and space are not by themselves enough to create solidarity or community. Put another way, the basis for solidarity is not the same thing as solidarity itself. Can we say that such solidarity is emerging at the global level? This is the linchpin of the whole communitarian argument.

As a preliminary matter, I would agree with commentators who see contemporary evidence of such emerging solidarity in our common response to global humanitarian crises, needs, and atrocities, and even in our failures to respond. Put another way, insofar as our failures to respond to humanitarian crises abroad, when we have both knowledge and capacity, provoke shame and outrage, even such failures illuminate the growing sense that we both could have done something and *ought* to have, which together

[52] Garcia, *Global Community*, *supra* note 9, at 27.

render such a failure an injustice.[53] This level of response, even if at times still limited, weak, and inadequate, suggests an emerging sense of solidarity or sense of community at the global level, which for all its weaknesses would not have happened at all one hundred years ago.[54]

However, to more fully evaluate whether solidarity and/or community are emerging from our mutual knowledge and the recognition of our shared risks, we need to look more carefully at *how* we are responding, which brings me to my second point, about the globalization of institutions.

c. Globalization and Shared Traditions, Practices, and Understandings. The communities of knowledge and risk I outlined previously are increasingly becoming a community of shared traditions, practices, and understandings concerning how we respond to such knowledge and risks. These responses grow, both spontaneously and institutionally, out of our perception of shared needs and interests, our capacity to help and to

---

[53] *See* PETER SINGER, ONE WORLD: THE ETHICS OF GLOBALIZATION, 156–158 (2004) (citing example of 1970s humanitarian crisis in Bangladesh).

[54] Bruno Simma and Andreas L. Paulus list Rwanda and Somalia as examples of a weak solidarity which can suggest either that the concept of global community is either half-full or half empty. They decide it is half full, asking "After all, who would have cared – and how – a hundred years ago." *The International Community: Facing the Challenge of Globalization*, 9 EUR. J. INT'L L. 276 (1998). *See also* Sarah Joseph, *Social Media, Human Rights and Political Change*, 35 B. C. INT'L & COMP. L. REV. 145 (2012).

harm, and our awareness of each other's plight – in short, our understanding of globalization as interlocking our fates.

It would be a mistake to understate the reality of conflict over social practices and values, which contributes at least at the rhetorical level to actual political conflicts today.[55] However, globalization has also been a powerful force for developing widely shared practices at many levels. To begin at the cultural level, many have noted the harmonizing tendencies of globalization toward a more homogeneous popular culture.[56] Short of homogenization, culture is being "de-territorialized," due to cross-border human and cultural migrations characteristic of contemporary globalization.[57] At the ethnographic level, globalization is breaking down the very notion of territorially distinct, epistemically unique "cultures" or "communities" due to "social and economic processes that connect ... even the most isolated of local settings with a wider world."[58]

Moreover, regardless of what state we find ourselves in, we are increasingly a part of global social networks such as

---

[55] Huntington's "clash of civilizations" may be overstated, but the reality of conflict between groups with different normative communities is undeniable, even if it might be more accurately explained as a clash between tradition and modernity, or local control and globalizing capitalism, or developed versus underdeveloped.

[56] *See, e.g.,* Richard Barnet and John Cavanagh, *Homogenization of Global Culture,* in THE CASE AGAINST THE GLOBAL ECONOMY, 71–77 (J. Mander and E. Goldsmith, eds., 1996).

[57] *See* Berman, *supra* note 46, at 512, and sources cited therein.

[58] *Id.* (citing Gupta and Ferguson).

multinational corporations (MNCs), NGOs, and enterprises such as global scientific cooperation. Such shared enterprises build and constitute their own epistemic communities across national boundaries, all of which contribute to the development of such shared traditions and practices as can support global community.[59]

Developments in international law itself have fostered a role for international law as a community-building force. At the level of positive law, the postwar growth of universally recognized international human rights has played a particularly important role in international law's status as a global set of shared practices and understandings.[60] More recently, commentators suggest that, at least at the political level, there is an emerging consensus, or shared understanding, around the importance of markets and even democracy as well.[61]

---

[59] *Id.* at 500; GUNTHER TEUBNER, NETWORKS AS CONNECTED CONTRACTS (2011). Indeed, Manuel Castells has argued that globalization is bringing about a new form of nation-state, the "network state," whose principal duty is to successfully manage on our behalf this web of networks. MANUEL CASTELLS, THE POWER OF IDENTITY 242–273 (1997).

[60] Terry Nardin, *Legal Positivism as a Theory of Global Society, in* INTERNATIONAL SOCIETY, *supra* note 40, at 17–35.

[61] This consensus can be seen at the level of positive international law. *See, e.g.,* Thomas Franck, *Emerging Right to Democratic Governance,* 86 AM. J. INT'L L. 46 (1992). From a normative perspective, this can be seen as building upon an underlying normative consensus, insofar as the world's leading religious and philosophical traditions can be said to converge around this triad.

To more fully illustrate this critical element of emerging global community, I would like to focus on two particular types of contemporary shared practices – markets and meta-state institutions – as highlighting the interplay between globalization and our community-building responses to interconnectedness of various kinds.

i. Shared Understandings and Practices about Markets. Insofar as globalization is creating a global market society, this in itself is a shared practice or set of practices, albeit quite complex, contributing to a global community of shared understandings about socioeconomic organization.[62] At this point in world history, it is possible to say that virtually all people live in some form of organized market economy. Globalization has been both a facilitator and accelerator of this trend, and not without significant controversy.[63] However, for our purposes here, it is the ubiquity of the market itself that is significant from the perspective of shared understandings and practices, not its controversial nature.

The widespread use of the market does not, of course, mean that all countries have identical interests with respect to markets, or identical forms of market society. To take just

David R. Mapel, *Justice Diversity and Law in International Society*, *in* INTERNATIONAL SOCIETY, *supra* note 40, at 247.

[62] Hurrell, *supra* note 28, at 42.

[63] The global market economy is one of the most controversial aspects of globalization, for good reason. *See, e.g.,* JOSEPH STIGLITZ, GLOBALIZATION AND ITS DISCONTENTS (2002).

one example, the United States and Germany (two of the world's most developed countries) practice advanced capitalist forms of market economy that differ in important ways such as competition policy, labor-management relations, tolerance level for economic inequality among citizens, and social welfare policies, even in these otherwise similar market societies.[64] The contrast is even more marked when one ventures beyond the United States versus Western European market society and looks at Asian capitalism, even Chinese capitalism.[65] In fact, markets have been touted on instrumental grounds precisely because they can facilitate efficient transfers among people who do *not* necessarily share identical conceptions of the good.[66]

Nevertheless, *market society* has certain attributes – the need for bureaucratic regulation, recognition of private property, and functioning civil courts, to name a few – which by virtue of their significant spillover effects, contribute to the formation of important shared interests among participants.[67] Raymond Aron has called such liberal pro-market

---

[64] *See* POLITICAL ECONOMY OF MODERN CAPITALISM (Colin Crouch & Wolfgang Streeck, eds., 1997) (comparing Anglo-American, European, and Asian models of capitalism).

[65] *Id.*

[66] MANDLE, GLOBAL JUSTICE, *supra* note 1 at 130. This is one of the more promising aspects of a global market. The more sinister aspect is a global race to the bottom through deregulation.

[67] *See, e.g.*, DON SLATER & FRAN TONKISS, MARKET SOCIETY: MARKETS AND MODERN SOCIAL THEORY 92–116 (2001) (surveying the range of institutions which markets require and/or are embedded in).

norms the "germ of a universal consciousness" insofar as they have come to be held in common by developed and developing market states.[68]

One category of shared interests around markets is particularly significant for the purposes of this chapter: the interest in regulating the market through institutions. Most market societies have experience in developing domestic institutions capable of supplementing and mitigating the rigors of capitalism, for example, by compensating the "losers" through some form of wealth transfer. But what is truly distinctive about the emerging global economy is the shared recognition of the need for institutions that regulate the market at a transnational level. This is but one aspect of a larger move toward meta-state institutions at a global level.

ii. Shared Understanding of the Need for Meta-State Institutions. Perhaps the strongest evidence of an emerging global community involves our recognition of a shared need to look to institutions beyond the state, in order to frame an adequate social response to many of the problems and challenges we face. In other words, the need for increased global governance is itself a shared understanding, and the reality of global governance by its nature constitutes a shared practice.[69]

[68] Stanley Hoffman (citing Raymond Aron), *Clash of Globalizations,* in THE GLOBAL TRANSFORMATIONS READER, *supra* note 29, at 106.
[69] It is useful at this juncture to recall the point I discussed earlier, that understandings and practices can be debated and contested without

Globalization's many aspects are together pushing us toward increased cooperation at the meta-state level. Returning to Rawls's account of the circumstances of justice, the human response to these circumstances is to enter into systems of social cooperation for mutual advantage. Through this cooperation we create "society," in particular the "basic structure" – the institutions we employ to allocate resources and opportunities, and which thereby directly affect our life prospects. Through globalization, social regulation is increasingly conducted through a complex partnership, consisting of states and their constituent units, international organizations, and nonstate actors through mechanisms such as the market, all regulated or established through international law.[70]

By leading us to create new institutions and shift responsibility for many social allocations to the meta-state level, globalization is creating a global basic structure.[71] Through globalization we find ourselves in precisely the sort of cooperative venture for mutual advantage that is the subject of

> that necessarily rendering them not "shared" – this has to be so or there are in fact no communities at all, which would be incoherent.
>
> [70] "[T]he institutions and quasi-formal arrangements affecting persons' life prospects throughout the world are increasingly international ones – international financial institutions, transnational corporations, the G8, the World Trade Organization ... " JONES, GLOBAL JUSTICE, *supra* note 20, at 8.
>
> [71] For an interesting analysis of the issues presented by the possibility of a global basic structure, *see* Simon Caney, *The Global Basic Structure: Its Nature and Moral Relevance* (unpublished paper) (on file with the author).

justice, and sharing the fruits of social cooperation (trade opportunities, for example) through meta-state institutions such as the WTO and the European Union.

This move to the meta-state level could be seen as *merely* tending toward the creation of global society, which in the communitarian view does not go far enough for global community. However, I would like to suggest four ways in which this shift toward the meta-state level has profound communitarian consequences.

First, this shift indicates that the communitarian assumption of bounded distributive communities no longer holds at the nation-state level, necessitating a shift to a "higher" or "more inclusive" level of community in which all relevant distributive decisions are taken – the global level. Recall that Walzer describes the political community of justice as one "capable of arranging [its] own patterns of division and exchange, justly or unjustly."[72] When a community is no longer capable of fixing its own patterns of division and exchange, it is no longer sufficient to analyze the justice of that community with sole reference to itself.[73] In other words, unable to fix its own distributions entirely itself, the community is not capable of delivering its own justice. We must therefore look to that further level of institutions that is affecting that community's distributions, and to its justice.

[72] WALZER, SPHERES OF JUSTICE, *supra* note 15, at 31.
[73] This also resembles the point raised earlier about the tenability of Rawls's assumption of self-contained national distributive communities, in his analysis of domestic justice. *See* RAWLS, A THEORY OF JUSTICE, *supra* note 11.

This is precisely the effect of globalization.[74] In Hurrell's words, "[I]ntegration and globalization have undermined the boundedness of political communities whose particular cultures, traditions and ways of living are given so much weight by communitarians."[75] From a distributive justice perspective, globalization is revealing domestic society to be an incomplete community (even as it renders domestic society so), incapable of securing the overall well-being of its members by itself, thus prompting us to look to a higher level of community as part of group efforts to secure well-being. The many anti-globalization protests focused on the Bretton Woods institutions, for example, indicate the growing awareness that these institutions are increasingly constraining allocative decision making at the national level, as well as themselves engaging (through the allocation of trade benefits, crisis financing, and development aid, for example) in positive distributive functions.[76]

---

[74] *See* Alberto Tita, *Globalization: A New Political and Economic Space Requiring Supranational Governance* 32 J. WORLD TRADE L. 47, 49 (globalization leads to internal pressures on states as traditional macroeconomic policy tools "become less and less capable of being determined at a national level by democratically elected governments").

[75] Hurrell, *supra* note 28, at 36.

[76] It is in this sense that Teubner characterizes such protest movements as "parasitic" (though I would choose a different word): "They presuppose specialized institutions with high problem-solving potential, which they accuse of over-specialized tunnel vision and can provoke into innovations." Gunther Teubner, *Global Private Regimes: Neo-spontaneous Law and Dual Constitution*

Second, globalization is forcing us to look to international institutions such as the UN and the WTO for global policy solutions, and this has an inherent community-building effect. The role played by common institutions sharing a common language in building polities out of disparate peoples has long been recognized in international relations as well as domestic politics as "nation-building."[77] For example, in the United States we reinforce our shared identity as a nation when together we look to the federal level for resource allocations and policy responses, as in the case of natural disasters or security crises. Similarly, our tendency to look, at least in part, to meta-state institutions for responses to social and environmental problems globally reflects a shared understanding that such institutions play an increasingly prominent role in formulating or channeling social policy decisions and orchestrating social welfare responses, and that few states can act without them on any important social issue.[78]

---

of Autonomous Sectors in World Society?, in GLOBALIZATION AND PUBLIC GOVERNANCE 71–87 (Karl-Heinz Ladeur, ed., 2000). On the (re-)distributive potential of the Bretton Woods institutions, *see, e.g.,* Frank J Garcia, *Global Justice and the Bretton Woods Institutions, in* THE FUTURE OF INTERNATIONAL ECONOMIC LAW 23 (WILLIAM J. DAVEY & JOHN JACKSON, eds., 2008).

[77] *See, e.g.,* Hurrell, *supra* note 28, at 39 (state institutions tremendously important in creation and development of national communities); Will Kymlicka, *Territorial Boundaries: A Liberal Egalitarian Perspective,* in BOUNDARIES AND JUSTICE 249, 256 (David Miller & Sohail H. Hashmi, eds., 2001).

[78] *Id.* In this sense, even the anti-globalization protests contribute to the community globalization is creating, insofar as they take up

Third, the role of institutions in global regulation – economic and otherwise – is itself increasingly recognized as a source of norm-creation and shared understandings. Again in the words of Andrew Hurrell, "Once created, institutions act as platforms for on-going normative debate, for the mobilization of concern, and for debating and revising ideas about how international society should be organized."[79] For this reason, such institutions themselves can "move different states and societies towards 'shared understandings of the meaning of social goods.'"[80]

Fourth, this shift to meta-state institutions represents the emergence of a shared understanding with respect to regulating global social conflict. This reflects the distinction between first- and second-order social understandings in both Walzer and Miller with respect to how we manage conflicts over "shared" understandings in domestic communities, and suggests how globalization may be creating a broader shared understanding with respect to how we manage conflicting claims. As I have discussed, one answer communitarians give to the reality of conflict over understandings in domestic communities is to change the level of analysis to "understandings about understandings," or

one part of a larger global debate over the most humane ideology for global market society.
[79] Hurrell, *supra* note 28, at 42. A current example of this idea is reflected in the critique of the UN for failing to interfere in the Syrian crisis. *See, e.g.,* Saira Mohamed, *The UN Security Council and the Crisis in Syria,* 16 ASIL INSIGHTS (March 12, 2012).
[80] *Id.* (citing Walzer).

"shared public cultures," which might help resolve the problem but also casts the community's identity in a different light. When viewed this way, it may be said that communitarians are actually linking justice to a kind of shared institutional culture rather than a true community of shared primary beliefs.[81]

If so, this shift to meta-state institutions has profound consequences for global justice. Quoting again Hurrell's excellent article:

> [T]he density, scope and complexity of the agreements, norms, and rules in which states and societies are already enmeshed provide some basis for positing a community interest or an agreed set of purposes and values against which new substantive norms may be judged – the idea of an objective community interest or of the common interest of global society.[82]

When global social relations involve conflicts between incomplete national communities of justice over allocative decisions, globalization bumps us up a level, invoking a new shared understanding that the meta-state level is the place to resolve this conflict, according to new understandings regarding appropriate distributions, and norms in general,

[81] Perhaps what communitarians are identifying when they speak of the common good, is really a commitment to this second-order set of understandings about disputes, the rules about rules, the public culture.

[82] Hurrell, *supra* note 28, at 41.

at the global level. Insofar as these global practices deepen and extend, we see stronger shared traditions and practices of global social policy formation and allocative decision making. In the development of new forms of meta-state institutional governance, we are developing a new form of shared understanding, or rules about rules, at the global level.

d. Globalization and the Pace of History. Thus far I have not commented on the role of shared history in forming communities of justice. Communitarians like Walzer cite "time" as a key ingredient in the formation of community out of a hodge-podge of shared experiences and cooperative activities, the raw material of mutual self-interest; and in a similar vein Miller writes of the importance of shared history.[83] Thus one objection to the claim that the changes discussed earlier are forming some kind of global community is simply that it may take more time – that at the global level, even granting the changes I have suggested, there has simply been too little shared history for these changes to ripen into communitarian-style solidarity.[84]

One effect of globalization's transformation of time and space may be to change the role of time in the creation of community, making global community possible at a

---

[83] *See, e.g.,* MICHAEL WALZER, JUST AND UNJUST WARS: A MORAL ARGUMENT WITH HISTORICAL ILLUSTRATIONS 54 (3rd ed., 2000); MILLER, ON NATIONALITY, *supra* note 20, at 23–24.

[84] There has been plenty of history (colonialism comes to mind) but little of it "shared" in the sense communitarians mean.

relatively fast pace. Communitarians mention time or history as a necessary ingredient in community for two reasons: first, and less important, as a substitute for a more thorough explanation of the formation of communal bonds ("time" as a sort of magic wand to wave in the place of a detailed understanding of causation); and second, and more significantly, because a period of time has generally been considered necessary for social contact and social knowledge to attain the sort of cumulative intensity necessary for the creation of more intimate bonds.

This is where globalization's effects on time and space in many significant human social relations may come in. Because of globalization, it may well be that the process of building intense social bonds can occur at a much faster rate, meaning that a common life might be shaped more rapidly during periods of globalization than otherwise thought possible. Thus it may be quite possible to see global community emerge in a matter of decades.[85]

Second, I would like to suggest that globalization narratives themselves function as the sort of constitutive myth, which historians cite as essential in actually creating the

[85] We find a hint of acknowledgment of this changing nature of the pace of change itself, in Walzer's comparison of the fall of communism with the "fall" of medieval Christendom: the time span of the former is much shorter than that of the latter, "as befits the rhythms of modernity." MICHAEL WALZER, THICK AND THIN: MORAL ARGUMENT AT HOME AND ABROAD 47 (1994). I am suggesting, in this sense, that the rhythms of globalization may be even faster.

identity these myths already assert.[86] As David Miller points out in his discussion of nationality, the very concept of nationality in the operative sense depends upon a myth of shared history, often masking actual social processes of domination and conquest.[87] This invention of a "communal national past" is an essential element in the formation of a national identity and becomes part of the identity itself once established.[88]

Similarly, the many divergent globalization narratives at work in the present historical moment can play a vital role in creating a globalized world as a matter of identity. To begin with, the complex social forces of globalization themselves lead us to consider whether we are imagining the right community – isn't the globalization debate itself the beginning of imagining a community larger than the nation state?[89]

[86] *See* Berman, *supra* note 46, at 516–518 (discussing states as "imagined communities" and the shift through globalization to community "imagined" at the global level).

[87] The mythological aspect of national histories is one basis for objecting to nationalism as justified partiality. JONES, GLOBAL JUSTICE, *supra* note 20, at 159–160. Here I would like to accept for the time being this mythological aspect of historical narratives and explore its relation to globalization narratives.

[88] MILLER, ON NATIONALITY, *supra* note 20, at 122–123, citing Anthony David Smith, THE ETHNIC ORIGIN OF NATIONS (1986); *see also* Berman, *supra* note 46, at 123, citing ERNEST GELLNER, THOUGHT AND CHANGE 168 (1964) (nationalism is not "the awakening of nations to self-consciousness: it invents nations where they do not exist.").

[89] *See* PETER SINGER, ONE WORLD: THE ETHICS OF GLOBALIZATION 171 (2004) (citing Anderson's work on imagined communities).

Moreover, to engage in the globalization debate, even to contest globalization, is to reinforce the subjective formation of a globalization identity, which shares many of the same features of national identity already discussed. We discover ourselves to be together in an ineluctable social-historical process, in which our interests are bound up with each other, and which distinguishes us from others.[90]

However, and this is a crucial difference, because social membership in a global community is comprehensive, the "Other" we are distinguished from in globalization narratives is not the Other of a rival contemporary political community, but the Other of a pre-global past.[91] In other words, our identity is no longer based solely on nation versus nation, but on global versus pre-global.

Using the literature of imagined communities,[92] Berman argues that the very fact that our national community "identities" have been constructed suggests that changes in global social relations can in the same way lead to new imagined communities at the meta-state or global level:

[90] *See* Berman, *supra* note 46, at 490.
[91] If correct, this means that history is changing (but not ending!) such that those seeking alternatives to globalization are seeking to live in the past, rather than in an alternate present, becoming Luddites rather than Soviets.
[92] *See, e.g.,* Benedict Anderson, Imagined Communities 6 (1991) (nation-states are "imagined communities" because "the members of even the smallest nation will never know most of their fellow-members, meet them, or even hear of them, yet in the minds of each lives the image of their communion").

[I]f communities are based not on fixed attributes like geographical proximity, shared history, or face-to-face interaction, but instead on symbolic identification and social psychology, *then there is no intrinsic reason to privilege nation-state communities over other possible community identifications that people might share.* Thus the very same conception of community upon which the nation-state relies also provides the basis for critiquing the hegemony of the nation-state as the only relevant community under discussion.[93]

Thus, to borrow an illustration from United States history, we may come to see the "pre-globalized" world in the same way we in the United States see the Thirteen Colonies under the Articles of Confederation: partly as history, partly as myth, entirely in the past, but contributing still to our shared sense of identity.

e. Recapitulation. I have argued that in global social relations today we see, emerging both intersubjectively and at the regulatory level, the constitutive elements of a limited global community. I submit that globalization itself is in the process of creating a new global identity, consisting of shared understandings, practices, and traditions capable of supporting obligations of justice. Members of this global society are increasingly aware of each other's needs and circumstances, increasingly capable of effectively addressing these needs,

---

[93] Berman, *supra* note 46, at 518 (emphasis in original).

and increasingly contributing to these circumstances in the first place. They find themselves involved in the same global market society, and together these members look to the same organizations, especially those at the meta-state level, to provide regulatory approaches to addressing problems of global social policy. These organizations, in addressing such needs, are involved in allocating the benefits and burdens of social cooperation, such as rights, opportunities, privileges, membership, and resources, activities that have been traditionally understood in the domestic sphere to make justice both relevant and necessary.[94]

All of this is not to argue that global community has emerged fully formed, with the richness and force of national community. Hurrell cautions us that "whilst the idea of a global moral community is not entirely illusory, the elements of deformity [in contemporary global social relations] provide good grounds for arguing that it is certainly fragile and cannot bear too much weight."[95] Nevertheless, the problem – and the opportunity – are clear: paraphrasing Domingo, society is globalizing, but states (and international law) are merely internationalized.[96] What can we reliably say at this point?

---

[94] In Rawls's terms, we see at the global level institutional arrangements that "define men's rights and duties and influence their life prospects, what they can expect to be and how well they can hope to do." RAWLS, A THEORY OF JUSTICE, *supra* note 11, at 7.

[95] Hurrell, *supra* note 28, at 46.

[96] RAFAEL DOMINGO, THE NEW GLOBAL LAW (2010).

In the words of Paul Berman, we can at least say that "these ideas of space and community [do] complicate the presumed naturalness of nation-state communities."[97] Moreover, we can say (with Hurrell) that:

> [s]hared and institutionally embedded understandings as to what constitutes justice and injustice are no longer confined within national communities. In examining the changing structure of international society we surely are dealing with "an identifiable set of institutions whose impact on the life chances of different individuals can be traced." (quoting Miller)[98]

Taken together, it is my contention that these developments allow us to begin to speak in important ways of limited degrees of community, or "spheres of justice" to borrow Walzer's phrase, with respect to different issues, institutions, or sets of social relations within the global social space. Thus we can speak of "limited global community" as embracing that level of "community" necessary to support relations of justice, even if it does not manifest that level of community necessary to speak of "global community" in the fullest communitarian sense.[99]

It is in this sense that I have sought to establish that traditional communitarian objections to the possibility of global

---

[97] Berman, *supra* note 46, at 516.

[98] Hurrell, *supra* note 28, at 43.

[99] When Domingo speaks of "global community" he intends it in this latter, totalizing, aspirational sense. DOMINGO, *supra* note 95, at 102–103.

justice are being weakened by globalization itself. In doing so, I have deliberately refrained from arguing for a particular substantive view of global justice. My goal, instead, has been to suggest why globalization is itself changing the very nature of the phenomena that moral and political theories of global justice seek to explore. Thus my main effort has been to establish a link between our evaluation of the claims of communitarian theory, and our empirical evaluation of the social changes of globalization.

However, three quite serious questions remain: first, whether the sort of limited community I propose is really coherent as a normative community; second, whether global social relations will ever achieve the sort of thick community Walzer and others argue is necessary for global justice; and third, should such objections be overcome, what a communitarian approach to global justice would actually look like. I will take these questions in reverse, beginning with the third question here and saving the first two for my remarks concluding this chapter.

4. *What Would a Communitarian Theory of Global Justice Look Like?*

If one is willing to accept, even provisionally, that globalization is leading in some manner or degree to the emergence of a global community of some kind, then the stage is set for an examination of a communitarian approach to global justice. However, this undertaking poses quite a complex set of questions. If the central tenet of communitarianism is that justice flows from community norms, practices, and understandings, then what exactly are the norms, practices, and understandings of the partial or limited community I am positing here? Moreover, what is the effect of the limited aspect of this global community on the feasibility (or even identifiability) of such norms?

A complete account of the extent of shared global norms, practices, and understandings is beyond the scope of this book.[100] However, I will offer a few general observations here in order to illustrate the implications of this approach. To begin with, we should not expect a communitarian theory of global justice at this time to be as comprehensive as a domestic theory of justice, since there is still no comprehensive community at the global level. Instead, we might find something resembling Michael Walzer's "thin" approach to global justice, consisting only of those areas of overlap among normative communities.[101] The core to Walzer's approach is that it is built on a principle of mutual recognition rather than persuasion.[102] Walzer's mistake, as I have argued earlier, is not in what he catalogs, which is fundamental, but what he leaves out – that globalization renders thickness and thinness a dynamic set of properties, and trends toward thickening. Nevertheless, something like this comparative

---

[100] Interesting and promising beginnings of such an account include DOMINGO, *supra* note 95; Berman, *supra* note 46.
[101] MICHAEL WALZER, THICK AND THIN, *supra* note 84.
[102] *Id.* at 17.

study of norms is certainly a key element in discerning the contours of a global communitarian account of justice.

Alternatively, we might find that insofar as there is limited or partial community, its members already share a clearly identifiable set of normative commitments (even if not comprehensive). One example is the view often expressed by commentators that the global market reflects principles of economic liberalism, due to the liberal ideology of its institutions and key actors.[103] Insofar as that is true, we might find that a liberal theory of economic justice, first considered in Take One as limited to the foreign policy of liberal states, might be sustainable with regard to *all* participants – states and institutions alike – in the specific global community of the global market.[104] In other words, we might find that a liberal theory of economic justice is an appropriately pluralistic theory of global economic justice for the global economic "community" because the global economy has been fashioned

---

[103] Thus extending at a global level Polanyi's Market Society argument. *See* KARL POLANYI, THE GREAT TRANSFORMATION (1944). Whether or not optimally performing markets naturally reinforce liberal principles is a debate at least as old as Adam Smith. *See* ADAM SMITH, AN INQUIRY INTO THE NATURE AND CAUSES OF THE WEALTH OF NATIONS, chapter III (arguing that the economic and political potential of the French-British relationship was best served by freeing – not regulating – trade between the two rivals).

[104] We might even find, in the end, that communitarian changes in global social relations make cosmopolitanism sustainable bit by bit – a sort of creeping cosmopolitanism – insofar as we see emerging pockets of liberal community.

along liberal lines and reflects a consensus among participants on this basic point about socioeconomic organization.

Much more work needs to be done on these and other such questions. Sketching out the contours of an answer requires us to draw upon both traditional domestic political theory, and the many innovative studies of our new global social and legal reality currently under way, to capture the emerging norms of these new communities and envision the next generation of global institutions and doctrines capable of delivering this global community's global justice.[105] For the moment, let me offer this set of suggestions regarding what kind of global justice commitments a communitarian approach to global justice might support at this stage, drawing upon the work of Messner and others on a "global minimal ethics."[106]

As has been well documented, globalization is challenging and transforming traditional political and legal concepts that have hitherto organized social relations at an international level, in particular the role of states and the nature

[105] *See generally* SASKIA SASSEN, TERRITORY, AUTHORITY, RIGHTS: FROM MEDIEVAL TO GLOBAL ASSEMBLAGES (2006); DOMINGO, *supra* note 95; PAUL SCHIFF BERMAN, GLOBAL LEGAL PLURALISM: JURISPRUDENCE OF LAW BEYOND BORDERS (2012).

[106] Messner, *supra* note 44, at 33. Here I am thinking in more general terms, along the lines of what sorts of norms, albeit "thinner" ones, could reflect the broadest possible support from a limited "global" community. A particular, deeper, "sub-community" of globalization, such as the global market, might be able to support a "thicker" set of norms, as suggested above.

of boundaries.[107] Historically, the dominant view of the role of the state in international law has been as a sovereign actor acting in its unitary self-interest. Beginning with the postwar human rights movement and intensifying through globalization, social processes and increasingly regulation as well are occurring on a transboundary networked basis. These dynamics have been challenging and transforming this understanding of the state as agent in the sense of actor, to the state as agent in the sense of one who acts on behalf of another, in an increasingly rich multipolar and networked environment. That "other" consists of the range of individuals, groups, and national communities that states represent on the international level.[108]

These changes have implications throughout domestic and international politics and social relations. To begin with, states have traditionally used territorial boundaries and social boundaries, such as the concept of citizenship, to determine whether and how such factors as people, goods,

[107] *See, e.g.,* DOMINGO, THE NEW GLOBAL LAW, *supra* note 105 at 55–57 (the globalization of social relations forcing a globalization of law); KENICHI OHMAE, THE END OF THE NATION STATE (1996); *but see* ANTHONY HOPKINS, *The History of Globalization – and the Globalization of History?,* in GLOBALIZATION IN WORLD HISTORY 19, note 43 (and sources cited therein) (2002) (globalization is itself the product of nation-states and can flourish only if nation-states remain strong).

[108] Hurrell, *supra* note 28, at 41. Or, depending on one's view, that other is the transnational capitalist class. *See* B.S. Chimni, *International Institutions Today: An Imperial Global State in the Making,* 15 EJIL1 (2004).

money, and ideas will move through *their* space – whether they are "in" or "out," with all that this implies.[109] Boundaries have therefore played an important distributive role, in allocating the resources, rights, and opportunities that flow from one's status as "in" or "out."

Because of globalization, the very notion of what is "national" and what is "international" or "global" is undergoing a change, as even "national" institutions can often be understood more accurately as horizontally integrated components of a transnational system than as vertically accountable components of a traditional "state."[110] This implies, among other things, that a state's legitimacy will increasingly depend on its ability to successfully deliver social goods to the people and groups it represents by managing, not resisting, such transboundary networks.[111] When a state exercises such agency, it is increasingly to be guided by emerging notions of a transnational sense of the public good.[112] All of this is profoundly changing our understanding

---

[109]   One example is Guantanamo – the U.S. decision to move prisoners outside our territorial boundaries in order to deny them the protections such boundaries would extend graphically illustrates on a global stage the absurdity of a territorially determined package of basic rights. *See, e.g.,* Matthew Ivey, *A Framework for Closing* Guantánamo *Bay*, 32 B.C. Int'l & Comp. L. Rev. 353 (2009) (the very act of exploiting the gaps and loopholes of the current system, illuminates the emptiness of its moral reasoning).

[110]   *See* Saskia Sassen, *The State and Economic Globalization: Any Implications for International Law?*, 1 Chi. J. Int'l L.109 (2000).

[111]   Manuel Castells, The Rise Of The Network Society (2000).

[112]   *Id.*

of boundaries – they are to be managed by the state for the good of the individuals and groups it represents according to some emerging notion of the global public good.

This has profound implications for not only the law of territorial boundaries but for international law and its role, and makes it possible to ask what sorts of rights and institutional structures can be said to exist in this transboundary space, which we are calling here a partial or limited global community. If a global community with some notion of global public good is emerging, at least in a limited form, then it needs something like a global public law to structure it.[113]

This is the fundamental transformation that globalization is effecting in international law: shifting it from the public law of interstate relations, to the public law of a global community.[114] This change works in both directions,

---

[113] Global public law can be conceptualized as the organization of the structure of powers, duties, and limits of meta-state governance and its officers; relations of the meta-state levels of governance (international organizations) to the midrange (states) and to individuals; and the definition and exercise of powers of meta-state governance for the public good. Alternatively, one can think of it as the regulatory system for delivery of global public goods. *See generally* PROVIDING GLOBAL PUBLIC GOODS (Inge Kaul et al., eds., 2003).

[114] *See* DOMINGO, THE NEW GLOBAL LAW, *supra* note 105 at 121 ("Global law ... does not yet constitute a legal order in the strictest sense, but it is called to become one"); Benedict Kingsbury, *International Law as Inter-Public Law,* in MORAL UNIVERSALISM AND PLURALISM (Henry S. Richardson & Melissa Williams, eds., 2009); Berman, *supra* note 46; I say more about this in Garcia,

as international law is itself a force facilitating regulatory globalization and the interconnection of disparate legal communities.[115] Such a shift at the global level resembles the emergence at the regional level of a "European" law and a "European" economic community out of the many disparate states involved in the European integration process; a new legal order both facilitates and emerges out of a reconstituted (and constitutive) set of socioeconomic and political relationships.[116]

What can we say about the content of such a global public law? This, too, requires much work, something along the lines of a comparative study of public law and a legal anthropology of globalization.[117] Let me begin here by suggesting a

Globalization and the Theory of International Law, supra note 7, at 21.

[115] Paul Schiff Berman, *Global Legal Pluralism,* 80 S. CAL. L. REV. 1155 (2007).

[116] Indeed, Hurrell cites the European Union's evolving *acquis* as an example of the sort of shared community-building understandings that transnational institutions can build. Hurrell, *supra* note 28, at 43. The foundational treatment of evolution is of course J. H. H. Weiler, *The Transformation of Europe, 100* YALE L. J Symposium: International Law, 2403 (June 1991). For a recent overview of this process that emphasizes the role of legal institutions, *see* Vlad Perju, *Reason and Authority in the European Court of Justice,* 49 VA. J. INT'L L. 307 (2009).

[117] Benedict Kingsbury's global administrative law project has, of course, been central to this kind of development. *See, e.g.,* Benedict Kingsbury, Nico Krisch, and Richard B. Stewart, *The Emergence of Global Administrative Law* (N.Y. Univ. Pub. Law and Legal Theory Working Paper Group., Paper No. 17, 2005).

minimum core of rights that plays an important role in this emerging global public law, even though all these rights are not equally realized at this stage.[118] I call this minimum core the "Global Basic Package": a basic bundle of political, social, and economic rights, safeguarded through global law and delivered in a partnership between global and national institutions, in much the same way that political, social, and economic rights are safeguarded by Federal law and delivered through a variety of federal/state partnerships in the United States.

This list can be drawn in a variety of ways. For example, Andrew Hurrell cites emerging norms around safeguarding peace and security, managing common challenges (such as the environment or the global economy), and promoting common values (such as self-determination, human rights, and democracy).[119] Rafael Domingo places dignity, liberty, and equality (including addressing economic inequalities) at the center of global law.[120] Charles Jones offers three core values: subsistence, liberty, and physical security.[121] Brian Barry adds to this a list of "vital interests" such as clean drinking water, sanitation, clothing, shelter, medical care,

---

[118] This substantive approach complements but differs from a more procedural approach such as Berman's collection of tools for managing a global legal pluralism. *See* Berman, *Global Legal Pluralism, supra* note 115, at 152–194.

[119] Hurrell, *supra* note 28, at 41.

[120] DOMINGO, *supra* note 95, at 139–142.

[121] JONES, GLOBAL JUSTICE, *supra* note 20, at 4.

and primary education.[122] Importantly, Deacon adds political participation to this list, albeit in a more expansive concept of global citizenship.[123]

I suggest that at a minimum, the Global Basic Package as it is emerging consists of the following four elements: security, subsistence, liberty, and voice.[124] These are widely recognized in human rights instruments, multilateral treaties of various kinds, global and domestic political relations, civil society, and political theory.

With respect to security and subsistence, international human rights law recognizes a core commitment on the part of the global community to ensure and, if necessary, deliver food, shelter, and some minimum level of security as a function of our basic human rights. Because in reality this often amounts to very little, however, commentators such as Jean Elshtain have argued that there is still no equivalent to the state for such matters.[125]

---

[122] Brian Barry, *International Society from a Cosmopolitan Perspective* in INTERNATIONAL SOCIETY: DIVERSE ETHICAL PERSPECTIVES 144 (DAVID R. MAPEL & TERRY NARDIN eds.) (1998); *see also* Stanley Hoffman, *Clash of Globalizations, supra* note 67.

[123] On global citizenship and the basic package, see Robert Deacon, *Social Policy in a Global Context* in INEQUALITY, GLOBALIZATION AND WORLD POLITICS 238–247 (ANDREW HURRELL AND NGAIRE WOODS EDS.) (1999).

[124] The brief overview that follows is drawn from an earlier preliminary run-through of some of these issues. *See* Garcia, *Globalization and the Theory of International Law, supra* note 7, at 21–26.

[125] Elshtain cites Arendt's point that the only meaningful site for citizenship remains the state. Annual Meeting of American Political

With respect to liberty, human rights law offers some limited guarantee of liberty from unlawful detention, and international economic law (through the WTO) offers some liberty to exercise economic rights. Petersmann, for example, notes the interrelated and unstable nature of political and economic liberty and the emergent (but as yet incomplete) framework for protecting both through international human rights law and international economic law.[126]

The consensus is less clear with respect to voice. Although several core human rights instruments recognize the right to political participation, not all people live in functioning democracies, and there is still no consensus on the role of political representation or voice at the global level, on economic matters or otherwise. B. S. Chimni notes "strong resistance from powerful states to put in place a transparent and democratic decision-making process."[127] However, many commentators point to an emerging human right to democracy at a national level (with international consequences), and the movement for increased participation and transparency at multilateral as well as national levels

Science Association Panel, *Theorizing Globalization in a Time of War: Challenges and Agendas* (September 2, 2004).

[126] Ernst-Ulrich Petersmann, *Constitutional Primacy and 'Indivisibility' of Human Rights in International Law? The Unfinished Human Rights Revolution and the Emerging Global Integration Law,* 5 INT'L ECON. GOV. AND NON-ECON. CONCERNS, 211, 217–218 (2003).

[127] *See, e.g.,* B.S. Chimni, *supra* note 108, at 3.

suggests a recognition of voice at a global level, even while its expression and protection are imperfect and uneven.[128]

One limitation affecting all elements of this approach is the lack of any effective mechanism for global wealth transfers at the scale necessary to support the global basic package. This limitation reflects in part the emergent nature of any consensus on a global community of justice, even at the partial or limited levels posited here, and the tendency to revert to nationalist perspectives around zero-sum issues such as resource allocation and security.[129] This continues to be one of the most "deformed" (to use Hurrell's term) aspects of contemporary global social relations, as globalist norms compete with statist enforcement models: we still need to rely on effective state power to manage economic crises and effect global wealth transfers – hence, their underdevelopment at the global level.[130]

---

[128] Voice is tied to the emerging global economy as well, and may also be driven by it. Jay Mandle and Louis Ferleger refer to this as the need for institutional mechanisms for control, one of two fundamental elements (the other is compensation) of the regulation of a global market society. Jay Mandle and Louis Ferleger, *Preface: Dimensions of Globalization*, 570 ANNALS AM. ACAD. POL. & SOC. SCI. 8 (2000).

[129] Interestingly, Chimni sees this as linked to the democratic deficit in international governance – the more democratic the system, the greater the pressure for wealth redistribution, as those facing massive inequalities far outnumber those more fortunate (or powerful). *Supra* note 108, at 3.

[130] Hurrell, *supra* note 28, at 44.

When viewed in this light, any consensus over shared norms of global justice is clearly a work in progress; however, this debate over the possibility and contours of global justice itself reflects the communal process of deliberation over possible shared understandings, and shared institutions, which is itself both evidence of and constitutive of such community. Moreover, there is an emerging outline of areas of agreement from perspectives as diverse as natural law, communitarianism, and cosmopolitanism as has been noted by scholars such as Barry and Miller.[131] From this perspective, both proponents and opponents of global justice, even from a more stringent communitarian perspective, are not so much debating its possibility as they are participating in its constitutional convention, so to speak.

If this is so, then the historical moment we are in is the emergence of a consensus over global justice. Its evolution will be incremental and will involve work at the theoretical, doctrinal, and institutional levels. Continuing the work of "thickening" this model of global communitarian justice in economic and noneconomic matters will require, for example, a sustained reexamination of core international legal doctrines and institutions, such as boundaries, sovereignty, legitimacy, citizenship, and the territorial control of resources, from the perspective of emerging global polities.

---

[131] MILLER, NATIONAL RESPONSIBILITY AND GLOBAL JUSTICE, *supra* note 27, at 50.

B. Contributions and Limits of This Model

The principal advantage of this approach is that it tries to directly address the question of global justice by articulating a basis for a global normative community. On this view, globalization itself is in the process of creating a new global community, consisting of shared understandings, practices, and traditions capable of supporting obligations of justice at a global level. Members of this global web of relationships are increasingly aware of each other's needs and circumstances, increasingly capable of effectively addressing these needs, and increasingly contributing to these circumstances in the first place. They find themselves involved in the same global market society, and together they look to the same organizations, especially those at the meta-state level, to provide regulatory approaches to addressing problems of global social policy.

Having established a basis for global norms, this approach also offers the opportunity to reflect on what such norms might look like. Depending on the degree of global community one can identify, global norms may resemble "thick" domestic theories of justice, such as Justice as Fairness, "thinner" models of global justice along the lines of the global minimal ethics approach sketched out earlier, or the thin level of consensus in extreme cases posited by Walzer. In either case, what is significant is that such norms are understood to apply to all global participants because they are justified by reference to the community relationships they are all a part of and they are all building, through their global activities.

Moreover, these norms can also be applied directly to international institutions qua institutions, a significant improvement over the limits of Take One. These institutions are involved in meeting the globally shared needs of their communities through the allocation of the benefits and burdens of social cooperation such as rights, opportunities, privileges, membership, and resources: activities that have traditionally been understood in the domestic sphere to make justice both relevant and necessary. Within a global community, limited or otherwise, there would be some degree of shared understanding as to the nature of such institutions and their role in justice.

One important drawback to this approach, however, is that it tangles the question of global justice in controversial claims about the changing nature of global social relations. On this point, Hurrell is worth quoting at length:

> We are faced with the old difficulty of relating empirical accounts of an increasingly unified world to normative accounts of the emergence of a world community. However dense and intense economic exchange may be, it does not translate easily or automatically into a shared awareness of a common identity, a shared community or a community ethos. This is especially true given the massive inequalities within contemporary global capitalism. There is also a real danger in tying notions of moral community too closely to networks of economic interaction, particularly when so

many of the world's most vulnerable people are precisely those who are excluded or marginalized from integration processes that are misleadingly described as "global."[132]

There is an interesting analogy here to the history of international law itself. For several centuries, international law was mired in a theoretical dispute over whether it was law at all, which largely turned on the fact that international society did not look like domestic society, and then-contemporary models of law were drawn from domestic society: no international sovereign, no international law.[133] In a similar sense, Take Two embroils the global justice debate in contentious analogies to domestic political communities.

For international law, the way out of this dispute was, in effect, to look out the window and see that a lot of law abiding was going on, regardless of the theory.[134] In other words, we had to recognize that reality had bypassed theory. Something interesting, important, and different was in fact going on.

In a similar sense, it is costly to suspend or condition action on the many pressing tasks of global justice while we debate whether we are seeing global society, global

---

[132] Hurrell, *supra* note 28, at 36.

[133] *See* DOMINGO, *supra* note 95.

[134] In the famous words of Louis Henkin, "Almost all nations observe almost all principles of international law and almost all of their obligations almost all of the time." LOUIS HENKIN, HOW NATIONS BEHAVE: LAW AND FOREIGN POLICY 47 (2d ed. 1979) (emphasis omitted).

community, or global justice.[135] We do not see communitarian accounts of global justice in the literature, let alone communitarian-based critiques of existing global distributive institutions. The fundamental work necessary for such an account has yet to be done at a global level because the necessary preconditions to such an account are still in contention. Take Two can be useful in helping us get to the point of global justice, but may not yet be much help in telling us what global justice might look like.

To suggest the potential that this approach might have, I have sketched out an outline of a "global basic package" or "global minimum ethics" approach to such an account. However, this work is by its nature very preliminary and highly debatable, particularly when compared to the mature levels of political theory and, by extension, accounts of global justice, possible in other approaches such as cosmopolitanism or the liberal internationalism of Take One, each of course bringing its own limitations to the project. It may be true, as I have suggested, that the debate over the possibility of global justice is not simply a delay on the road to global justice but is itself part of the constitutive process of recognition and consolidation of the emerging global community's consensus with respect to shared practices and understandings. However, the bottom line is that the hard substantive work is still ahead.

---

[135] *See* AMARTYA SEN, THE IDEA OF JUSTICE (2009) (arguing in favor of a more pragmatic, less theoretical (and divisive) approach to global justice).

3

Take Three

Global Justice as Consensual Exchange: Consent, Oppression, and the Nature of Trade Itself

Thus far we have considered two approaches to the question of global justice. The first, Take One, unilaterally extends domestic principles of liberal justice to transboundary justice problems, transforming the question of global justice into an inquiry into the possibilities and obligations of justice as the foreign policy of liberal states. Take Two examines the nature of global social relations and argues that even assuming stringent communitarian standards for justice, some degree of global community is in fact emerging, at least enough to support an inquiry into principles of justice at least in some aspects of global social relations. Foremost among these is the global economy, with international economic law and its institutions as a complex system of shared practices and understandings.

Both approaches bring important strengths into the global justice project. Take One operates within the world of well-understood normative concepts and can be applied to transnational justice problems without first establishing a basis for shared principles of justice, an advantage in an environment of normative pluralism. Take Two embraces the effects of globalization on transboundary social relations, captures something of the underlying transformation under way in the global social space, and begins to frame a basis on which to seek truly transboundary norms for transboundary justice. Thus each contributes something vital and has an important role in any global justice inquiry.

Equally important, however, both present difficulties with respect to the key issue of establishing an effective basis from which to constrain others. Insofar as global justice advocates seek grounds on which to assert normative claims against powerful international or transnational actors, they must pay attention to, and are ultimately limited by, the theoretical justification for such claims. Such advocates would find themselves dissatisfied by both Take One and Take Two. The liberal internationalist view does not offer a basis for claims that bind anyone beyond liberal states (a necessarily limited number), leaving the question of global justice ultimately to unilateral action by such states and the political process of the global policy-setting institutions they seek to influence. The global communitarian view seeks to transcend this problem by arguing for the emergence of some form or degree of global community capable of supporting truly global normative claims, but by doing so situates global justice squarely in the middle of controversial empirical and theoretical claims about globalization and its effects on global social relations, and our nascent understanding of what such claims might even be.

This problem stems in part from the fact that both Take One and Take Two represent an "external" approach to the question of justice in international economic law.[1] The essential characteristic of all external approaches (and most current approaches are external) is that they take a particular normative theory and apply it to a body of law.[2] They are "external" because the theory underlying the analysis is not "legal" in origin but comes from moral theory, political theory, or some other branch of social theory that concerns itself with fairness.[3]

Any reader interested in law, policy, and law reform will recognize that there is nothing particularly exotic about the idea of an external critique of law; it is the most common

[1] See Frank J. Garcia & Lindita Ciko, *Global Justice and International Economic Law,* in RESEARCH HANDBOOK ON GLOBAL JUSTICE AND INTERNATIONAL ECONOMIC LAW (John Linarelli, ed., 2013) (contrasting external and internal approaches).

[2] The extensive Rawlsian literature sampled in Take One offers a paradigmatic case of an external approach common to both domestic and international law.

[3] A wide range of social theory concerns itself with justice and is therefore relevant to any domestic or, potentially, global justice inquiry. For an excellent introduction *see* KARL R. SCHERER, JUSTICE: INTERDISCIPLINARY PERSPECTIVES (1992).

form of normative critique of domestic law. However, the external critique of international law is somewhat less developed (and less successful) than external critiques in areas of domestic law, for many of the reasons we have seen in Takes One and Two. Most political theory is developed in a domestic context, which means that it must be adapted to an international social context.[4] This adaptation/extension must be justified – the fact that the relevant social and economic relations occur across national boundaries raises numerous complex and contentious issues having to do with asserting transboundary moral obligations, which we inevitably must do with an external critique of a transnational system of law such as international economic law. In particular, one must be concerned with establishing the transnational validity of the normative theory one seeks to import within a new and different social and epistemic context, or the resulting transnational critique will not have transnational validity. Domestic political theory does not gain this validity simply by being applied to a transnational body of law.[5]

---

[4] Caney's book on global justice is an important recent exception. SIMON CANEY, JUSTICE BEYOND BORDERS: A GLOBAL POLITICAL THEORY 10–12 (2005). He sets out to create a truly global political theory. However, in my view his cosmopolitan approach raises the issues discussed in the Introduction.

[5] *See* Frank J. Garcia, *Developing a Normative Critique of International Trade Law: Special & Differential Treatment* 5–22 University of Bremen TranState Working Paper No. 66, 2007, *available at* http://www.sfb597.uni-bremen.de/pages/pubApBeschreibung.php?SPRACHE=en&ID=76 (discussing in the context

What if instead there is another avenue toward what we call global justice, beginning with the fact that both trade and trade law are on the leading edge of globalization and constitute a ubiquitous, if not universal, form of contemporary social interaction? Rather than seeking to import first principles into economic law, we could begin closer to participants' immediate experience of economic interactions or to the nature of international trade law itself and look there for a basis for mutually agreed regulation. Would this allow us to evade both the limits of particular normative communities and the ambiguity of emerging global social relationships? Such are the questions that this third "take" on the question of global justice seeks to address.

A. The Model

1. *Internal Approaches to Law's Normativity*

I want to begin the analysis by situating Take Three within this larger context of internal versus external approaches to law's normativity. Instead of starting from first principles as in traditional applications of political theory to international economic law, internal approaches begin with a radically different starting point: *within* the phenomenon of economic relations and their regulatory structure, and not outside them. In contrast to a traditional "external" approach in

of Rawlsian liberalism the necessary adjustments to transpose domestic political theory into a transnational context) [hereinafter Garcia, *Normative Critique*].

which normative principles are derived extrinsically to the system in question and then applied, the "normative" principles in an internal approach flow directly from the structure and mandate of the system or the nature of its underlying social interactions and objectives.[6]

Lon Fuller's epochal book *The Morality of Law* offers an illustrative parallel. In this book Fuller sought to develop an alternative approach to the question of law's morality, distinct from the dominant natural law theories that were clearly external in the sense discussed here. Fuller asked of law in general the same question that internal approaches seek to ask about international economic law: what are the principles inherent in the system that must be respected if the system is to operate as a system of *law* and not as something else that just looks like law? These principles are the "internal" morality of law.[7]

With respect to trade law, an internal approach to trade and justice could begin with trade law *as a system*, examining the mandate and formal structure of an organization as well as its members' expectations, following, for example, Aaron James's structural equity approach.[8] Alternatively,

---

[6] *See, e.g.,* RICHARD MILLER, GLOBALIZING JUSTICE: THE ETHICS OF POVERTY AND POWER (2010) at 71 (distinguishing "deliberations with a goal of justice internal to the regime from deliberations with external goals").

[7] *See* LON L. FULLER, THE MORALITY OF LAW (1964).

[8] Aaron James, *Global Economic Fairness: Internal Principles* in GLOBAL JUSTICE AND INTERNATIONAL ECONOMIC LAW (Carmody, Garcia, and Linarelli, eds., 2012), [hereinafter James, *Internal Principles*].

one can begin with the nature of trade *as an experience*, looking at the core constitutive elements of the underlying social interaction, such as the role of consent in trade. In both cases, the goal is not to apply an external normative principle but to seek to articulate those principles inherent in each that must be respected if trade is to be trade and if trade law is to function optimally to achieve its intended social purpose. Before turning to the consent theory I will present in this chapter, I want to further illustrate the internal approach through a closer look at recent work by James and by Chios Carmody that can be taken to represent this new approach.

In "Global Economic Fairness: Internal Principles," James examines principles of fairness inherent within the global economic system by virtue of its being a particular kind of shared social practice, namely, the international practice of mutual reliance on a shared market. James distinguishes three subsequent principles of structural equity in trade relations. The first principle concerns the harms from trade, namely, that measures be taken by states to alleviate the specific adverse impacts attributable to free trade. An example of this principle is the controversial trade adjustment assistance (TAA) provision attached to the legislation introducing the U.S. free trade agreements (FTAs) with Korea, Panama, and Colombia into the U.S. Congress.[9]

[9] *See, e.g.,* International Center for Trade and Sustainable Development, *US Trade Agreements with Colombia, Korea, Panama Face New Setbacks,* 15 *Bridges Weekly* (June 2011).

The second principle requires that the gains from trade be equally distributed within a society, or in manner acceptable to all members of that society, and concerns primarily national systems for social allocation such as the tax code and employment policies. The third principle is simply the second principle applied between states, so that all societies mutually relying on this market share equally in the gains of trade or distribute those gains in a manner acceptable to them all, through mechanisms such as the principles of Special and Differential Treatment (S & D) in the WTO system discussed in Take One.[10]

These three principles comprise "structural equity," the manner in which an institution or system such as the global trading system distributes its advantages and disadvantages in order to achieve equitable results, equitable as understood within the system itself. They are "internal" because in each case they are derived from the structure of existing arrangements and the expectations of its participants, rather than any a priori normative theory.[11] They form the basis for evaluating its practices and offering policy recommendations, without needing to secure in advance some level of agreement on the relevance or applicability of external normative theories.

Chi Carmody's recent work on the WTO can also serve as an example of the internal approach, here limited specifically to the WTO as an arrangement among member states.

[10] *See* Take One *supra* pp. 88–92.
[11] James, *Internal Principles, supra* note 8 at 102–107.

The aim of the WTO is "to preserve the basic principles and to further the objectives underlying the multilateral trading system."[12] The WTO agreements have established a series of rights and obligations for WTO members and created a series of expectations in these members. The organization seeks to protect these expectations through various channels exemplified by the Dispute Settlement Understanding (DSU), which governs the adjudication of disputes on alleged non-compliance and, if necessary, enforces obligations through the authorized application of unilateral sanctions (called the suspension of concessions).

One of the most widely recognized structural defects in the DSU system is that it depends ultimately on the effectiveness of these sanctions, which in turn depends on the relative market size of the sanctioning and sanctioned states and their capacity to absorb the economic effects of sanctions, which are felt by both the sanctioning and sanctioned states.[13] An authorized suspension of concessions is generally effective in bringing a party into compliance with its WTO obligation in cases brought by developed countries, with large markets that are significant to the

---

[12] Paragraph 5 of the preamble to the Agreement Establishing the World Trade Organization.

[13] *See, e.g.,* CHENG-YAN TUNG, CROSS-STRAIT ECONOMIC RELATIONS IN THE ERA OF GLOBALIZATION: CHINA'S LEVERAGE AND TAIWAN'S VULNERABILITY (2007). Philip I. Levy, *Sanctions on South Africa: What Did They Do?* Economic Growth Center, Yale University, Discussion Paper No. 796 (1999) *available at* www.yale.edu/growth_pdf/cdp796.pdf.

sanctioned state and which can absorb the higher costs of the sanctioned goods to domestic consumers. However, the same mechanism is not as effective when a developing country, with its small and highly trade-dependent market, is awarded the right to suspend concessions against a larger noncomplying state, both because its consumers can ill afford the higher costs of the sanctioned goods, and the volume of trade with the noncomplying state is simply too small from that state's point of view for the sanctions to have any appreciable impact.

In the view of Carmody and others, this is an unjust result.[14] The difference is that for Carmody this is an internal issue, not the result of an evaluation according to external criteria of justice and fairness. It is internal because this failure reflects a frustration of member expectations based in the agreements themselves, through an ineffective means of dispute settlement. It is a justice issue, because as Carmody points out, WTO "[j]ustice is ... about maintaining the distribution of expectations [of trade related behavior] which is equal; the ethos is justice-as-equality."[15] Thus we are talking about justice and fairness as an intrinsic part of the WTO itself, because these are expectations of the members incorporated as integral parts of the system itself.

---

[14] *See, e.g.,* United States – Measures Affecting the Cross-Border Supply of Gambling and Betting Services (DE285)

[15] Chios Carmody, *A Theory of WTO Law,* 11 J. INT'L. ECON. L. 527, 542 (2008).

Thus the analysis of internal principles of fairness or structural equity in a system simplifies the deduction of standards of justice to evaluate that system. From this example we can see that fairness as equality between members is such a standard in the WTO. However, we should not assume that this conclusion merely reflects a stealthily imported liberalism on the part of the analyst. Equality is *not* an intrinsic part of all international organizations, as, for example, in organizations such as the IMF in which members have *structurally* unequal voting power. Moreover, different organizations and different regimes could derive different standards even from similar internal principles such as fairness – fairness need not mean equality. Within the World Bank and the IMF, for example, access to funds is not formally equal: progressivity in the form of preferential and concessional lending to the least developed borrowers is an important internal operating principle, thereby making *inequality* an internal principle of justice in the service of fairness within such organizations.[16]

2. *Consent as an Internal Approach*

The work of James, Carmody, and others illustrates the diversity of approaches to the internal normativity of trade law.

---

[16] *See* Frank Garcia, *Global Justice and the Bretton Woods Institutions*, 10 J. INT'L ECON. L 481 (2007) [hereafter Garcia, *Global Justice and the Bretton Woods Institutions*]. (evaluating, but from an external viewpoint, the unequal access to development capital and trade currencies as an important element of justice).

In this chapter, I will pursue a different internal approach, built around the notion of consent and its function in economic transactions.[17] This analysis is based on the nature of economic exchange and our language for it – something of a phenomenology of trade, or an analysis of its essential nature – that aims to stay close to experience.[18] I will look at how economic interactions themselves have certain intrinsic requirements or characteristics that both support and require what we might otherwise describe as behavior that is just. In this way, it is hoped that the law can strengthen what is already working and wrestle with what is not working in such experiences in a manner that participants from any normative tradition would recognize intuitively as prudent, even necessary.

In this Take I am arguing that "consent" is that essential characteristic making economic exchanges "trade" rather than theft, coercion, or exploitation. Such a proposal is not far from ideas that are already part of the conversation about law and justice. Brian Barry suggests, for example,

---

[17] This approach is based on an ongoing project involving the role of consent in trade law. *See* Frank J. Garcia, *Is Free Trade "Free"? Is It Even "Trade"? Oppression and Consent in Hemispheric Trade Agreements*, 5 SEATTLE J. FOR SOC. JUST. 507 (2007) [hereinafter Garcia, *Free Trade*].

[18] For Martin Heidegger, language and experience are interwoven – they arise at the same time. "[O]ur access to the world and to anything that might show up within the world, is structured by language." Christina Lafont, *Heidegger, Language and World-disclosure*, 45 INQUIRY 185, 185 (2002).

that we ask of any rule or principle if it would emerge from a negotiation involving equality and freedom.[19] That is quite similar to the notion that it be a rule or principle freely consented to, since we assume that to be the case in negotiations involving equality and freedom. John Rawls's famous device of the Original Position can also be seen as an exercise to invoke our notions of consent: under the conditions he prescribes, what principles of justice would we consent to? Within liberalism as a whole we maintain that consent plays a normative role as the basis of the legal order itself, at least in the social contract model of liberal societies.[20]

What distinguishes the consent approach to trade from these other views is the idea that we attempt to come at the role of consent from the ground up, so to speak, basing the argument for the importance of consent in the nature of trade as we actually experience it, and that we extrapolate from this a set of benchmarks for actual trade agreements. In other words, in Take Three I am approaching consent not as an abstract quality, thought experiment, or theoretical requirement but as an active element both in an experience and in our legal concepts around that experience. The argument is that consent is essential to trade law, not for independent political or legal reasons, but because consent is inherent in the nature of the act in question.

---

[19] BRIAN BARRY, THEORIES OF JUSTICE 343 (1989).

[20] *Id.*, at 3–4; JOHN LOCKE, TWO TREATISES ON GOVERNMENT (Peter Laslett, ed., 3rd ed., 1988).

There is an extensive literature on the many roles that the notion of actual consent plays in the law.[21] Consent serves to invoke specific bodies of law such as the law of contracts, where the presence of consensual exchanges is what designates contract law as the relevant body of law, rather than, for example, the criminal law of theft or extortion.[22] Consent also plays a key doctrinal role *within* specific bodies of law, such as the criminal law of sexual relations, where a series of consequences to one's life and liberty depend upon a determination of consent, as defined by the law.[23]

Beyleveld and Brownsword open their comprehensive analysis of consent across many fields of law with an illustration of the changing law of consent in marital sexual relations. Under the early English common law, consent on the part of the wife was presumed in law by the state of marriage itself, illustrating the relationship between consent, power, and inequality in law that is also the subject of

---

[21] *See generally* DERYCK BEYLEVELD & ROGER BROWNSWORD, CONSENT IN THE LAW (2007) (reviewing this literature and analyzing the role of consent in public and private law).

[22] *See* ARTHUR LINTON CORBIN, CORBIN ON CONTRACTS §1.4 (rev. ed., 1993) (describing necessity of mutual assent – the so-called meeting of the minds: "If it is made clear that there has in fact been no such meeting of the minds, the court will not hold a party bound by a contract varying from the party's own understanding").

[23] *Id.* at 1–2.

this chapter, and law's role in either creating, reinforcing, or masking this relationship.[24]

What these consent doctrines have in common with the consent approach to trade is the shared idea that in any society that takes people and their choices seriously, consent will play a key role in the law.[25] Thus one could argue that to a degree, the notion of "trade" is a constructed concept in the same way that "contract" is a constructed concept: it reflects both a basic kind of behavior involving exchange or agreement, and a legal concept and related structure of enforceability, remedies, and rights in the law of a society that takes people and choices seriously when it decides which promises to enforce. Where the consent approach to trade may differ, as I will illustrate, is that there may be something "pre-legal" and therefore unconstructed about the role of consent in making trade "trade" and not something else. I am interested in examining how consent functions in the actual exchanges we undertake and in the agreements we negotiate about structuring such exchanges, for the normative implications that may follow.

This approach has important implications in the case of global rule making, which today means principally economic rule making through trade agreements. If we are

---

[24] *Id.* The common law's evolution with respect to consent in marital sexual relations also illustrates law's capacity for reform as our understanding changes.

[25] BEYLEVELD & BROWNSWORD *supra* note 21, at 3–4.

seeking to create a framework within which trade can flourish – as opposed to something else – then we should aim for and structure such negotiations so as to achieve and reflect such consent, rather than simply employ related notions of consent theoretical purposes.

Because I am ultimately interested in how the role of consent in trade should affect trade treaties, I also need to distinguish my use of consent here from the concept of state consent in international law and legal theory.[26] In international law, consent is a formal principle of legitimacy. As such, this notion of consent is important to the extent that trade law is part of international law and trade agreements are instruments under international law. However, as I discussed with respect to consent in political theory, I am not interested in the doctrinal role of consent as a formal requirement for the enforceability of international agreements. Instead, I seek through "consent" to grasp an elusive quality in trade arising from the nature of the social relationships formed through an exchange. Consent is the essential characteristic that makes such an economic exchange "trade" rather than theft, coercion, exploitation, or the like, and thus helps us distinguish between what *appears* to be trade from what *is* trade in the real meaning of the word.

---

[26] For an overview of consent in international relations and the role of consent as a legitimizing factor in international law, *see* Matthew Lister, *The Legitimating Role of Consent in International Law*, 11 CHI. J. INT'L. L. 663–91 (2011).

My aim is not to talk about the formalities of consent in international treaty law but to identify aspects of trade law and trade agreements that look and act like trade but are something else, and that damage the subject of trade because they do not reflect consent. When an act passes as trade but upon closer examination is not trade because it does not reflect consent, this act generates costs that impede the flourishing of trade and thus undermine the subject of trade.

The key to this approach being a part of the global justice project is the argument that a flourishing trade system that respects the consent of its individual and state participants will incidentally also be a more just system of global economic relations, since individuals and states will have fewer reasons to accept bad bargains and will instead negotiate and conclude more equitable bargains at the transactional and treaty levels. A truly consensual system of trade will therefore promote similar outcomes to what we seek to promote through the global justice debate, but through a route that ideally cuts across normative traditions and seems intuitively plausible to any market participant – through amplifying the scope for individual evaluations of equity to shape resulting economic relations.

In order to develop this model, in this chapter I will first look at the private level of individual transactions, utilize examples from private exchange, then focus principally on the social and regulatory aspects of trade – trade as a set of economic relations and as a system for governing such relations. I will begin by looking at some aspects of our language, concepts, and cultural experiences of trade as a human phenomenon, suggesting a preliminary definition of trade related to consensual exchange. I will then apply this model to international trade agreements, drawing my examples from United States hemispheric trade practice. This area of law offers us sharp portraits of the issues of consent and its absence, due to the marked inequality in bargaining power that characterizes trade negotiations between the United States and any other hemispheric trade partner. Through a brief examination of the Central America Free Trade Agreement's (CAFTA's) negotiation process and substantive law, I will illustrate how this approach can identify those elements of trade agreements that represent dynamics other than trade, such as predation, exploitation, or coercion.

By doing so, I hope to shed light on subtle but important dynamics in contemporary trade relations, particularly as they involve substantial inequalities in power among participating states (and not just the United States). These inequalities and their effect on trade rules and trade negotiations undercut global justice through their effects on the rules of the game and on the possibility of true consensual exchanges. If I am correct that an investigation into the nature of trade as a human experience reveals that many aspects of current trade law and policy mix what is ostensibly free trade with something else – exploitation, coercion, or predation – then this has important normative and pragmatic implications for global trade policy and offers us a radically different take on the possibility of and approaches to global justice.

3. *Investigation of Trade as a Human Experience*

Both our language and our collective experience of trade suggest many possible aspects or dimensions of that experience that merit further inquiry as we try to understand just what trade is.[27] This model begins with the notion of trade as a transaction rooted in a rich experience of encounter, risk, and inequalities in power.[28]

a. Trade as Exchange. To begin, trade can be seen as involving transactions. When we trade, we engage in a transaction – something changes hands, so to speak. I exchange a good with you for the good you have that I want. In this sense, trade is a basic everyday experience among people. It was none other than Adam Smith who noted "a certain propensity in human nature ... to truck, barter, and exchange one thing for another."[29] A more contemporary source, Amartya Sen,

---

[27] By speaking in the plural, I mean to invite the readers to consider whether they find what I say to be consistent with their own experience, rather than to presume I can speak for any of us or "all" of us in some definitive sense.

[28] The overview that follows is drawn from Garcia, *Free Trade, supra* note 17, at 507–510.

[29] ADAM SMITH, THE WEALTH OF NATIONS, BOOKS I-III 121 (Andrew S. Skinner, ed., Penguin Books 1999) (1776). I am indebted to Judith Wise for introducing me to this aspect of Smith's work.

puts it this way: "The freedom to exchange words, or goods, or gifts does not need defensive justification; they are part of the way human beings in society live and interact with each other."[30]

We also speak of trade, in a specifically international sense, as exchanges involving the crossing of geographic and political boundaries. This evokes other dimensions of trade, such as trade as exploration, where economic need rouses us out of the known into the unknown; and trade as adventure: will this gamble pay off? will the merchant ships arrive? will my fortune grow or be lost? One powerful evocation of this in Western literature is Shakespeare's *The Merchant of Venice*, in which the loss of Antonio's ships is one of the dramatic forces propelling the primary narrative.[31] This story, interestingly enough, is about another aspect of trade also quite relevant to this inquiry, namely, which kinds of exchanges we will and will not allow.

b. Trade as Encounter. The desire to exchange brings us into contact with one another; historically, we have crossed boundaries to engage in trade and it has meant encounters with the "Other."[32] Thus, trade is one of the prime forces in

---

[30] AMARTYA SEN, DEVELOPMENT AS FREEDOM 6 (1999).

[31] *See* WILLIAM SHAKESPEARE, THE MERCHANT OF VENICE (William J. Rolfe, ed., 1903) (regarding international trade and its vicissitudes).

[32] On the many ramifications of the Other, the canonical source is Edward W. Said's ORIENTALISM (1978).

bringing peoples in contact with other peoples on terms that might result in a mutually beneficial exchange. In this way, trade is a primal form of communication across difference, expressing who we are, what we make, what we want, and how we exchange.

One of the marvelous aspects of trade is that it can involve communication and exchange with the Other where there is no shared language, culture, or history – only the mutual desire to exchange. In this way, we can see that trade involves a form of what Stanley Cavell calls "acknowledgement" – the recognition that the Other exists as a separate, recognizable human person with the treatment due a person, even if we cannot directly or fully know the person's mind.[33]

Of course, encounters with the Other are not always beneficent. We can try to profit from the lack of shared language, or other information asymmetries, to engage in sharp dealing – trade as trickery or deceit. We have many colloquial examples of this, including offers to sell one another the Brooklyn Bridge, or the fable about Manhattan being "purchased" from indigenous Americans for a "handful of beads."[34]

Returning to *The Merchant of Venice*, the proposed flesh trade in the play already shows several of the negative

[33] STANLEY CAVELL, THE CLAIM OF REASON 329–426 (1979).

[34] *See* Peter Francis, Jr., *Beads and Manhattan*, *at* http://www.hartford-hwp.com/archives/41/415.html (last visited April 6, 2007).

dynamics of trade to be examined in this chapter: coercion; inequalities in social power; and the breakdown of acknowledgment along ethnic, religious, and gender lines. The most memorable speeches of the play are in fact calls for acknowledgment across and in spite of such differences.[35]

c. Trade as Domination. This raises another, more serious aspect of trade: trade as conquest. Obviously, I cannot mean this literally: conquest is conquest. However, even a cursory review of the history of trade offers examples such as the "trade" relations of the East India Company, for example, or the notorious "Unequal Treaties" between China and the West, that illustrate the fluid interrelationship between the concepts of commerce, conquest, and confiscation, allowing us to see a darker side of trade as domination under the guise of trading.[36]

Eduardo Galeano writes passionately how "Latin America's big ports, through which the wealth of its soil and subsoil passed en route to distant centers of power, were ... built up as instruments of the conquest and domination

---

[35] *See* SHAKESPEARE, *supra* note 31. I am indebted to Kim Garcia for pointing this out.

[36] *See, e.g.,* ANTONY ANGHIE, IMPERIALISM, SOVEREIGNTY AND THE MAKING OF INTERNATIONAL LAW (2005); Omar Saleem, *The Spratly Islands Dispute: China Defines the New Millennium,* 15 AM. U. INT'L L. REV. 527, 554–556 (2000) (documenting commercial exploitation, lack of reciprocity, and legacy of bitterness arising from unequal treaties); James Thuo Gathii, *Commerce, Conquest and Wartime Confiscation,* 31 BROOKLYN J. INT'L L. 709 (2006).

of the countries to which they belonged, and as conduits through which to drain the nations' income."[37] Anthony Anghie chronicles the way in which trading companies were used to assert sovereignty and extend the colonizing states' dominion over vast territories that the European states were not yet ready to administer directly.[38] Similarly, James Gathii documents the role of free trade concepts in legitimating Belgium's monopoly on exploitation of the Congo under the "freedom of commerce" principles agreed upon at the Berlin Conference.[39] By arguing that trade should be free, the colonial powers effectively left the stage open for unregulated exploitation of the Congo.[40] These examples sadly and vividly illustrate how trade can function as a form of dominance over the Other for economic gain.[41]

Once again, *The Merchant of Venice* offers us an eloquent window into these dynamics. Its secondary story line is also about domination, about choosing a woman not as a commodity but as a person.[42] Shakespeare makes the point that there is no marriage if the woman is a commodity, just

---

[37] EDUARDO GALEANO, OPEN VEINS OF LATIN AMERICA 197 (1973).

[38] ANGHIE, *supra* note 37, at 68.

[39] James Thuo Gathii, *How American Support for Freedom of Commerce Legitimized King Leopold's Territorial Ambitions in the Congo*, in TRADE AS GUARANTOR OF PEACE, LIBERTY AND SECURITY? CRITICAL, EMPIRICAL AND HISTORICAL PERSPECTIVES 97 (Padideh Ala'i et al., eds., 2006).

[40] *Id.*

[41] *Id.*, at 98 (citing SAID, *supra* note 33, at 3).

[42] *See* SHAKESPEARE, *supra* note 31.

as there is no trade if it involves domination. Viewed in this light, the play is also about the limits of the marketplace, as, for example, when Bassanio is given a ring he is not to give away.[43]

Historically, we can read the play as responding to a contemporaneous wave of globalization and the European approach to the "New" World, raising difficult and timely questions for Elizabethan England and for us. Can we deny our own and others' humanity for economic gain, involving, for example, slavery, the mines, and the *encomienda* system?[44] Does a "new" world mean it is all up for grabs, that maybe the old rules won't apply in this new economic space? Such questions are never far from the surface in international trade, up to and including contemporary globalization.

4. Investigating Trade as a Transaction

I would now like to take a few of these aspects of trade and further explore them to construct a preliminary picture of trade as a human experience.

a. Trade as an Exchange of Value. We engage in many types of transactions, whether involving money, goods, ideas,

---

[43] It has been suggested that this play shadows all our inquiries into trade, markets, and capitalism itself. *See* Sebastiano Maffettone, *Is Capitalism Morally Acceptable?* 1–2 (2005) (unpublished draft) (on file with the author).

[44] We hear echoes of Bartolomeo de las Casas here. BARTOLOMEO DE LAS CASAS, A SHORT ACCOUNT OF THE DESTRUCTION OF THE INDIES (Nigel Griffin, trans., 1992) (1552).

services, affinity, or information. However, if we think of what distinguishes trade from the many other exchanges we participate in, it is that trade involves a transfer of economic value. By "economic value" I mean, in a general sense, goods, services, or currency – as opposed to other qualities such as affection that have great value but are not economic in this sense. I am also not assuming any objective theory of value – for our purposes here, we can take value as determined by preferences and markets.

There are many different types of transactions involving a transfer of economic value, but not all of them are trade. For example, gifts are transactions involving a transfer of economic value, but one of their distinguishing characteristics is their unilateral nature: the gift-giver transfers something of economic value for nothing in return. In contrast, trade transactions are bilateral, or mutual, in nature, involving a *bilateral* exchange of economic value.

Theft is another type of unilateral transaction, helpful in clarifying the nature of trade. A theft involves an involuntary transfer of value. It could be said that theft is not trade because it is unilateral, but a simple thought experiment clarifies that this is not the essence of the distinction. A thief could give you a cheap watch in return for your wallet, but it would still be a theft despite its bilateral quality. We would not call this a trade, nor would we call it even a coerced exchange, as will be discussed later. The "exchange" element is cursory or symbolic only – the essence is the involuntariness of the transfer of the victim's wealth.

Thus, trade must also be voluntary, which introduces the key notion of consent – both parties must consent to the transaction or there is some element of theft. The role of voluntariness is reflected in our language.[45] We can speak of good trades versus bad trades in terms of meeting our goals, and yet we distinguish even bad trades from "rip-offs" or thefts. We would not refer to the experience of being robbed as a "bad trade," except in a deliberately ironic sense.

Another aspect to the voluntariness of bilateral exchange can be expressed through the notion of bargain. Bargaining, or the process of reaching mutually agreeable terms, is often a necessary element in reaching consent. Even when parties to an exchange do not actually bargain, the exchange presumes the freedom of both parties to consider and propose a variety of possibilities on the road to saying yes or no. Otherwise, if either of the parties was not able to bargain freely, the resulting transaction might still be voluntary in a basic sense, but something has been lost. This would be more akin to coercion than trade.

---

[45] I am of course working in English, as the language whose nuances I understand best. By saying "our language," I do not mean to assert that English is a universal language or that its terms are universally generalizable; I mean to invite the readers to assess these observations against their own language. Perhaps for commercial matters English is indeed a fairly generalizable language, but more than that I wouldn't want to suggest here (and I am not even sure about that). A definitive phenomenology of trade intended for an argument on global economic justice would need to undertake a linguistic interrogation of trade in many languages.

This notion of bargained-for consent is reflected in law through the concept of a "meeting of minds." The meeting of minds in contract law, even as a constructive notion, is key to the whole system for enforcing promises. If we look at the key justifications under which a contract is declared void or voidable – mistake, duress, or fraud – we see that they reflect the absence of bargained-for consent.

In summary, by examining our experiences and language of economic exchange, I have sketched out a notion of trade as consisting of voluntary, bargained-for exchanges of value among persons for mutual economic benefit.

5. What Is Not Trade, and Why

Based on this preliminary inquiry, several alternatives to trade (i.e., other economic interactions that we do not consider trade) can be examined in order to paint a fuller picture of what trade is and what it is not. In doing so, I rely primarily on the work of Simone Weil, the 20th-century French philosopher, known for her frank examination of the role of consent and its absence in distinguishing between economic transactions and economic oppression.[46]

---

[46] *See* Adrienne Rich, *For a Friend in Travail*, in AN ATLAS OF THE DIFFICULT WORLD: POEMS 1988–1991, at 51 (1991) ("*What are you going through?* she said, is the great question. / Philosopher of oppression, theorist/ of the victories of force"). "She" being Simone Weil, who wrote, "The love of our neighbor in all its fullness simply means being able to say to him: "What are you going through?" *See* SIMONE WEIL, WAITING FOR GOD 115 (Capricorn

a. Predation. In the previous discussion, I introduced the concept of theft as a contrast to trade. Essential to this distinction is the absence of consent on the part of the party surrendering economic value. Weil writes that one cannot seek consent where there is no power of refusal.[47] Thus, where there is no power to refuse, there is no trade because there can be no consent.

At the private-party level, contract law recognizes this difference through the concept of duress, a defense to the finding of a contractual obligation. In other words, where one party's consent to enter into a contract was not freely given but was given under some form of pressure, the law will not recognize this as a meeting of minds and will not find a contract.

In economic relations terms, the equivalent to theft – transactions that are not mutual and where consent is not present – can be called extraction or predation; add a political element and we call it economic dominance or colonialism. In these cases, an economic benefit flows from one party to the other but it is not mutual in a meaningful sense, and most important, it is not consensual. Rather, the economic benefit in these cases is achieved through power inequalities

Books 1959) (1951). Many thanks to Kim Garcia for introducing me to Weil and suggesting the connection between Weil's thought and trade.

[47] Simone Weil, *Justice and Human Society*, in SIMONE WEIL 116, 123 (Eric O. Springsted, ed., 1998) [hereinafter WEIL, *Justice and Human Society*].

as expressed by economic or military force.[48] Such transactions are not consistent with our concept of trade as outlined; they are, instead, a form of wealth extraction in the purest colonial sense.

b. Coercion. Short of predation, we can recognize a subtler weakening of consent, involving what I will call coercion. Coercion occurs when a transaction is mutual and in some basic way consensual, but something weakens the fullness or freedom of the consent, short of outright theft or duress.[49] This usually involves a restriction on the range of possible bargains that the parties are free, or not free, to propose and consider. Thus, coercion presupposes an inequality in bargaining power, where one party works to limit the range of possibilities "on the table," so to speak. The resulting agreement will be voluntary in an important sense, yet will be motivated less by a desire to commit to the bargain in

---

[48] *Id.* There remains the difficult issue of determining the limits of acceptable "influence" or persuasion between states (through forms of soft power, for example), which the discussion of coercion below only partly answers.

[49] *See* Robert Hale's groundbreaking essay *Coercion and Distribution in a Supposedly Non-Coercive State*, 38 POL. SCI. QUARTERLY 470 (1923) (even voluntary market exchanges can be coercive in the presence of disparities in bargaining power, resources or knowledge). I am indebted to Jeffrey Dunoff for introducing me to Hale's work. On the subtle distinctions between coerced consent and no consent at all, *see* BEYLEVELD & BROWNSWORD, *supra* note 21, at 345–346.

question than by "a desire to escape a more disagreeable alternative."[50]

As with duress, contract law also reflects this distinction. As Hale points out, since coercion is a market reality independent of the law, the law cannot eliminate coercion; at most, it can change the terms of coercion for better or worse.[51] For this reason, contract law provides particular protections for consumers and those with weaker bargaining power when they deal in what the law calls "adhesion contracts": contracts with commercial parties or manufacturers who possess greater bargaining power.

In such cases (when a dealer says "if you want this good, these are the terms and the only terms," leaving the consumer unable to negotiate), courts will look carefully before assuming the consumer consented to the adverse terms of the contract, even though in all other material respects it looks as if a contract was voluntarily entered into. The bargain may stand, and coercion may inevitably be a part of it, but under scrutiny and with moderation through law. Courts will not automatically void such a contract, as would be the case with duress, but they will look closely at the contract and may not enforce all of its provisions, particularly provisions such as a mandatory arbitration clause that gives away valuable legal rights and remedies.

---

[50] *Id.* at 472.
[51] *Id.* at 493–494.

c. Exploitation. I am principally relying on the work of Hillel Steiner to consider a third useful contrast, that between trade and exploitation.[52] In addition to the requirements that trade be a bilateral, voluntary exchange, Steiner adds a third element: that the two transfers are of roughly equal value. By rough equality, I mean (and I take Steiner to mean) that both parties consider the exchange *fair* – there is an appropriate relation, in their eyes, between what they are giving and what they are receiving. Where two transfers are not of equal value, yet the exchange is voluntary, Steiner characterizes this as evidence of exploitation.[53] Similarly, David Miller characterizes exploitation as the use of special advantages to deflect markets away from equilibrium, defined as exchanges involving equivalent value.[54]

Exploitation can have many causes, but the illustration Steiner offers is of a market for services in which the top bid, the one the service provider ultimately accepts, does not reflect the maximum possible value of the services. It is simply the top bid in that market at that time.[55] However,

---

[52] Hillel Steiner, Exploitation among Nations (2005) (unpublished manuscript) (on file with author) [hereinafter Steiner, Exploitation]; *see generally* Hillel Steiner, *A Liberal Theory of Exploitation*, 94 ETHICS 225 (1983–84) (analyzing exploitation in terms of prior rights violations).

[53] Steiner, Exploitation, *supra* note 52, at 2.

[54] DAVID MILLER, MARKET, STATE AND COMMUNITY: THEORETICAL FOUNDATIONS OF MARKET SOCIALISM 175 (1989) [hereinafter MILLER, MARKET, STATE AND COMMUNITY].

[55] *Id.* at 3.

Steiner does not rely on an objective theory of value to characterize the bid as inadequate.[56] Instead, he suggests that we look at other parties who might have bid, and perhaps bid more, but for various reasons did not.[57]

Among the reasons other parties may not have bid – reasons that may indicate exploitation – he includes the possibility that earlier rights violations occurred, such that the potential offerors either lacked the resources to bid, despite an interest in doing so, or were prevented from participating in the auction due to governmental interference.[58] In either case, the result for the service provider is that they accept a voluntary mutual exchange but for less than they might otherwise have received. In other words, the transaction is consensual and mutual, yet exploitative, because a potentially higher-paying third party was not able to participate in the auction.[59]

---

[56] Steiner has been criticized for this, though in my view unpersuasively. *See, e.g.*, MILLER, MARKET, STATE AND COMMUNITY, *supra* note 54.

[57] Steiner, Exploitation, *supra* note 52, at 3–4.

[58] *Id.* at 6.

[59] *Accord* MILLER, MARKET, STATE AND COMMUNITY, *supra* note 54, at 177, 186 (providing that it is in the nature of exploitation that the exploited party is unable to consider alternative, more attractive hypothetical transactions, due to the exploiter's use of unfair advantage). Miller considers the rights-violation theory of exploitation too narrow. For my purposes here, it is enough to note that such a case would be exploitation, even if, as Miller argues, other cases should also qualify. *See also* Garcia, *Developing a Normative Critique. Supra* note 5.

When applied to trade, this suggests that where certain third-party states and/or citizens are kept out of markets, or are economically unable to participate effectively in markets, an offeror suffers a detriment because he or she receives a lower bid from someone else. Therefore, the resulting exchanges between that offeror and the ultimate purchaser are not trade but exploitation.[60]

This differs from coercion in that the force, pressure, or rights violation occurs with respect to the third party, not between the two primary parties to the transaction. Nevertheless, this affects our evaluation of the consensual nature of the resulting transaction, in that the offeror's consent was again granted among a restricted range of choices.

To summarize, the essence of trade, as defined here, is consent to a voluntary, mutual, bargained-for exchange of roughly equal value. I have suggested three other types of transactions that, while they may look somewhat like trade, do not in fact meet the definition: predation, coercion, and exploitation. Participants in any of these three transactions

[60] Steiner, Exploitation, *supra* note 52, at 6. *See also* Richard Miller, *supra* note 6, at 60–62 (characterizing exploitation in international bargains as taking advantage of another's difficulty to secure agreements not otherwise possible). In the interstate context, we are again presented with the question of what level of interference is acceptable "pressure" and what rises to the level of exploitation. It is easier to mark the clear cases at one end of the spectrum (illegal use of force, human rights violations) than it is to map out the middle zone.

will see economic value exchange hands, and society may reap some economic benefit, but this occurs under conditions involving the absence or impairment of consent, which introduces its own costs and risks, including the risk that yet more societal benefit was left unrealized.

d. The Social Costs of Non-Trade. My concern over the distinction between trade and non-trade is not an aesthetic or conceptual one – the forms of non-trade we have discussed risk certain costs to those participating and to society at large. My concern here has nothing to do with moral principles but simply reflects an attempt to correctly evaluate our collective economic self-interest. Insofar as we make consensual bargains and not other kinds of exchanges, we preserve and enhance the opportunity to engage in future beneficial consensual bargains, and we reduce the social costs of overreaching. On the other hand, to the degree we engage in predation, coercion or exploitation, we may lose potential partners for future beneficial transactions, and we certainly increase the social costs of making and enforcing such bargains.

One way to begin to understand these costs is to look at the social psychology literature on justice. Psychologists are interested in studying our subjective human experience of fairness and unfairness, or justice and injustice, and the social consequences of perceptions of injustice.[61] Their

---

[61] *See generally* Kjell Tornbloom, *The Social Psychology of Justice,* in JUSTICE: INTERDISCIPLINARY PERSPECTIVES 177 (Klaus R. Scherer, ed., 1992).

research suggests that our emotional response to our perception of injustice is one of the most powerful motivators in the human psyche and can lead to emotions, judgments, and behaviors – indignation, resentment, hostility, and conflict, to name a few – that create personal and social costs.

This is quite relevant to our examination of trade and consent, because of the risk that being subject to predation, coercion, or exploitation – in a variety of ways, being forced to accept bad bargains or no bargain at all – will be perceived as the injustices that they are (in a subjective sense) and provoke precisely these same costly actions and reactions. Harder to quantify is the failure to thrive – for want of a better term – that an economic relationship subject to these forces will manifest, reminiscent of the suboptimal performance of Soviet-style command economies.[62]

For such reasons, our sense of whether we are engaged in trade or something else matters, not only to us as market participants but also to those concerned with the optimal performance of the market and with the minimization of social conflict over transboundary economic relationships.[63]

---

[62] *See, e.g.,* Alan A. Brown & Egon Neuberger, *Basic Features of a Centrally Planned Economy,* in INTERNATIONAL TRADE AND CENTRAL PLANNING FEATURES OF A CENTRALLY 404 (Brown & Neuberger, eds., 1968): Richard Rose & Ian McAllister, *Is Money the Measure of Welfare in Russia,* 42 REV. INCOME AND WEALTH, 75–90 (1996).

[63] *See generally* Frank J. Garcia, *Trade, Justice and Security,* in TRADE AS GUARANTOR OF PEACE LIBERTY & SECURITY? (Padideh Ala'I et al., eds., 2006).

The economic literature on game theory and on externalities – about which I will have more to say in the concluding chapter – also offers us ways to model and conceptualize the effects on others and on our future selves of certain kinds of opportunistic behavior. Put simply, if we are regulating trade to promote its flourishing and the attendant social benefits we would expect, then we have good reason to be concerned over the distinction between trade and non-trade, and the social costs of the latter.

6. *Application of the Model to Trade Agreements – CAFTA*

Based on this understanding of trade, I would argue that the policy goal of international trade law embraces more than simply eliminating economically distorting domestic legislation. The goal is to maintain an environment in which trade can take place and flourish, much as the goal of economic regulation in a domestic setting is to protect and promote a healthy market.

A consent approach to trade law suggests that in matters of global rule making, which today means principally economic rule making through trade agreements, we should structure such negotiations to achieve and reflect the consent of their participants, aiming for substantive rules that also protect and support consent at the private-party level. We should do this not as a way of confining trade within a particular view but as a way to promote its flourishing across the widest possible spectrum of individuals, transactions, and relationships.

First, this is going to require that we take the role of consent in trade negotiations seriously. If trade consists of voluntary, bargained-for exchanges, then the rules governing trade must preserve the possibility of bargained-for exchanges among private parties, and the rules themselves must be the fruit of such a bargain. If the rules of the game are not mutually agreed to, then any bargains struck under those rules are not fully free because they are not fully agreed to.[64] Without consent, agreements structuring economic exchange will be a form of oppression, or worse, predation.

This consent must go beyond mere recognition of the formal sovereign equality of states, the formal legitimacy of governments, and the formalities of ratification. In the context of trade agreements, an inquiry into consent must extend to difficult questions: whether the states have anything resembling equal bargaining power and what should be done if they do not; whether a negotiating government speaks for a meaningful range of affected citizens (or whether

[64] I leave for another day the important question of what degree of failure of consent at level one (interstate negotiations) fatally vitiates the possibility of true trade at level two (private-party contracts). I am grateful to my colleague Paulo Barrozo for raising this issue. I am also reserving for another day the trade relationship between the state and private parties, such as government procurement and procurement contracts, natural resource extraction and concession agreements, and the currently vexed subject of investor-state investment and investment agreements.

it speaks for its people at all); and whether a government has an adequate alternative to a negotiated outcome.[65]

Otherwise, we risk mistaking a mere form of consent for actual consent, a risk that is not confined to trade agreements. Beyleveld and Brownsword warn us that legal systems are prone to fictionalizing consent.[66] Similarly, Weil writes that in looking purely at the fact of voting, democratic theory readily mistakes true consent for a form of consent, which like any other form can easily be mere form.[67]

Bilateral and regional trade agreements by their nature are likely to present these issues most sharply, as the power inequalities can be most marked in this context. However, the WTO is by no means immune to the same dynamic.[68] The applicability of consent in a multilateral context such as the WTO has yet to be fully explored.[69] However, consent

[65] In negotiation theory, the latter is referred to as a party's BATNA, or Best Alternative to a Negotiated Agreement. If a party has no BATNA, it is in a very weak position. BATNA "is the only standard which can protect you both from accepting terms that are too unfavorable and from rejecting terms it would be in your interest to accept." ROGER FISHER & WILLIAM URY, GETTING TO YES 97 (1981).

[66] See BEYLEVELD & BROWNSWORD, *supra* note 21, at 337–338.

[67] WEIL, *supra* note 47, at 126.

[68] See, for example, James, *Internal Principles*, *supra* note 8; Carmody *supra* note 15; RICHARD MILLER, *supra* note 6; Lister *supra* note 26.

[69] See RICHARD MILLER, *supra* note 6, at 69–83, for an interesting preliminary account of "reasonable deliberations" at the WTO that focuses on coercion and exploitation.

is already a robust standard for evaluating justice and fairness in other aspects of international economic law, particularly in areas such as bilateral or regional trade agreements, investor-state investment agreements, and the generalized system of preferences, all of which are situations in which the number of parties is smaller and the potential inequalities greater.

In order to illustrate this dynamic, I will refer to the Central America Free Trade Agreement (CAFTA) – a recent trade agreement between the United States, five Central American states, and the Dominican Republic – for evidence of how the marked inequality in power between parties was used to vitiate or weaken consent, and the effects of this on the subsequent agreed terms for structuring "trade" between the parties. In this analysis, I am looking for examples of what is ostensibly free trade but in fact may be a form of coercion (no free bargaining), exploitation (no equivalent value), or predation (no consent).

There are two basic areas to examine when looking for aspects of trade agreements that preserve or jeopardize consent or reveal the degree of consent that went into their formation. First, we must look at the nature of the negotiations themselves, both with respect to the degree of consent *between* the parties, and the degree of consent *within* each party – in other words, to the representativeness (or not) of its government. Second, we must look at the terms of the agreement: what was substantively agreed to between the parties. The negotiation and substantive aspects of the inquiry are of course interrelated. For example, we would expect to see that the more unequal the bargaining power, the more the substance of the agreement would be one-sided as well.

a. Nature of the Negotiations. With respect to the nature of the negotiations, there are at least two issues: the problem of legitimacy stemming from the issue of underrepresented groups, and the problem of unequal bargaining power between states. Sadly, U.S. hemispheric trade negotiations offer us vivid examples of both problems, due to the historic lack of representativeness of the governments in most Latin American states, and the marked inequalities between the United States and all Latin American jurisdictions.

i. Theft and Lack of Representation. We cannot assume even in Europe or the United States, let alone most developing countries, that the government speaks for all affected sectors of society. This is a systemic issue in liberal theory, and the reason Rawls wrestles with the problem for liberal states of international relations with hierarchical states. The question, for Rawls and for us here, is how we can best take this absence of democratic representation within other states into account in our relationships with them, given our liberal commitments and our political necessities.[70] This issue is of special concern throughout the Central American

---

[70] JOHN RAWLS, THE LAW OF PEOPLES (1999).

region, where governments have a history of capture by elites.[71]

Lack of representation is particularly serious when fundamental economic decisions are being made, as in the CAFTA negotiations. One serious issue affecting the CAFTA negotiations is the problem of underrepresented groups. In Nicaragua, for example, during the CAFTA negotiations, there was widespread ignorance among most affected groups regarding what CAFTA would do, and there were allegations of a campaign of disinformation by the government. Many sectors of society were concerned that the new government only spoke for and negotiated on behalf of the moneyed interests, despite a recent history of social revolution.[72] Such dynamics raise the risk that for these sectors, the treaty and its resulting economic activity are neither mutual nor voluntary; the parties are not trading – something is being taken from them. In the terms of Take Three, the treaty does not create trade between the parties but a form of theft or extraction.

While no government can hope to represent the full range of affected citizens, in my view there is an essential, if complex, relationship between consent at the state level

[71] This problem has a long-standing history in Latin America. *See, e.g.,* THOMAS E. SKIDMORE & PETER H. SMITH, MODERN LATIN AMERICA 46 (2nd ed., 1989) (discussing exercise of political power by or for elites endemic to region); DECLINING INEQUALITY IN LATIN AMERICA: A DECADE OF PROGRESS (Luis F. Lopez-Calva & Nora Lustig, eds., 2010).

[72] *Garcia, supra* note 2, at 516

and representation at the domestic level. While one can justify this connection through liberal political theory, that is not my approach here. Rather, it seems to me that if individual consent is an essential element in trade transactions, then some form of consent, or at least representation, with respect to the process of framing the *rules* for trade, must be an element for the transactions occurring within those rules to be fully consensual and therefore truly trade.

Just how much of an element is of course an important issue that will require further study. At one level, it is important that there be at least some frank and open debate within a country's political institutions, as was the case in the Korean Assembly in connection with the recent Korea-U.S. FTA.[73] Many Latin American jurisdictions, in contrast, do not even rise to this level of public disagreement over trade, as in the case of Nicaragua.[74]

Of course, considering the degree (or absence) of political representation on the part of one's negotiation partner raises complicated issues of scope, criteria, and manageability for a negotiating state. In this respect, one can see how the traditional international law approach of accepting formal legitimacy and accreditation of diplomats does simplify

---

[73] *See, e.g.,* Channel News Asia, *South Korea-US FTA Takes Effect to Praise and Protest,* http://www.channelnewsasia.com/stories/afp_asiapacific_business/view/1189108/1/.html (last visited May 3, 2012) (FTA passed despite strong protests in the Assembly).

[74] Consultations by author with various elements in Nicaraguan civil society and the Nicaraguan trade negotiation structure, 2007.

matters, though at the expense of legitimacy. Under a consent approach, the cost is to the possibility of trade itself, versus theft or predation.

We may be able to borrow a tool from traditional political theory in this case: the importance Rawls places on there being a consultative mechanism may be a useful guide for how to address this problem under consent theory as well.[75] It may be that as an adjunct to trade negotiations with under-representative governments, we require that such governments form a special consultative mechanism for the purposes of that negotiation, not for reasons of political theory but to safeguard for ourselves the possibility of creating genuine trade with the social benefits it may bring, and to minimize the risk of creating non-trade with its attendant social costs.[76]

It is thus interesting to see how a consent approach leads us to issues also of concern under a traditional political theory approach, and that the range of solutions may overlap as well.

ii. Exploitation and Lack of any Real Alternatives. Turning to the relationship between the negotiating parties, we must consider whether the negotiation is conducted in a

---

[75] RAWLS, THE LAW OF PEOPLES *supra* note 70.

[76] This assumes, of course, that our government is interested in increasing consultation in its trading partners' governments, and not in taking advantage of its absence, under the misguided view that the latter would be in the U.S. national interest.

manner that promotes or respects consent on both sides of the table. One issue concerns the presence or absence of viable alternatives for Latin American trade development to continued or deeper engagement with the United States. The absence of such alternatives contributes dramatically to the other party's bargaining power, which in the case of the United States was already significantly greater due to its many advantages of scale.[77]

The United States exercised its role as the regional hegemon throughout the past two centuries by restricting other states' opportunities in the hemisphere, which has continuing economic effects today.[78] Given this history of external domination by the United States of the southern hemisphere, both colonially and post-colonially, there is a genuine risk that other states in the region and elsewhere – states that might have offered more attractive alternative markets and sources of capital than the United States – may not have been able to do so. Nicaraguan government officials, for example, expressed the view that the CAFTA negotiations were influenced by the fact that the country did not have a real alternative to the treaty,

---

[77] *See* Editorial, *Harvesting Poverty: A New Trade Deal,* N.Y. TIMES, December 22, 2003, at A30 (asserting CAFTA's terms reflect asymmetry in negotiating power between the United States and the Central American region).

[78] SKIDMORE & SMITH, *supra* note 72, at 5–7 (asserting that historic external domination has both threatened sovereignty and restricted available policy choices).

considering the dominant role the United States played in the Nicaraguan economy as the principal source of capital and markets.[79]

Expressed in the terms of Take Three, this raises the possibility that the treaty may be exploitative. More specifically, the risk is that the United States will exploit its position in this trade negotiation "auction," as its bid is the highest bid, either because other regional parties do not have the ability to effectively bid (due to the absence of sufficient economic development) or because other external parties have not been able to develop ties, levels of commerce, and investments to match the levels of the United States.

Such exploitation will influence the course of negotiations in several predictable ways. The chief risk, of course, is that the exploited party will accept suboptimal bargains since, on account of the exploitation, those are the best bargains on the table. This is compounded when the parties already operate from a distinct inequality in bargaining power, as is often the case in multilateral, bilateral, and regional trade negotiations involving developed and developing countries.[80] Moreover, these bad bargains have a disadvantageous intertemporal effect as well. Disadvantageous present negotiations impede better deals in the future, as

[79] *Supra* note 77.
[80] *See* John S. Odell, *Negotiating from Weakness in International Relations*, 44 J. WORLD TRADE 545, 546–551 (2010) (cataloging this inequality among trade negotiating states).

the rules agreed in an unequal regional trade agreement become the baseline for that relationship in the future, even if politics at the multilateral level allow for a better deal in principle.[81]

Negotiations among unequal parties, whether they involve explicit coercion or exploitation, need not always result in bad bargains. Scholars analyzing trade negotiations note a variety of strategies both "away from the table" and "at the table" which weaker parties can in fact pursue to attempt to offset this disadvantage. Odell focuses his analysis on moves "away from the negotiating table" such as coalition strategies and improving one's BATNA, since once one is at the table, many of the parameters of the negotiation are already set.[82] Rolland in turn analyzes the modalities of multilateral trade negotiations themselves and the effects that the overall negotiation structure and various kinds of issue linkages have on developing countries.[83] However, these strategies are far from perfect and the success stories are far outnumbered by the failures, which unfortunately become enshrined as treaty law.[84]

In the framework of this analysis, such a course of conduct results in agreements that are not "trade" agreements

---

[81] I am indebted to Sonia Rolland for pointing this out.

[82] Odell, *supra* note 80.

[83] Sonia Rolland, *Redesigning the Negotiation Process at the WTO*, 13 JIEL 65 (2010).

[84] *But see* Odell, *supra* note 80, cataloging some of the success stories.

but exploitation agreements, and creates rules which, due to their unbalanced nature, establish a framework for exploitative commercial relationships among the private parties bargaining within this exploitative framework.[85] What is then billed as a trade agreement liberalizing trade results in fact in an exploitation framework enabling and enhancing predatory opportunities.

Note that while an exploitative course of negotiations will create political and legitimacy costs for an exploiting liberal state, such is not our concern at the moment. From a purely self-interested point of view an exploitative course of negotiations will damage even the exploiter's long-term prospects in a repeated game (more will be said about this later).[86] One simply cannot afford to ignore the social costs of the resentment and conflict such a pattern tends to create among one's "trade" partners, which if nothing else will damage the long-term business and investment climate.[87]

b. Substantive Provisions. There is evidence to suggest that these dynamics that characterized the CAFTA negotiations have had their predictable effects in CAFTA's substantive

---

[85] For an interesting series of reflections on the interrelationship between international commercial treaties and the facilitation, or frustration, of individual choice within the framework they create, *see* Anne-Marie Slaughter, *International Law in a World of Liberal States*, 6 EJIL 1, 19–20 (1995).

[86] See *infra* Conclusion.

[87] *Supra* note 63.

provisions as well. Inequality in bargaining power and the problem of legitimacy manifest themselves in treaty terms that reflect impaired consent and proceed to impair the consent of others.

Key substantive areas of a treaty to examine for an investigation and evaluation of the effects of nonconsensual bargaining include the following: the treaty's dispute resolution mechanism; the structure and timing of market access available to the parties; the extent and nature of domestic law reform mandated by the treaty; and the existing provisions, if any, for special or differential treatment.

i. Coercion, Exploitation, and the Terms of Market Access. The terms and timing of market access can speak volumes about a weaker party's capacity to protect its markets from external competition before local industry is ready. Moreover, when we look at which sectors are excluded by whom and why, we get a more complete picture of the weaker party's ability, or lack thereof, to bargain for what it wanted and needed.

To take the agriculture sector as an example, CAFTA eliminates the protections in place for regional small-scale farmers and agricultural workers in several key sectors such as rice and yellow corn, exposing them to immediate competition from highly subsidized U.S. agricultural products.[88] However, the United States assiduously

[88] CAFTA, Annex 3.3, Tariff Schedule of the United States Aug. 5, 2004, *available at* http://www.ustr.gov/Trade_Agreements/

maintained protection of sugar, one of its most sensitive sectors that had been of interest to Central American exporters.[89] Moreover, in many of the sectors where CAFTA governments announced victories, their exports had either already enjoyed privileged access under the U.S. trade preference programs or are effectively blocked by sanitary or phytosanitary measures.[90]

Such one-sided bargains offer evidence of the disparity in bargaining power that plagues the treaty.[91] To explain the consent by Central American governments to such lopsided provisions, it may be helpful to employ the concepts of

Bilateral/CAFTA/CAFTA-DR_Final_Texts/Section_Index.html [hereinafter CAFTA]; Carlos Galian, *CAFTA: The Nail in the Coffin of Central American Agriculture*, in WHY WE SAY NO TO CAFTA 4 (Alliance for Resp. Trade 2004).

[89] *Id.* at 5; Annex 3.3, Tariff Schedule of the United States; *See* Galian, *supra* note 88; *see also* Elizabeth Becker, *Costa Rica to Be 5th Country in New Trade Pact with U.S.*, N.Y. TIMES, January 26, 2004, at A6 (reporting that the United States won its demand for opening Central American agriculture market to its exports while maintaining protection for sugar industry, of interest to the region).

[90] Galian, *supra* note 88, at 6.

[91] Editorial, *Harvesting Poverty: A New Trade Deal*, N.Y. TIMES, December 22, 2003, at A30 (asserting CAFTA's terms reflect asymmetry in negotiating power between the United States and the Central American region). Such allegations have also been raised about the WTO agreements and the Uruguay Round. *See* J. Michael Finger & Julio J. Nogués, *The Unbalanced Uruguay Round Outcome: The New Areas in Future WTO Negotiations* 3–4 (World Bank Pol'y Res., Working Paper No. 2732, 2001).

coercion and exploitation developed here. That such unbalanced market access provisions were agreed to by Central
American governments may suggest a coercive aspect to
the negotiation, in which the United States relied on the
Central American inequality in power to keep certain
options (such as liberalization of the sugar market) off the
table while pressing ahead for the concessions it wanted.[92]
We may never know the full details of the negotiations, as
all members of the CAFTA negotiations signed confidential-
ity agreements.[93]

Alternatively, or in tandem, consent by Central American
negotiators to such provisions can be evidence of exploitation, insofar as the United States relied on the absence of
other states able to offer Central America more attractive
terms in the "auction" for agricultural product market access
terms.[94] In either case, the one-sided nature of the market

[92] *See* James C. McKinley Jr., *U.S. Trade Pact Divides the Central
Americans, With Farmers and Others Fearful*, N.Y. TIMES, August
21, 2005, § 1, at 18 (reporting Central American negotiators lacked
sufficient leverage to extract needed concessions from the United
States, and faced implicit threat of loss of trade preferences).

[93] *See* CATHOLIC RELIEF SERVICES, *Transparency and Participation in
the Negotiations*, *in* FAIR TRADE OR FREE TRADE? UNDERSTANDING
CAFTA, *available at* http://www.andrew.cmu.edu/user/mtoups/
cafta_briefing_final_dec03.pdf (last visited March 17, 2007).

[94] It will be interesting to see how the recently increasing Chinese
presence in Latin America will affect such negotiations and their
outcomes. This theory would predict more balanced agreements
as a result, but it will be very difficult to reopen treaties such as
CAFTA for adjustment, and the United States is rapidly sewing

access provisions in agriculture suggests that the treaty may not truly reflect or create free trade in this respect.

Even those terms that may at first appear to be U.S. concessions tend to prove otherwise upon further inspection. Concessions on textiles have been widely trumpeted as one of the premier benefits conferred on the Central American nations by CAFTA.[95] However, the CAFTA textiles rules include safeguard provisions allowing the United States to unilaterally impose tariffs if there is a surge of textile imports that have the potential to hurt domestic manufacturing.[96] Such safeguards are standard in trade agreements and, by themselves, do not suggest an absence of consent. However, the United States has already used the threat of invoking this safeguard in the case of imported socks in an attempt to renegotiate a term of CAFTA.[97]

---

up the entire region in a network of bilateral and regional agreements, presenting future regional leaders with a fait accompli.

[95] CENT. AM. DEP'T AND OFF. OF THE CHIEF ECONOMIST, LATIN AM. AND CARIBBEAN REGION, WORLD BANK, DR-CAFTA: CHALLENGES AND OPPORTUNITIES FOR CENTRAL AMERICA 4 (2005).

[96] *See* OFF. OF THE U.S. TRADE REP., CAFTA FACTS–TEXTILES IN CAFTA (2005), *available at* http://www.ustr.gov/assets/Trade_ Agreements/Bilateral/CAFTA/Briefing_Book/asset_upload_ file583_7185.pdf.

[97] At the behest of the textile lobby, the United States demanded either the delay of duty-free importation of socks despite existing treaty provisions or, alternatively, the modification of their rule of origin requirements in order to protect the U.S. sock manufacturing industry. *See Pension Bill Including Trade Provisions Faces Uncertain Path in Senate*, INSIDE U.S. TRADE, August 4, 2006.

The manner in which the safeguard provisions have been invoked in this renegotiation illustrates the aspects of U.S. trade negotiations that jeopardize consent. In this case, under special-interest-based congressional pressure, the Bush administration invoked a lawful provision in an unprincipled manner, as a threat to attempt to force a change in the terms of a previously negotiated trade agreement. Such an attempt to change a previously negotiated agreement is coercive.

If this were a case in private law, such modifications would most likely be held invalid under traditional contracts doctrine. If we consider contract law as a proxy for domestic notions of fairness, application of the Restatement is a useful exercise to measure how fair U.S. negotiation practice is by its own standards. The Restatement Second of Contracts states that "[a] promise modifying a duty under a contract not fully performed on either side is binding if the modification is fair and equitable in view of the circumstances not anticipated by the parties when the contract was made."[98] In this case, a modification made under threat is hardly fair, and the circumstances invoked – that CAFTA would lead to an influx of imported socks – hardly unanticipated (indeed, that is the purpose of a safeguards clause in the first place). Therefore, any modification to CAFTA made on this premise would be invalid and would not be sustained in court.

[98] Restatement (Second) of Contracts §89(a) (1981).

Although a domestic contract law example such as this one does not map literally onto the contours of an international treaty, it does illustrate how U.S. trade policy is not always consistent with notions of justice inherent in domestic private law. Stated differently, the rules at home are not the same as the rules abroad.[99]

ii. Coercion and Law Reform. If we are investigating consent, we should also take a close look at those aspects of trade agreements that mandate law reform to determine who benefits from these reforms and how they were agreed. For example, the CAFTA services chapter requires Costa Rica to undertake significant substantive revisions of its agency and distribution law.[100] These revisions can be seen as an end-run around the protections that such laws typically include for agents and distributors in the event of termination, to the benefit of foreign – in this case, United States – principals.

The treaty requires Costa Rica to enact new laws that will not presume that such commercial relationships are exclusive, whereas under Law No. 6209, such contracts were implied to be exclusive.[101] The treaty also requires new laws

---

[99] I am indebted to Daniel Blanchard for his elaboration of this point.

[100] *See* CAFTA, *supra* note 88, Annex 11.13, §A, pts. 1–6 (mandating changes to Costa Rica's Law No. 6209, "Law for the Protection of the Representative of Foreign Companies").

[101] U.S. COM. SERVICE, U.S DEP'T OF COM., DOING BUSINESS IN COSTA RICA: A COUNTRY COMMERCIAL GUIDE FOR U.S. COMPANIES 2006 at 10 (2006).

mandating that termination by the principal absent any breach of obligation by the representative is nevertheless to be considered termination for just cause (provided there is notice), thus waiving all rights of the agent or distributor to indemnification for unjustified termination. Under Costa Rica's old law (which reflected the traditional approach to safeguarding Latin American commercial representatives), Costa Rican representatives had been broadly protected against termination, subject only to statutory grounds for "just cause."[102] Finally, all such contracts will now be deemed subject to private arbitration unless expressly subject to litigation, even though under Law No. 6209, access to Costa Rican courts could not be waived by contract, even with explicit arbitration clauses.[103]

Although one can legitimately debate whether Costa Rican law was more protective than necessary,[104] those are matters of domestic policy, and the changes required by the United States go beyond simply conforming Costa Rican law to modern hemispheric standards. These changes soften provisions found particularly onerous by U.S. firms, such as

---

[102] *See* David R. Martinez, *At Termination, Independent Sales Reps are Anything But*, 7 LATIN AM. L. & BUS. REP. 19 (1999).

[103] *Id.*

[104] Interview with Prof. F.E. Guerra-Pujol, Catholic University of Puerto Rico, in Bogotá, Colom. (May 19, 2006); *see also* Salli A. Swartz, *International Sales Transactions: Agency, Distribution and Franchise Agreements*, *in* NEGOTIATING AND STRUCTURING INTERNATIONAL COMMERCIAL TRANSACTIONS 15–19 (Mark R. Sandstrom & David N. Goldsweig, eds., 2nd ed., 2003).

restrictions on their freedom to terminate agreements without cost, and they limit important rights previously enjoyed by Costa Rican citizens, such as access to the courts.

This imposition of arbitration is particularly noteworthy for two reasons: first, because it appears quite self-serving, given that the United States already influenced Costa Rica toward adopting a U.S.-style arbitration code through its influential role in the 1997 overhaul of Costa Rica's arbitration system[105]; and second, because it seems opportunistic, given that under U.S. domestic law, the imposition of arbitration through contracts of adhesion is one ground for their unenforceability.[106] In other words, one of the places where private firms exercise their unequal bargaining power over consumers is by imposing arbitration instead of litigation. Ironically, the United States used the treaty negotiation

---

[105] Elizabeth Thomas, Commercial Arbitration in Costa Rica, (2005) (unpublished manuscript) (on file with author) (documenting the U.S. role in reforming Costa Rican arbitration law to its own way of thinking, arguably giving U.S. parties an advantage).

[106] Although the Federal Arbitration Act favors the enforcement of arbitration agreements, they are still subject to challenges under state law principles of unconscionability. Generally, to be unenforceable a contract of adhesion must be both substantively and procedurally unconscionable. Given that under CAFTA arbitration may be implied by law, those agreements are arguably already procedurally unconscionable. Thus, if these were U.S. contracts, absent the unique imprimatur of Federal law, their enforceability would depend solely on the ability of their substantive terms to withstand strict scrutiny. *See generally* Thomas H. Oehmke & Joan M. Brovins, *The Arbitration Contract – Making It and Breaking It,* 83 AM. JUR. PROOF OF FACTS 3D 1 (2007).

process to impose such measures on Costa Rican parties *as a class*, acting as an agent of the U.S. manufacturers *as a class*, provisions that U.S. courts themselves would be reluctant to enforce in parallel private law circumstances at home.

When viewed in this light, the fact that the Costa Rican government would agree to strip protections from agents and distributors, and to impose U.S.-style arbitration on a class of private parties through treaty law, may be evidence of coercion at the state level, which also creates a coercive effect on private parties. In this sense, CAFTA might be considered an adhesion treaty.[107] Here, CAFTA fails both aspects of free trade: it does not preserve the bargained-for exchanges among private parties, and in this instance, it is not itself a voluntarily bargained-for exchange among states.

iii. Coercion and Dispute Resolution. Another revealing aspect of trade agreements is the manner in which their dispute resolution provisions are structured. Informal nonbinding consultations, while apparently neutral, favor the more powerful party because the outcome is not determined by law but by power. Thus, while the WTO's binding dispute settlement process has been key to several victories by developing countries, in NAFTA and CAFTA the dispute

---

[107] See Corbin, *supra* note 24 at §1.4 (noting the origin of the term "adhesion contract" was the international law term for a treaty that states must accept or reject despite having no voice in formulating its provisions).

resolution provisions allow disparities in economic power to influence outcomes.

CAFTA disputes involving the United States are subject to the wishes of the most powerful party: the United States. When the dispute resolution implementation provisions are examined closely, it is clear that the provisions echo the NAFTA-style preference on the part of the United States for nonbinding dispute resolution.[108] In other words, the arbitral panel's final report is not implemented as a legal decision; rather, it is the basis for a settlement by the parties, which need not track or implement the panel report at all.[109] Moreover, should the losing party fail to honor its commitments, or the prevailing party refuse to accept a settlement short of full implementation, the prevailing party's only recourse would then be suspension of equivalent benefits.[110] However, it is well documented that such suspensions are particularly inadequate in agreements between states with great economic disparities, because the markets of small economies are simply too small for such measures to create

---

[108] *See generally* Frank J. Garcia, *Decisionmaking and Dispute Resolution in the Free Trade Area of the Americas: An Essay in Trade Governance,* 18 MICH. J. INT'L. L. 357, 378–83 (1997) (analyzing NAFTA dispute resolution mechanism).

[109] CAFTA, *supra* note 88, art. 20.15. It is true that the parties can elect to pursue a claim in the WTO instead, where they have overlapping rights, but this is of no help where the rights are unique to CAFTA, and in any event does not alter the essentially nonbinding nature of CAFTA dispute settlement per se.

[110] *Id.* art. 20.16, pt. 2.

any real economic incentive for a country like the United States to change its policies, and the domestic cost to the imposing state is too high.[111]

7. *Recapitulation*

I am proposing in Take Three that instead of beginning with traditional normative theory as an avenue toward global justice, we begin with an examination of the nature of trade itself, our language, and our experiences in economic exchange. I am suggesting that such an examination reveals trade to consist of mutual and consensual exchanges of roughly equal value – and that the proper goal of international trade law is to safeguard the conditions for such exchanges, thereby ensuring that we are actually involved in trade and not some form of predation, coercion, or exploitation. This implies a need for change in our approach to trade negotiations and to the social costs of trade rule enforcement.

Analyzing CAFTA as representative of hemispheric trade agreements where power inequalities are perhaps most intense furnishes numerous examples of negotiation behavior and substantive trade provisions that suggest predation, coercion, or exploitation rather than trade. In talking about such issues and their social consequences, we

---

[111] *See generally* Gregory Shaffer, *The Challenges of WTO Law: Strategies for Developing Country Adaptation*, 5 WORLD TRADE REV. 1s77 (2006) (surveying challenges to developing countries).

have reached key elements of the global justice agenda, but through a different doorway.

B. Contributions and Limits of This Model

Because internal approaches to justice in international economic law are relatively new, it is worth offering some methodological reflections on this approach, before proceeding to the customary analysis of the strengths and weaknesses of Take Three for the purposes of the global justice project.

1. *Methodological Considerations*

As with any external approach to normative issues in law, there are important methodological considerations when carrying out an internal normative analysis of trade law. First, it is important to identify carefully the relevant internal features of the sociolegal system in question and to justify one's selection of those features. For example, why does James focus on the legal-theoretical framework of the trading system when seeking to identify trade's internal principles of fairness? Why does Carmody focus on justice-as-equality for WTO Members in his theory of WTO law? Why is consent, among other possible constitutive elements of trade as an experience, foregrounded in the consent approach to fair trade? One might call this a requirement to justify the inductive reasoning underlying an internal theory of fair trade. Paying careful attention to such questions is key to establishing a sound basis for the analysis and prescription to follow.

Second, and related, is a concern to carefully articulate the normative significance of these features. In other words, the persuasiveness and impact of an internal approach depends upon the clarity and cogency of the principles one draws from the system or underlying concept under analysis. One could call this a requirement to carefully justify the deductive aspect of an internal approach, as one seeks to deduce from the sociolegal features one has identified their normative implications.

Finally, a unique characteristic of internal approaches is their strong interdisciplinary aspect. By looking at the legal-theoretical framework of institutions of international trade, or trade itself as human experience, we must take into account discussions that traditionally would fall within the domain of political science, economics, literature, psychology, anthropology, and other disciplines. In fact, the internal approach to trade is in part an attempt to bridge the gap between these disciplines and to overcome the persistent lack of connection between global justice theorists and the realities of the international trade regime.[112]

Ultimately, the value of any internal approach must be judged by the same standard applicable to traditional external approaches: how effectively does it identify serious

---

[112] *See, e.g.,* Tesón and Klick, *Global Justice and Trade*, in GLOBAL JUSTICE AND INTERNATIONAL ECONOMIC LAW: CHALLENGES AND OPPORTUNITIES (Chios Charmody, Frank J. Garcia and John Linarelli, eds., 2011) [hereinafter GLOBAL JUSTICE AND INTERNATIONAL ECONOMIC LAW].

injustices in contemporary international economic law, and how persuasively does it suggest the ways international economic law should be negotiated or reformed.

Looking ahead, one can expect, as the internal approach develops and matures, that there will be other methodological issues to consider and new internal approaches with which to enrich our arsenal of justice tools. One interesting area for future work involves undertaking a more explicitly phenomenological account of trade law.[113] Another important area is to develop a more explicitly cross-cultural or anthropological study of trade as a human experience, testing intuitions developed from a Western view across the range of human experience. I will have something to say about both issues next and in the concluding chapter.

2. *Substantive Evaluation*

Recalling the discussion in the Introduction concerning modes of justice discourse, I am characterizing the approach in Take Three as representative of the Transactional Mode of justice. In this mode, justice is seen as specific to the requirements of a particular transaction or exchange between the participants. It does not depend on the actor's own commitments (the Integrity Mode) or the existence of any enduring social relationship between the participants (the Relational Mode) other than the transaction itself. Instead, the requirements

[113] *See, e.g.,* Teresa Goodwin Phelps & Jenny Ann Pitts, *Questioning the Text: The Significance of Phenomenological Hermeneutics for Legal Interpretation*, 29 ST. LOUIS U. L. J. 353 (1985).

of justice (here understood as a transaction that is satisfactory to both parties) will depend on the nature of the transaction itself and its own requirements.[114] The Transactional Mode is thus evocative of older "just price" theories of fairness in economic exchange, which I would also characterize as within this mode. However, the Transactional Mode does not commit one to a substantive conception of justice in transactions, be it an "external" standard such as just price theory, or an "internal" standard such as consent or structural equity. What this mode *does* do is direct the justice inquiry to the transaction itself.

The specific approach I use in Take Three, by focusing on the nature of trade itself, gives us a basis on which to regulate globally that, unlike cosmopolitanism or global communitarianism, does not depend on a prior normative consensus or on the presence of certain kinds of social relations (other than economic transactions themselves, of course). Instead, it begins with an articulation of trade as a human experience and therefore identifies the appropriate regulatory goal of trade law: protect an environment in which trade can take place, and not predation, coercion, or exploitation.

The strength of Take Three is that it may achieve some of the goals of the first two takes without the weaknesses. If we cannot all agree on norms of economic justice, and we have not yet become a single global community of justice, what is our best avenue toward increasing the fairness of

---

[114] There is thus a close relationship between the Transactional Mode and the internal approach to thinking about trade and justice.

our global economic relationships? It may be that we safeguard the consent of the parties, and trust them not to enter into unfair bargains when they do not have to. This may reflect the advantages of a Transactional Mode as much as the strengths of any specific internal approach such as consent. In other words, I am suggesting that approaching justice as Transactional may offer unique advantages in a plural context in which actual participation in a global market may be the single most widely shared social experience in the global social space.

Second, by highlighting consent, Take Three emphasizes a criterion very congenial to liberalism, but not by arguing for it as a matter of political theory. Instead, it grows out of a close analysis of the meaning of our concept of trade itself. Moreover, by focusing the law on maintaining a healthy regulatory environment for economic exchanges, this goal is articulated in a manner that is very congenial to business actors and economic interests generally: the law exists to support and protect a vigorous market, and markets exist in part to facilitate transactions between parties whose cultures and interests do not necessarily align.[115]

Third, by pointing us toward consent, Take Three gives us a good policy metric or benchmark (in much the way that

---

[115] Indeed, as noted in Take Two markets have been favored on instrumental grounds precisely because they can facilitate efficient transfers among people who do *not* share conceptions of the good. Jon Mandle, *Globalization and Justice*, 570 ANNALS AM. ACAD. POL. & SOC. SCI. at 130 (2000).

Liberal Internationalism did with the Difference Principle) through which to evaluate trade rules and trade agreements. Do they grow out of a consensual process? Does a treaty represent the effective consent of states? If so, does this consent include at least representation if not the consent of all of the affected groups in those states? Do the substantive rules protect the consent of private parties? If so, are they the sorts of rules that freely bargaining parties would have agreed to?

These inquiries require us to pose difficult questions with respect to negotiations: whether the states have anything like equal bargaining power; whether a negotiating government speaks for the full range of its citizens; and the presence or absence of a government's BATNA – whether it has an adequate alternative to a negotiated outcome.[116] If we fail to consider such questions, we risk mistaking the presence of formal consent for actual consent.[117] These are not easy questions, but they are manageable – at least, we are used to working with them in traditional governance outcomes.[118]

---

[116] As discussed, if a party has no BATNA, it is in a very weak position. For an interesting account of an apparently successful effort on the part of Mexico to improve its BATNA with respect to oil in the NAFTA negotiations, *see* Odell, *supra* note 80, at 553.

[117] Echoing Weil's concern that democratic theory often mistakes true consent for a form of consent, which can easily, like any other form, be mere form. *See* WEIL, *Justice and Human Society*, *supra* note 47, at 126.

[118] Such issues arise in a range of institutional settings, both transnational and domestic. *See, e.g.,* JONATHAN G.S. KOPPELL, WORLD

One weakness of Take Three is that, like global communitarianism, it grounds the inquiry into global justice in a readily contestable claim. In Take Two, the claim involved the nature of globalization and its effects on social relationships at the global level. Here, the claim involves the nature of economic exchange and my exegesis of it, which could be challenged as idiosyncratic, simply wrong, or as particular to the language-world of English-speaking Western participants in trade. This challenge deserves further study. However, it may be that the intuitions underlying this account are more general and could be matched to the experience and language of other participants in economic exchange from other cultures and legal systems – the cross-cultural phenomenon of trade across language worlds suggest this may be so.

A second kind of limit to Take Three may be that, like Take One but for different reasons, it does not give us a basis on which to constrain other parties in a hard, formal sense, nor would it necessarily furnish a basis on which to argue for significant wealth redistributions of the sort that feature prominently on most global justice agendas.[119] I will take each of these points in turn.

RULE: ACCOUNTABILITY, LEGITIMACY AND THE DESIGN OF GLOBAL GOVERNANCE (2010); ISEULT HONOHAN, CIVIC REPUBLICANISM (2002).

[119] It may be that Take Three resembles liberal internationalism in another, paradoxical respect: by focusing on the consent of states, Take Three may also reinforce the primacy of states and hence trend more towards international justice rather than global

One criticism of Take Three from the perspective of political theory is that this approach does not offer a basis other than self-interest on which to ground obligations. Therefore, mistaken notions of self-interest and short-term opportunistic behavior can lead parties, including trade negotiators, to establish something other than trade but call it "trade" nonetheless, beyond the reach of the arguments of political theory. This goes back to the root of Hobbes's objection to the possibility of transnational justice: without a central sovereign to enforce social norms, we cannot overcome the collective action problems associated with reaching global justice and are left with self-protection as the only rational strategy.[120]

However, by appealing directly to economic self-interest, this approach may in fact offer more, not less, than traditional approaches to justice. Tools such as game theory (which I will address more directly in the Conclusion) allow us to model the self-defeating aspects of opportunistic behavior in repeated games (once one has understood that trade is a repeated game and not a one-off game, as is also the case with many other aspects of international relations). With this in mind, the consent approach gives us a basis on which to articulate a more accurate view of self-interest, as protecting the basis for future bargains. We can do this

justice. I leave further exploration of this possibility to another day, and I am grateful to Jeffrey Dunoff, for raising this issue.

[120] Thomas Nagel, *The Problem of Global Justice*, 33 PHIL. & PUB. AFF. 114, 113–147 (2005).

without resorting to hortatory or ethical language which may neither be shared in terms of norms, nor effective in view of the seemingly weightier pull of economic self-interest (albeit misunderstood).

Another objection from many points within the global justice debate might be that the consent approach does not establish a basis for large-scale wealth redistribution efforts of the sort that form a part of nearly every characterization of global justice, in view of the enormous disparities of wealth, opportunity, and life prospects that we find ourselves in. This is a fair comment, but it misunderstands the aim of this approach (and forgets the point that we need *many* theories of justice to perform *many* tasks within the global justice project – no single theory will do it all). While it is true that the consent approach does not aim at distributive justice in the traditional sense (beyond promoting the conditions for fair economic transactions), the aim of this approach is rather to establish the regulatory framework to protect consensual bargains, which themselves over time can build a more just economic order one transaction at a time, so to speak.[121]

---

[121] This approach echoes the dramatic plea by cotton-exporting African countries that if developed countries would only end their market-distorting practices, letting the cotton trade operate in a true market framework, they could keep their (redistributive) foreign aid and let the market do its work. *See, e.g.,* Mary Robinson, Africa Needs Fair Trade not Charity, YALE GLOBAL ONLINE (August 23, 2005) available at http://yaleglobal.yale.edu/content/africa-needs-fair-trade-not-charity-0 (last accessed February 23, 2012).

Thus Take Three does offer a basis on which to regulate global trade toward substantively fairer transactions, but one that does not presuppose or enforce a normative consensus. Instead, it identifies consent as essential to the object of regulation itself: a thriving market for economic exchanges. This may well have the power to attract support through an appeal to self-interest, which in the long run may be more significant than the power to compel obedience. Moreover, insofar as it offers an alternative route to addressing fairness issues that is rooted in the nature of economic exchanges and not in extrinsic notions of fairness, rooted either unilaterally or globally, Take Three offers a different basis and justification for trade regulation than either Take One or Take Two, that may evade some of the limitations inherent to those Takes. Whether or not this can be a basis for an improved system of trade agreements will be further explored in the concluding chapter.

Conclusion

A. Where Have We Been?

This book began with the question of how to articulate claims for global justice in a normatively pluralistic, globalizing environment. I have posed the question in a manner that assumes there will be no single comprehensive approach, and instead aims at identifying the strengths and weaknesses of each of the featured approaches (as well as a few others I touch upon).

In the Introduction I distinguished between the concept of justice on the one hand, and the many specific conceptions of justice that particular theories of justice embody. Throughout the book I have also tried to discern several core modes or rhetorical strategies of justice discourse that underlie a wide range of different theoretical approaches and make themselves felt below the level of theory, so to speak. Identifying and analyzing the modes of justice discourse in this way introduces a further distinction beyond concept and conception that is not so much about the substance of justice as it is about the way we think about it and speak about it, which is partly about what gives rise to the need for justice, partly a flavor of what justice means or represents, and very much about inspiring us or moving us to action.

In this concluding chapter I want to step back and review the ground we have covered for the possible insights to be gleaned, both about the current state of the global justice debate and about possible next steps at the level of theory and action. Understanding both how we talk about justice and the role that particular theories, with their advantages and disadvantages, can play in the overall project of advancing global justice, can help us toward a more effective, comprehensive, and inclusive conversation than currently seems possible.

1. Rhetorical Modes of Justice: Understanding What We Talk About When We Talk About Global Justice

In this section[1] I would like to revisit the notion of modes of justice, with the perspective gained by discussing several of

---

[1] In titling the section I am paraphrasing the title of Noah Richler's marvelous memoir/political essay on the competing rhetorics of war and peace in the post-9/11 Canadian identity, WHAT WE TALK ABOUT WHEN WE TALK ABOUT WAR (2012), which also informs the spirit of this exercise.

them in connection with the three Takes presented earlier. As with the project as a whole, the goal is not to identify a single ideal or correct mode for conversations about justice – such a thing is not possible – but instead to see how the different modes of justice discourse themselves influence the global justice conversation.

In Take One, we looked at one approach to these issues: frame global justice as a foreign policy commitment of liberal states, and leave it to their unilateral actions and multilateral advocacy to establish a liberal vision of justice at the global level, to the extent possible. This Liberal Internationalism approach also introduced one mode of justice discourse, Justice as Integrity, in which what matters is how we act – consistently or not – with reference to our own principles and commitments, not how we think others should act.

This approach has the principal benefit of sidestepping the problem of truly *global* norms and working within established channels of state action. However, this comes at the cost of limiting the reach of global justice to liberal states and whatever policy goals they can secure outside their community through their international relations efforts. I suspect this limitation is actually inherent in the underlying mode of Justice as Integrity, whatever the substantive conception of justice we frame in this manner, liberal or not. We can accomplish a great deal if we understand and act upon the implications of our own principles as they affect our treatment of others, but we also run into the limits inherent in their being *our* acts, and in the finite membership of our normative tradition. I shall have more to say about this shortly, but for the purposes of this recapitulation, it is for such reasons that I ultimately characterize Take One as "international" justice.

In Take Two, we approached the question of global justice from a different direction, namely, by examining whether globalization is sufficiently changing the nature of global social relationships so as to make a truly "global" justice possible at least in some areas of global social life, despite the reality of pluralism. I framed the issue in terms of the present theoretical debate between cosmopolitans and communitarians over the possibility of global justice, given the nature of existing transnational social relations and the purportedly communal nature of justice.

Cosmopolitanism also introduced us to the Universal Mode of justice discourse characteristic of how many theories of justice are rhetorically framed: advancing a specific conception of justice as universally applicable because it is grounded in principles that are universal in scope, therefore applying equally (and forcefully) to all people everywhere. The reasons for its universal applicability will vary according to the substantive conception of justice in question – our equal human dignity in the case of cosmopolitanism, or, for example, our equal status as children of God in a Christian theistic theory of justice – but what these conceptions share in common (and what characterizes the Universal Mode) is their purported universality.

In contrast, the communitarian theory of justice introduced us to a different mode of justice discourse, Justice as Relationship, which is characteristic of the rhetorical approach underlying Take Two. In this mode, which again can be employed in connection with a variety of substantive theories, justice is framed as function of the presence or absence of specific kinds of relationships understood to have normative significance. In particular, I discussed two variants: Justice as Shared Enterprise, which underlies the contractarian form of relational approaches, and the Communal mode associated with communitarian theories of justice.

Take Two developed according to the communitarian theory of justice, which understands justice as rooted in the shared traditions, practices, and understandings of a specific community as to who gets how much of what social goods. The question therefore became whether globalization allows us to articulate global justice on communitarian terms, as the shared traditions, practices, and understandings of a global community with respect to who gets how much of what social goods.

This approach has the advantage of taking globalization and the possibility of truly global norms seriously and building upon one of the most promising aspects of globalization, namely, its potential contribution toward increasing basic justice for a larger and larger share of the world's people. However, by linking the realization of global justice to the continued evolution of transnational social relations at an ever-deepening level, Take Two ties global justice to the resolution of debates over the nature and extent of global social relationships. This reflects a limitation inherent in the Relational mode of justice discourse: the argument shifts to the presence, absence, or correct characterization of the relationships the theory puts forward as generating justice obligations. In terms of our global justice project, the risk is that we may not yet reach communitarian standards, and it is not very clear how we know when we do (there is no properly "communitarian" theory of global justice yet, perhaps for this reason), yet much work on transnational socioeconomic problems needs to be done in the meantime.

For these reasons, I outlined a third approach to the problem of global justice, one that aims to be more truly "global" than liberal internationalism, yet on a basis that can perhaps avoid unnecessary theoretical entanglements and delays, by appealing to pragmatism and self-interest in its pursuit of economic fairness rather than explicitly normative principles. This "internal" approach (most approaches are "external," applying political theory to international economic law) relies on a close examination of the nature of international trade, that quintessentially interconnecting experience, and the possibilities trade offers precisely because it takes place across lines of cultural, linguistic and social difference – in other words, within the world as we find it.

Thus Take Three approaches the question of global justice through an examination of the phenomenon of economic exchange and our language for it. Through this avenue, "trade" is characterized as consisting of voluntary, mutual, bargained-for exchanges of roughly equal value. This allows us to then characterize the regulatory purpose of international trade law (deferring, for the time being, the question of its broader applicability to international economic law more generally), as safeguarding and promoting the conditions necessary for such exchanges to flourish. Protecting the true consent of those involved – both negotiating states and transacting private parties – is therefore a principal means to this end.

This Take also introduces us to a further distinct mode of justice discourse, the Transactional Mode: justice as specific to the nature of particular transactions, exchanges, encounters, or interactions. This mode is independent of, but compatible with, other modes of justice such as the Relational or Universalist: regardless of whether our transaction partner is in an ongoing communal relationship with us, and regardless of whether and how our partner in the exchange is embraced within the scope of our universalist theories, the nature of what we happen to be doing with them brings its own intrinsic requirements. The quintessential example of this is our decision to barter with, rather than rob, the Other: we don't call this, except in an ironic sense, as theft by another name – we call it trade.

The advantage of this Take is that, by adopting a "bottom-up" approach to characterizing the normative goal of trade law, we can arrive at something like global economic justice (read as "fair transactions") through a market-oriented consensual process that parties from any normative tradition could recognize and support as essential to the proper functioning of the global economic system. This also reflects the advantages of an internal approach to justice, as outlined in the previous chapter: the principles that emerge are familiar to participants and require no extrinsic normative justifications or commitments.

Thus each Take brings to the global justice conversation several distinctive contributions and shortcomings, and at the same time illustrates the strength and weaknesses of the rhetorical mode it speaks in. Analyzing and comparing the rhetorical modes underlying these three Takes and others suggests that some of the issues and conflicts arising in the global justice debate may come not so much from our substantive conceptions of justice, but from the rhetorical strategies we adopt to conceptualize and argue them. In fact, we can see that one common source of disagreement stems not from Universalist claims or the Universal Mode in itself, but from another mode often traveling in their shadow.

As was discussed earlier, cosmopolitanism is generally framed in the Universal Mode of justice – Justice as principles that apply universally to all. The Universal Mode of justice discourse is not unique to cosmopolitanism – virtually any theory of justice can be articulated in this mode. What matters is that the principles are discussed and advanced as universal in scope, with universal validity and – perhaps most problematically – universal binding force.

It may appear that Universal Modes of justice discourse have no place in a pluralistic global environment, with its reality of different, competing universalist views about human nature, society, and justice, but in fact I don't believe this is so: most if not all of us hold or have held some view or other in this manner without a problem, and insofar as this is itself a "universal" phenomenon, it must have its place. The difficulty does not lie with Universalism per se. It is certainly true that people can confuse the universalism of their rhetoric or beliefs with the actual level of agreement – or disagreement – about these principles on the part of others, and it is also sadly true that people operating through a Universal Mode of discourse can also be committing acts of intolerance or cultural hegemony, but these are mistakes or pathologies of the Universal Mode. In the case of the global justice debate, I suspect that the problem does not lie with the universalism of such views or even these mistakes and pathologies, but rather with something else that often travels with Universalist theories and can be confused with them – a focus on the behavior of others. In order to explain this, we need to revisit Take One.

Take One introduced us to the Justice as Integrity mode. This mode characterizes justice as a matter of acting consistently with our own principles and commitments with respect to behavior toward others, regardless of who they are or what they might think is just, and whether or not we agree or disagree on such principles. In particular, Justice as Integrity does not try to tell others how they should act. That is a matter for their own integrity.

Focusing our arguments on how others should act based on our view of justice is more properly a function of what I call Justice as Discipline. In this mode, one talks about and thinks about justice as a tool for changing and controlling the behavior of others. Note carefully the difference: a Universalist conception of justice such as cosmopolitanism may include beliefs and judgments about how other people should act (one might consider that as inherent in the Universal Mode, and perhaps in justice itself). However, that does not necessarily mean that in a Universal Mode one considers it *right* or one's *privilege* to discipline or sanction others on the basis of their failure to act according to our own principles. *That* is what I am calling Justice as Discipline.

The challenge, of course, is that confronting what we believe to be injustice – strongly and persistently – is what the global justice debate, and all justice theory, is about, and as this often involves challenging the acts and decisions of others, the distinction between confronting injustice and employing the mode of Justice as Discipline can be elusive at times. Nevertheless, there is a difference. There is no question that as part of making the world a more just place, we are often called upon to label what others do as unjust. However, the key to the difference between a conversation or debate and a rupture or a crusade is all in *how* we talk about it, and what we are then led to do.

First, in my view, it would be best if we proceeded most carefully in situations where the conduct of others is the subject, being sure we have thoroughly reviewed our own responsibilities according to whatever theory of justice we hold. The proverbial splinter in the other's eye and log in our own echoes here.

Second, when we address the injustice of others' acts, it is vitally important that we couch our appeals, and denunciations, in theoretical and rhetorical modes best calculated to appeal to them and convict them, rather than simply using the modes we ourselves find most convincing. For example, if the target of our admonishment understands justice in a relational mode, then it would be most effective to appeal to any shared relationships, rather than simply invoke our particular Universalist view if it happens not to be theirs. Alternatively, we can take the time to understand their Universalist views well enough to frame our arguments in terms of their principles.

This is the heart of the difficulty with what I am calling the Justice as Discipline mode or strategy, and it is in the end simply good lawyering: if one seeks to persuade or reform, don't make the mistake of simply sounding off loudly with the Universalist theory one holds and finds compelling.

Take the time to find out what particular theories or modes would be most compelling to one's audience, and frame one's arguments about *their* behavior in those terms.

This means that in debates over global justice, the real key if one is committed to a pluralistic approach or at a minimum one accepts that the world is pluralist, is not so much to prove a Universalist theory wrong as to take care to point out – and disagree with – the rhetoric of Justice as Discipline when it is being employed, and to resist the temptation to take action in a Justice as Discipline manner. Disciplining others is what is least effective in a pluralistic environment, not holding one's beliefs about justice – or anything else – in a Universalist manner.

Perhaps we have come around to the virtue of tolerance, but through a different doorway, as the antidote to Justice as Discipline. It is critically important for the global justice debate, and for justice on a global level, that we chart a path forward that allows one to simultaneously hold universalist views, in a tolerant manner, yet be energetically engaged in fighting injustice on a global level without needless head-on attacks on the wrongness of another's universalist views.

If this is right, then it suggests that a sensitivity to the rhetorical modes in which we talk about justice and what they imply can be very helpful in avoiding unnecessary conflict and finding common ground in the pursuit of justice. If we are going to deliberately speak about justice in many voices, we can then pay attention to how each voice rings and how well (or not) they harmonize together.

Understanding the rhetorical conflict between Justice as Discipline on the one hand, and any one of a number of theories of justice or other modes such as the Universal Mode, is but one of the insights possible through a comparative and pluralist approach to justice theory. Additional insights are possible through Sen's plural grounding approach to justice theory, as a method for extending the comparative analysis inherent in this book to more explicit conclusions about justice theory.

2. *Plural Grounding*

In *The Idea of Justice*, Amartya Sen establishes an important procedural principle that he calls "plural grounding." By this he means that in our ordinary discourse about justice (more often really about injustice), we tend to employ rhetorical strategies that offer multiple bases for judging a situation to be unjust.[2] It is only within the realms of philosophical argument (of a certain kind)[3] that we tend instead to attempt to establish a single triumphant and exclusive ground for articulating both justice and injustice.

---

[2] Amartya Sen, The Idea of Justice 2 (Belknap Press 2009).

[3] As discussed in the Introduction, Sen distinguishes between two distinct approaches to justice: what he calls "transcendental institutionalism," in which the goal is to describe the social characteristics of "perfect justice" as he calls it; and "realization-focused comparison" in which the goal is to increase justice/decrease injustice through comparisons among societies as they already exist "or could feasibly emerge." *Id.* at 5–7.

In Sen's view this is a mistake, and it has more than rhetorical consequences. Insofar as ideas allow us to evaluate situations and then act accordingly, it is of course important to have the best, sharpest, most powerful ideas possible. However, if the process of sharpening and challenging ideas of justice devolves into a theoretical exclusivism, the intellectual debates this engenders draw attention and energy away from the accurate and effective characterization of present, grave injustice. Such distractions prevent or delay both the moment of conviction and the moment of action that are meant to follow from the sustained, broad-based examination of manifest injustice.

Instead, rational accounts of injustice are by nature plural and are meant to be employed in a strategy of plural grounding, whereby we develop a fuller, nuanced understanding of an unjust situation and what makes it so, and in the process uncover reasons for remediation that a wide variety of persons may find compelling. The plural grounding approach thus takes into account two important aspects of human discourse: different reasons appeal to different persons, and sometimes we need several different reasons in concert to reach conviction.

Put in this light, contemporary philosophical debates over global justice resemble medieval and early modern attempts to philosophically demonstrate the existence of God. Centuries of intellectual energy went into attempting to establish which proof of the existence of God was stronger or more effective than all the rest, while often ignoring the reality of how people tend to approach such questions: different arguments persuade, or not, different persons, and no one argument can hope to convince everyone. The most any argument can do is open the rational possibility of God's existence for the right person at the right time. Here, plural arguments for justice can together move us in a similar fashion from consideration to action – or that is the hope.

It is important to clarify at the outset that a plural grounding approach is not the same as simply failing to reason carefully or thoroughly about injustice, or assuming a kind of unreflective approval with respect to all assertions about justice – quite the opposite. Sen expects that rigorous tests of rationality will be applied to each different kind of argument about injustice. Rather, the plural grounding approach is about a shift in expectation – we do not argue with the goal of establishing the supremacy of a single idea of justice; instead, we argue with the goal of developing the most comprehensive diagnosis of injustice possible and the best set of reasons for doing something about it.

So, if we adopt Sen's view of plural grounding, how does this clarify the relationship between the three different approaches to global justice outlined here (and others we have not examined)? In order to begin answering these questions, I will examine and compare each Take along three axes: its distinctive diagnosis of injustice, its distinctive rationale for action, and its distinctive benchmarks or criteria by which to choose a course of action and evaluate progress. I will then examine how each Take illustrates its distinct rhetorical mode of justice discourse, and the implications these modes have for the global justice project.

a. Reasoned Diagnoses of Global Injustice. First, we can see that each Take presents a specific reasoned diagnosis of global injustice, a distinctive account of the problem to be addressed: the nature of an injustice and its root causes.

i. Take One: Global Injustice as Unjustified Inequalities. Liberal internationalism begins, as does its underlying theory of domestic Justice as Fairness, with the fact of natural inequality and its social consequences. As human beings we are morally equal yet differentially endowed, and insofar as social institutions make allocative decisions according to these natural inequalities, we become socially unequal. Unless such socially created inequalities are justified (through something like the Difference Principle), they violate our moral equality.

On this view, global injustice stems from two basic categories of causes: domestic institutional failures and international institutional failures. At the domestic level, when domestic institutions fail to fulfill the conditions of Justice as Fairness, such failures create injustice at two levels. First, they adversely affect the fairness of conditions within their own borders for their own citizens. Second, given the interconnectedness of global socioeconomic relations, such decisions create externalities for other states.

At the international level, states make and carry out decisions through international institutions that reinforce natural inequalities and thus create or reinforce unjustifiable social inequalities at an international level. Unless informed by a liberal theory of justice, decisions made through international institutions such as international law (through the interpretation and application of doctrines such as sovereignty and *terra nullis*) and the Bretton Woods institutions (such as the IMF and its conditionality practices) reinforce natural and social inequalities among both people and states, thereby contributing to an unjust global order. Such decisions can often be traced to domestic *political* failures, but as the decisions operate through the instrumentality of international institutions, such causes are better treated as a distinct category.

Given the reality of pluralism, liberal internationalism responds differently to these two sources of global injustice. With respect to domestic institutional failures, it first depends on the state in question. In the case of failures by a liberal state's own institutions, its citizens have complete responsibility and a full range of direct responses at both political and private levels.

Where the injustice is attributable to the domestic institutional failures of other states (whether liberal or nonliberal), the range of responses depends on whether the other state is liberal or not. Liberal states and their citizen-consumers are engaged in a richly textured web of relationships with each other and are subject to many of the same kinds of persuasion, on account of their shared liberal values and their reputational interests.

In the case of failures on the part of nonliberal states such as burdened states (states with severe institutional and developmental challenges), there is little that can be done directly if liberal states are to respect the limits of their own liberal consensus regarding the primacy of liberty (here read as nonintervention). Instead, liberal states must decide (and Rawls attempts to guide us through this in *The Law of Peoples)* the appropriate limits of aid, advocacy, influence, and leverage in their relationships with nonliberal states.

With respect to the second cause, institutional failures at the international level, liberal internationalism can respond vigorously with respect to the actions of liberal states, articulating the foreign policy obligations of a liberal state with respect to what it can and should do regarding the transnational distributive effects of its own policies and the policies of the multilateral institutions it participates in. In the case of institutional failures attributable to the decisions or actions of nonliberal states (the role of China or Russia in UN Security Council votes comes to mind), once again there are limits to the effectiveness of a liberal state's advocacy, influence, or leverage. Such situations present some of the most difficult international relations challenges facing liberal states today.

In summary, Take One understands global injustice as attributable to institutional failures, addressable at different levels in different ways depending upon the locus of failure. Many of the arguments about global justice within this perspective have to do with assigning responsibility to the "correct" level for such failures, as, for example, in the neoliberal debates over the responsibility of domestic governments versus international agencies such as the IMF or the Inter-American Development Bank in cases of persistent underdevelopment such as Latin America.

ii. Take Two: There Is No Truly "Global" Injustice, Just the Suffering of Others. Turning now to Take Two, a global communitarian account of the causes of global injustice begins with a different account of our natural condition – our social embeddedness – and its implications for the justice of our social relations. On this view, human beings require community in order to form an identity and to determine what justice means. Each community therefore finds its own justice, and the members of that community are responsible for supporting each other as co-venturers in this shared project.

On this view, there is no global justice or injustice as those terms are commonly used. Instead, what we *call* global "injustice" has two distinctly different causes. First, there is the inescapable fact that different political communities have achieved different levels of success or failure in supporting the life projects of their members. Given that political communities differ in their definitions of justice, the success of their institutions, and the resources they command to fulfill their individual or national projects, we will inevitably see differences in the wealth, opportunities and life prospects of different states and their citizens.

Interestingly, in this aspect the diagnosis of this Take resembles the first branch of the diagnosis offered by liberal internationalism – the failures of domestic institutions. However, the implications are radically different: from this perspective, such conditions do not amount to a *global* injustice – just a great deal of suffering and inequality occurring in communities other than our own (speaking from the liberal, developed states' perspective).

It is also important to note that there is no second "international institution" branch to the diagnosis of injustice offered by Take Two. International institutions do not operate in the realm of justice from a communitarian perspective, because they are outside of and independent from political community. They fulfill, or not, their treaty-based functions as established and influenced by the powerful contracting states in charge. They may happen to achieve results which, from a domestic point of view, comport with one theory of justice or another, but that is incidental and a byproduct of the politics of that moment and the normative commitments of powerful or effective member states. There are, therefore, no failures of justice at the level of international institutions. States may of course oppose or frustrate each other's national projects and the life projects of other citizens through their transnational actions, but it is not "injustice" – just unfortunate international politics.

This leads me to suggest a second, more complicated reason for "injustice" that is more properly speaking a consequence of this view rather than a tenet of it. I am speaking here of a misunderstanding about the nature of social relations in this era of globalization, which I have argued distorts the communitarian account of the possibility of global justice. As was discussed in Take Two, in the traditional communitarian view justice stops at the border of political communities, and since there is no overarching global community supporting global justice, there is no global justice (or injustice). Instead, we stand by and watch each other's national projects succeed or fail (helping or hurting as the politics of the moment dictate), while doing our best to maintain our own.

However, insofar as globalization is working a change in social relations such that our fates are increasingly interlinked and shared practices and understandings are in fact emerging, then (speaking as a communitarian) our theory of political community has been overtaken by events, and we are in fact in relations of mutual responsibility without fully recognizing this (whether innocently or intentionally). In other words, because of globalization the problems of inequality and the suffering of others are now "our" problems, and insofar as we fail to recognize this, or act on it, we are perpetuating (and participating in) global injustice, since justice at some level is now possible between national political communities.

This failure, delay, or reluctance to acknowledge an emerging global community and the responsibilities (and opportunities) it creates therefore becomes a second distinct cause of global injustice. I recognize, however, that this is a controversial and emerging view, which communitarians might reject as inaccurate about social reality, and cosmopolitans as mistaken about justice and therefore unnecessary or mischievous.

iii. Take Three: Coerced Bargains on a Global Scale. This brings us to Take Three, an internal approach based on the notion of consent. This Take offers a radically different diagnosis of "injustice," rooted in something we are already familiar with: our experience of trade and its pathologies and our misunderstandings about what makes trade "trade." When we look closely at trade we see that its essence is voluntary mutual bargained-for exchanges of value. The regulatory function of trade law, therefore, should be to protect such exchanges and establish a framework to promote their flourishing.

Instead, we find that we have misled ourselves about the nature of trade and the object of trade law and have focused on freedom from distorting governmental regulation rather than on the nature of trade and its pathologies. Among other things, this elision allows us to pursue short-term opportunistic strategies we think will work to our advantage, without the restraining effect of law on such behavior. Thus through "trade" law, we have been protecting and enhancing coercion, predation, and exploitation in the guise of trade, thereby undermining the conditions for consensual bargains and the more equitable global economic order such bargains would constitute at a basic level.

Returning to our theme of plural grounding, we can see from this preliminary investigation how a plural grounding approach offers a richer menu of social analysis than any single theory of justice and injustice could offer. We have three different diagnoses of injustice and its causes, looking at natural inequalities, social distributions, the nature and limits (and evolution) of community and its relationship to justice, and the differences between mutually beneficial bargains and various forms of economic opportunism.

Seen in this light, it seems only too clear that a phenomenon as complex as global injustice should have multiple causes and need multiple reasoned diagnoses if we are to richly and accurately evaluate the nature of the problem and reach conviction as to necessary action.

b. Distinctive Rationales for Action on a Global Level. In addition to offering a reasoned diagnosis for injustice, each Take offers a different kind of reason *for* justice, or rationale for corrective behavior, which is the second element of a plural grounding approach. Why, on each of these accounts, should one do anything about global injustice?

i. Take One: Justifying Inequalities at the Global Level. For liberal internationalism, the core reason for action depends upon a prior set of moral intuitions. Insofar as we are convinced of our moral equality, and the arbitrariness of the distribution of natural abilities (i.e., we don't "deserve" what we are born with), then the principles of Justice as Fairness are both powerful and compelling. We see everywhere patterns of social distribution that create or reinforce natural inequalities we cannot square with these moral intuitions. At the global level, we recognize our complicity in the various distributive decisions made through international law and institutions.

Therefore, if we are committed to our moral intuitions, we must take action to address injustice both within our own societies and, to the extent we can, within other liberal and nonliberal societies. Our aim in all cases is to justify social inequalities according to their benefit to the least advantaged of us and rectify those that cannot be justified. Paraphrasing Rousseau, it is intolerable that persons are born equal yet everywhere are treated unequally. To fail to act would be to betray our core principles.

This is a very powerful set of reasons for action with respect to injustice. The complication here is the basic question of pluralism: what do we do about the fact that others may not share all – or any – of our moral intuitions or our commitment to principles of moral equality, or may reason differently from them? Put another way, the world as we find it is divided into different normative and political communities and traditions, to some degree coextensive with different sovereign states or groups of states, within which peoples are pursuing very different social projects with different principles of justice and different allocative effects.

Faced with this set of circumstances, and going back to the basic problem presented in the introduction, we have two choices: act *as if* our own view is shared, or accept the reality of pluralism and adjust our sights downward, confining our arguments and actions to our own normative community and its unilateral reach. The latter is the option that distinguishes liberal internationalism from cosmopolitanism: limiting this vision of justice to those states that already share these moral commitments at the level of core political values. Thus for liberal states, Take One offers a compelling call to action and activism at the international level, but without any presupposition of a shared view. We accept that our reasons for justice are compelling for us and us alone, and we proceed as well as we can.

ii. Take Two: Recognizing Solidarity Beyond Our Borders. Take Two offers a very different reason for action in the face of injustice, or more properly, suggests the emergence of a new and compelling reason for action: we may well be in the process of becoming a global community at least in some areas of global social relations, and may therefore already be responsible for each other's well-being at a global level, in ways we hitherto thought only applied to our co-nationals.

On this view, the reason for justice is the deepening of our global social interconnectedness and our consequent responsibility for the effects of our actions and decisions on many others. We may be discovering that we are after all our brothers' and sisters' keepers on a global level.

This Take thus offers its own compelling rationale for action – interconnectedness and the possibility of global solidarity. In the long run, this may well be the *most* compelling reason for action against injustice on a global level. However, at the moment it roots action in a controversial and contestable claim about global social relations – the possibility of global community.

iii. Take Three: Preserving the Possibilities Inherent in Future Bargains. In keeping with its different point of departure, Take Three offers a very different kind of reason for action, not in the strictest sense about justice at all. Instead, what this approach suggests as a reason to act is the need to protect consent as an essential element in trade, lest trade become something else, whatever we then call it: coercion, predation, or exploitation.

The reasons we want to protect trade and not these alternatives have nothing to do with moral principles but simply reflect a correct evaluation of our own economic self-interest. Insofar as we make consensual bargains and not other kinds of exchanges, we preserve and enhance the opportunity to engage in future beneficial consensual bargains, and we reduce the social costs of overreaching. On the other hand, to the degree we engage in predation, coercion, or exploitation, we may lose potential partners for future beneficial transactions, and we certainly increase the social costs of enforcing such bargains.

Thus by protecting the conditions for what makes us and others better off, we also promote what we characterize in another mode as "just behavior," and thereby over time contribute to a more just global economic order. Justice and self-interest align in the difference between real trade and its pathologies. Despite the attractive possibility of disproportionate short-term gains due to overreaching, we only gain from trade in the long run if it is truly trade, so therefore we had better protect consent. "Fairness" is not an ideal but the fruit of an authentic process of real bargaining that yields concrete economic benefits, so it is in our own interest to protect the conditions for real bargains.

Thus each Take sets out a distinctive reasoned diagnosis of the nature of injustice and offers a distinctive rationale for justice. In doing so, each Take thereby suggests a different model for the relationship between injustice, justice, trade law, and pluralism. In keeping with the turn away from transcendental institutionalism (following Sen),[4] these models are not intended to be models of an ideally just society; instead, they are meant to diagnose particular injustices and persuade us to act on them, thereby moving social conditions further from injustice, as defined by each

[4] *Id.* at 5–7.

particular model. But how do we evaluate whether we have succeeded, according to each model, in making the world less unjust/more just? This is the third and final element of the plural grounding approach as developed here.

c. Benchmarks for Global Justice. For plural grounding to ultimately work, each Take on global justice should yield criteria for identifying social alternatives as more just/less unjust than other alternatives. Applying this to our three Takes, we see the following kinds of criteria emerge.

i. Take One: The Global Least Advantaged. For liberal internationalism the criterion is straightforward (and comes right out of Justice as Fairness): does a particular rule, institution, or arrangement (in other words, a particular piece of the basic structure) comply with the Difference Principle? Does it justify social inequalities by making them work to the benefit of the least advantaged? Does a particular reform, innovation, or initiative render the basic structure more compliant? Does it lessen the scope for arbitrary factors to influence social distributions? If the answer to any of these forms of the question is "yes," then our action has reduced injustice.

If the answer is "yes" for some affected persons, and "no" for others, then the situation is more complicated. This is the liberal dilemma: how to evaluate a course of action that benefits some least advantaged persons while disadvantaging other least advantaged persons – do we simply count? At a policy level something like a utilitarian calculus often occurs, but at a theoretical level that is problematic. In this context, the problem highlights the limits of a liberal internationalist approach.[5] I suspect the decision would be made according to political calculations (since it is a state-based approach): are the advantaged persons our citizens or the citizens of our allies? How powerful is the state whose citizens would be disadvantaged and what political costs could they impose on us? This is hardly the best way to determine questions of transnational justice, but it is really the default way given the nature of international relations today and for the foreseeable future (human rights aside – to an extent). Thus liberal internationalism does not move the ball too far down the field in this respect.

Returning to the Difference Principle, as I illustrated in Take One with reference to Special and Differential Treatment, this kind of criterion can very usefully be applied to regulatory systems such as trade law. Doing so helps us evaluate the justice or injustice of trade law, and whether our attempts at addressing this (through Special and Differential Treatment, for example) are more or less just. In other words, we can evaluate our remediation policies themselves according to the Difference Principle, which can help us design or reform them as needed. Moreover, the widespread use of this criterion in evaluations of domestic policy means that we have much experience to draw on in making such evaluations.

---

[5] I am indebted to Sonia Rolland for raising this issue.

ii. Take Two: Global Solidarity and the Global Basic Package. The question of criteria for justice and injustice is more complicated with respect to Take Two, since the normative work in elaborating a global communitarian theory of justice is perforce less developed, given its emergent nature. As I discussed in that chapter, both the evolutionary nature of the global social relations at the core of this approach, and the "glass half-full/glass half-empty" quality characterizing the emergence of communal bonds, means we do not yet have much clarity with respect to the content of a communitarian theory of global justice. Nevertheless, we can make a beginning.

First, with respect to justice as a communal good – identified and sustained by and within a community – we can look at one sort of basic criterion going to the health of such a community: does a particular rule, practice, or institution acknowledge connection, community, and responsibility? Does it build solidarity? Does it enhance our ability to care for our fellows?[6] If the answers are yes, then that rule/practice/institution is supportive of justice as that community defines it. If the answer is no, then the rule/practice/institution is undermining justice, or at least the conditions under which it thrives within that community.

---

[6] The echoes here to feminist theory and the ethics of care are probably not an accident insofar as both converge on the centrality of community and connection. See, e.g., VIRGINIA HELD, THE ETHICS OF CARE (2005) (exploring the ethics of care as an alternative approach to traditional theories of justice in a range of settings including globalization and international relations).

A second way to look at global justice through this lens, as I sought to illustrate with the Global Basic Package concept, has to do with the nature of the emerging normative consensus with regard to shared understandings and practices as to what makes a global arrangement just or unjust. Through an outline of what a Global Basic Package might look like, I suggested that the current state of this consensus consists of at least rudimentary levels of entitlement to security, subsistence, liberty, and voice. Therefore, one kind of criterion for evaluating the justice or injustice of a given arrangement, assuming I am right about this, is the degree to which the arrangement enhances one or more of these core values without harming the others.

To take an example from international economic law, we can ask whether an effort to reform the voting and quota allocation rules of the IMF enhance the voice of IMF participants. According to at least one scholar (and IMF director), the answer (given current reform proposals) would be yes for some states (the less developed countries, or LDCs), and possibly no for others (the newly industrialized countr(ies) [NICs] who would lose voice).[7] This of course mirrors the liberal dilemma expressed earlier: how to act when the effects of action are mixed? It is interesting (and significant) that we come to the same problem from two different theoretical perspectives: this highlights the need for broadly shared

---

[7] *See, e.g.*, Hector Torres, *Reforming the IMF – Why Its Legitimacy Is at Stake*, 10 J. INT'L ECON. L., 443–60 (2007).

criteria that guide action when action inevitably yields a multitude of often-conflicting effects.

Analyzing such reforms in this manner gives us a way to articulate their effects in terms of emerging norms which, on this theory, may be held in common across lines of nationality and levels of development. Those are the sorts of inquiries that a global communitarian approach to justice would require and make possible.

iii. Take Three: Protecting and Promoting Consent at the Global Level. Finally, with respect to consent, the benchmark is relatively straightforward, as was the case with Take One as well: does a particular rule/practice/institution establish, protect, or enhance the possibility for real consent? If we treat consent as an example of an internal approach to trade and justice, then the benchmark question can be similarly broadened out: how well does a particular rule/practice/institution respect the particular internal principle of justice in questions? We can ask this both with respect to the process whereby it has become a rule/practice/institution, and with respect to the substantive regime it establishes for private party conduct. If so, then by protecting the conditions for consent, it advances the possibility of real trade and contributes to a flourishing market. If not, then it establishes something else altogether – predation, coercion, or exploitation – and the social costs attendant to such practices.

As with Take One, I sought to illustrate through trade law what a metric such as consent might look like in application, by analyzing the CAFTA treaty along the lines of its support or damage to consent. The result was rather ominous: in many respects, CAFTA and treaties like it are the result of a coercive or exploitative process, and create rules which themselves facilitate predatory, coercive, and exploitative transactions by private parties.[8]

The solution is less clear: is the process of bargaining for the treaty so flawed that the treaty as whole must be scrapped? Or can the substantive rules be amended, or reinterpreted, such that the treaty can promote a zone of more consensual bargains within its jurisdiction? Is the domestic distribution of gains from trade so skewed, or the domestic regime so nonrepresentative, that a fairer bargain for the state as a whole is not likely to lead to fairer outcomes for its citizens? To what extent can we remedy such situations by simply reinterpreting provisions of existing, flawed treaties? These questions need further study (and I will return to them in the final sections of this chapter), but at least

---

[8] Unfortunately the same can be said regarding the emerging network of international investment treaties and their effects on social values. *See* Javier Perez, Myriam Gistelinck & Dima Karbala, *Sleeping Lions International Investment Treaties, State-investor Disputes and Access to Food, Land and Water,* OXFAM DISCUSSION PAPERS (May 2011); Lindita Ciko, *Customary International Law and Treaty-based Investor-State Arbitration* (unpublished paper on file with the author).

a consent approach points out what the questions are, and suggests what a less unjust outcome might look like.

This completes our review of these three Takes from a plural grounding perspective. We have seen how each offers a particular reasoned diagnosis of injustice, which together paint a more comprehensive view of global injustice than any one theory alone can do. Each offers distinctive rationales for action that may appeal to different people for their own different reasons but together can establish a compelling call to action. Finally, each offers distinctive benchmarks for whether our actions in response are addressing global injustice in a measurable, positive direction, along a range of metrics.

The question now becomes what this type of comparative analysis of modes and conceptions of justice suggests about where we should be going next, both with respect to the theory of global justice, and to the law, policy, and practice of our efforts to remedy global injustice and promote global justice.

B. Where Might We Be Going?

In this section, my goal is to turn from a comparative study of these three Takes on global justice, in which the aim was to shed light on how we talk about and analyze global justice, to a more prescriptive inquiry into how these Takes might suggest useful next steps at the level of both theory and practice. In other words, I would like to draw implications from this analysis both for the evolution of global justice theory and for our efforts to reform institutions and policies. In terms of the latter, my aim is less to apply these theories to specific concrete injustices – which I did to some extent for illustrative purposes in each chapter – and more to look synthetically at how analyzing international economic relations through these three Takes might suggest next steps in the evolution of the global economic system *as a system*.

1. *The Uneven State of Contemporary Global Justice Theory*

Extrapolating from Sen's plural grounding approach, we can say that different theories of justice are meant to play different roles not just in the process of analyzing injustice and convincing us to act, but in the larger process of envisioning and creating a more just order in a pluralistic world. We can use Rawls's typology of states as liberal, hierarchical, or illiberal to begin to ask what kinds of work each theory can do within this panoply.

We can also benefit from Wilfried Hinsch's concept of "moral federalism," a structure within which different principles of justice do different but complementary kinds of work at different levels within the system (in particular, the national and the transnational).[9] For Hinsch, there is no reason in principle why domestic and transnational principles of distributive justice need to be identical. Indeed, allowing for divergent but compatible conceptions of justice may be

[9] Wilfried Hinsch, *Global Distributive Justice*, 32 METAPHILOSOPHY 58, 59 (2001).

more consistent with the pluralist nature of global society, and with liberal values of autonomy.[10]

Take One articulates a vision of liberal justice that, for the liberal community of states, is global justice itself. In other words, Liberal Internationalism would be Global Justice if all states were liberal. This typifies a whole range of theories, and theorizing, about global justice, in that it takes a domestic theory of justice and extrapolates from it to what global justice might look like, if global social space were like domestic social space. Because of this key assumption and analogy, liberal internationalism applies directly and fully only to liberal states that share the same basic political framework and commitments. But within that community, liberal internationalism is global justice.

With respect to nonliberal states – both hierarchical and illiberal states in Rawls's ordering – Take One shifts gears and becomes a guide informing the foreign policy of liberal states toward these other states. Specific policies or arrangements with liberal states might take different forms for hierarchical versus illiberal states, given that different relationships are possible and normatively justifiable with

[10] *Id.* at 60. Hinsch maintains that divergent *domestic* conceptions of justice must be balanced by a shared *global* conception of justice, but this does not entail that all societies support global justice for the same reasons – presumably, their support for such a shared conception will be grounded in the rationales distinctive to their own domestic traditions, thus preserving the importance of pluralism – and plural grounding – even in Hinsch's stricter model of global consistency.

each given their differences. But in either case, the theory no longer works as a theory of global justice – it has become a theory of the foreign policy obligations of liberal states in a pluralistic world. The theory does not explain or predict what a just relationship within or between such communities would look like[11] – only how liberal states are to act in its absence.

Thus Take One and the approaches it exemplifies – and, I suspect, any theory that operates in a Justice as Integrity mode – helps us achieve two important goals: theorizing about the global justice obligations of states that share core political commitments, and theorizing about the obligations of such states toward normatively different states. Both are important and useful elements within the larger process of global justice, but even taken together they do not allow us to theorize about the full range of global justice issues and opportunities.[12]

In Take Two, we looked at a different approach to global justice, based on an evolutionary model of global community, and a distinct mode of justice discourse, the Relational approach to justice. In one respect, this Take is similar to liberal internationalism, in that we began with a domestic

---

[11] Except, of course, in the sense that the theory dictates that such states become liberal states in order to be just, but then we are violating our presumption in favor of pluralism, or states as we find them.

[12] Cosmopolitans, in particular, are bound to be disappointed by this approach.

model of justice – the communitarian approach this time – and extrapolated from it to what global justice might look like (or what global social relations might need to look like in order for there to be global justice).

However, Take Two differs in two crucial respects: (1) it does not assume that global social relations are identical to domestic social relations (that transdomestic societies would have to be identical to domestic societies); and (2) it does not assume a static model of social relationships – in fact, it assumes the opposite as its starting point. The strength of the approach in Take Two is to attempt to capture in a dynamic sense the evolutionary nature of global social relations and to explore what theoretical and normative possibilities for global justice such changing social relations create.

Thus in Take Two we have a model for what a more truly global approach to global justice theory might look like, in that it takes seriously the fact that global social space is not like domestic social space, and also takes seriously that global social space is changing in important ways. This means that domestic political theories might still have something to say about global justice, but in a reconstituted global social sphere, not a naively imagined global domesticism.

In this sense, Take Two offers an important supplement to Take One, insofar as it takes globalization into account and lays a foundation for analyzing the normative implications of this emerging order. However, just as with Take

One, there is a contingency, but of a different sort. Whereas in Take One a truly *global* justice depended upon all states being liberal (unlikely), in Take Two global justice depends upon all states (or, more accurately, their people) becoming part of a global *community* (controversial and possibly unattainable). The very fact that this is an emerging order means that we may not yet be at the point where a truly global theory of justice works in this new social space, even for economic relations (despite my arguments in Take Two), and we may not be there for a long time, if ever.

Putting the two Takes together, this means that for domestic justice and for transnational justice among similar states we have a well-theorized model with a limited reach, but for global justice we have an under-theorized model with problematic assumptions but potentially greater reach. Thus we can see that existing theories do some of the work well (theorizing liberal justice on a transnational level), and leave other aspects of the work – namely, constructing an inclusive system of global justice among a pluralistic set of states – less well developed.

Put in communitarian terms, the problem is that we have only begun to explore what the shared understandings of such a set of states/political communities might be (or even whether they might have any). Given the current state of global social relations, we may only be able to *begin* to do so. Nevertheless, there are some tantalizing signs of development here. Gillian Brock, for example, suggests that there are new lines of convergence between cosmopolitan and communitarian views.[13] Miller acknowledges some areas of agreement at least with respect to the priority of protecting everyone's vital interests before the nonvital interests of any particular person or group.[14]

Similarly, Walzer has tried to demonstrate a zone of overlap among different theories of justice at least with respect to grave injustices.[15] In this sense, Walzer's work resembles Sen's plural grounding approach. However, there is one crucial difference between Walzer's efforts and what I am proposing here. In *Thick and Thin*, Walzer's model is essentially a static one, taking both theory and social reality as he finds them today and charting the overlap that we happen, fortuitously, to discover. This is no small feat and thank goodness for the fortuity, but Walzer misses a critical opportunity. The zone of overlap is not static, and globalization itself plays a key role in intensifying these processes.

For this reason, I am arguing that what we really see is a dynamic process of emerging consensus around shared understandings in a newly constituting global social space. This means that one of the key tasks for global justice theory is to try to determine what those understandings might

---

[13] GILLIAN BROCK, GLOBAL JUSTICE: A COSMOPOLITAN ACCOUNT 246–65 (2009). Brock allows for the possibility of more extensive duties to co-nationals within a cosmopolitan framework, similar to Tan.

[14] DAVID MILLER, NATIONAL RESPONSIBILITY AND GLOBAL JUSTICE. 46–50 (2007).

[15] MICHAEL WALZER, THICK AND THIN (2006). I discuss his approach more extensively in Take Two.

be and the extent of consensus, a possibility Walzer does not contemplate (and would probably discount).[16] In a sense, Take Two is Walzer plus a time path and a driver – globalization, as a mechanism for the creation and deepening of shared norms.

This kind of comparative analysis is only just beginning and is likely to prove quite contentious for some time, if the debate surrounding the nature, extent, and status of human rights law today – a functional parallel – is any indicator. The audacity of the claims of human rights – indeed the very concept – and the resistance it provokes from political realists and political despots alike, have made the entire set of issues surrounding their status in law quite complex and contentious. In a similar way, the notion of a global community and its norms is likely to provoke a long and complex investigation and debate. I do conclude Take Two with a preliminary outline of some of the contours of this convergence, but there is much more to be done on this. In the meantime, is there a basis for theorizing a more just global order despite the imperfect and incomplete nature of these relationships or this set of understandings?

One possibility is to begin the work of something like an anthropology of global justice – an effort to determine what we can say about an emerging consensus regarding basic justice in this limited/emerging global economic community. As I said with respect to Take Two, if the global justice

[16] *See* SEN, *supra* note 2; WALZER, *Supra* note 15.

debate is precisely where the emerging consensus of this new community is being established, then we can use the concept of a Global Basic Package I outlined in that chapter and also look at the extent to which each approach to global justice supports elements of this Global Basic Package, as an experimental method to study the extent of any global consensus on justice.

Another possibility is to build such an order around an entirely different basis. The consent approach itself might offer a way to ground efforts to promote global justice in a truly global manner, namely, in a presently shared consensus about the importance of trade, and commerce generally, but based on a more accurate view of what such trade really consists of, and how best to encourage its flourishing. This road to a more just global system involves establishing a framework of consensual bargains and letting the rest play itself out. This may be the contribution a consent approach makes to our "moral federalism."

2. *Establishing a Global Framework for Consensual Bargaining*

My aim in this final section is to consider how a consent approach to international trade law may serve not only as a way to analyze the differences between trade and something else, thereby clarifying the proper role for trade agreements, but also as a basis for establishing a kind of global economic framework that promotes and stabilizes more equitable socioeconomic relations among people and states. If consent can lead us toward these kinds of relationships, we may thereby achieve at least some of the goals of the global justice movement but in a different manner, pending further evolutions to come from other directions, such as liberal internationalism (as the politics of global justice mature) and global communitarianism (as the relationships of global interconnectedness deepen).

In considering rather skeptically the possibility that there are degrees of mutual responsibility on a spectrum of transboundary relationships, Nagel considers the possibility that simply being involved in a network of international trade and trade agreements might give rise to one such level of obligation.[17] However, in dismissing this possibility, he doubts "that the rules of international trade rise to the level of collective action needed to trigger demands for justice, even in diluted form. The relation remains essentially one of bargaining."[18]

This is precisely where a consent approach can make an important contribution to the general debate on global justice and international trade law. The fact that international trade – and international trade rules – are the fruit of bargaining is precisely what allows us to look at the sorts of bargains they strike among states, the sorts of bargains they facilitate or obstruct among private parties, and the relationship of all of this to the core of a true trade transaction: consensual bargaining itself.

---

[17] Thomas Nagel, *The Problem of Global Justice*, 33 PHIL. & PUB. AFF. 114, 141 (2005).

[18] *Id.*

Put another way, I would argue that it is an impoverished view of trade, and a misunderstanding of the nature of its bargains, which allows Nagel to dismiss the possibility of trade law as a basis for collective relationships of mutual responsibility, on the basis that it involves "mere" bargaining. Doubtless it will be a different kind of responsibility, not so much that of political theory as that of mercantile law: the need to strike and protect fair mutual bargains if one hopes to continue bargaining in the future. However, this relationship between self-interest and fair bargains is precisely the reason to hope that a consensual treaty relationship can contribute to more equitable economic relationships.

Recast this way, trade agreements can do more than simply promote fair bargains, important as that is: they can begin to answer the larger question we face of how to construct a more just global economic order within conditions of pluralism. A network of truly consensual trade agreements can serve an important ordering role in global socioeconomic relations, by establishing a pragmatic, commerce-based rule of law among peoples who do not necessarily share any other sociopolitical loyalties. In order to explore this further, I want to draw on two earlier precedents in international law, *jus gentium* and *lex mercatoria*.

a. Classical Antecedents to Contemporary Opportunities. Within the Roman legal system there developed a system of *jus gentium* or the law of peoples, as the answer to a particular set of needs within the Empire. The Roman legal system embraced a particular kind of legal pluralism. For Roman citizens there was Roman law, the most highly developed system of private law of its time. For conquered peoples, Rome did not extend the benefits of Roman law, largely allowing whatever customary legal system they had developed to remain in force, subject only to traditional imperial constraints on fiscal matters.[19] This left a significant gap, namely, the rules that would apply to relations between Romans and foreigners in such matters as commercial transactions, contract disputes, property transactions, injuries, and so on.

For such matters, Roman law developed the *jus gentium*, a set of pragmatic rules based in part on Roman law but also on custom and mercantile practice.[20] This body of law provided the necessary basis in the rule of law for orderly relations among these groups, without either absorbing all peoples into the Roman legal system as citizens (politically and culturally impossible) or leaving relations between

---

[19] A. ARTHUR SCHILLER, ROMAN LAW: MECHANISMS OF DEVELOPMENT 538–539 (1978).

[20] *See* HENRY JAMES SUMNER MAINE, ANCIENT LAW 47 (SCHOLARLY PUB. OFFICE, U. OF MICH. LIBR. 2005) (1861) ("The expedient to which [the Romans] resorted was that of selecting the rules of law common to Rome and to the different Italian communities in which the immigrants were born.... [T]hey set themselves to form a system answering to the primitive and literal meaning of *Jus Gentium*, that is, Law common to all Nations. *Jus Gentium* was, in fact, the sum of the common ingredients in the customs of the old Italian tribes, for they were all the nations whom the Romans had the means of observing, and who sent successive swarms of immigrants to Roman soil").

Romans and non-Romans to the state of nature (socially costly and out of keeping with the Roman legal spirit).[21] The result was a body of law that addressed the distinctive legal and social characteristics of the time, which are interestingly also similar to key features of today's globalization and its pluralistic legal environment.[22] We live within a global legal framework in which there is no single universal system of law, politics, or public order that claims comprehensive jurisdiction or allegiance.[23] Instead, as during the Roman and post-Roman periods, we have commerce between people of different countries and legal cultures who do not share a single legal or political system, leading Hedley Bull

---

[21] See ADOLF BERGER, ENCYCLOPEDIC DICTIONARY OF ROMAN LAW 528–529 (AM. PHIL. SOC'Y 1991) (1968) ("[I]us gentium appears ... as the product of the political and economic growth of the Roman state. Contact with foreign territories in the Mediterranean basin that were gradually conquered, commercial relations with those nations and the necessity of considering their legal customs in Roman courts when transactions were concluded in Rome, the jurisdictional activity of the praetor peregrinus, created expressly for the latter purpose and given the power to recognize transactions which the Roman ius civile did not recognize – all this promoted the development of a new legal system beside the formalistic ius civile, which was not accessible to peregrines. The formalism of the ancient law had to be sacrificed in favor of international trade and the peregrines had to be admitted to Roman institutions.")

[22] For similar reasons, Domingo begins his fascinating monograph on global law with an examination of the jus gentium. RAFAEL DOMINGO, THE NEW GLOBAL LAW 3–11 (2010).

[23] See generally PAUL SCHIFF BERMAN, GLOBAL LEGAL PLURALISM (2012).

and others to call this the "new medievalism."[24] We need a set of rules that bring stability and order to these economic relationships, without presupposing a single shared political or legal system or normative framework, much as the *jus gentium* did within Roman territory.[25]

For a similar set of reasons, *lex mercatoria* arose among the mercantile community as a response to the need for orderly management of private commercial relationships when participants did not share a political community or legal system, were doing business beyond the range of any such system, and/or were suspicious of the ability of any national legal system to understand or effectively resolve their commercial disputes. All that such people had in common was that they were merchants trying to carry out transboundary commercial relationships.

It was on this shared basis – economic self-interest and the need to carry out sustained transboundary commercial relationships – that the mercantile community developed what we now call the *lex mercatoria*: a body of mercantile custom governing the formation and enforcement of bargains and the resolution of commercial disputes.[26] What

---

[24] HEDLEY BULL, THE ANARCHICAL SOCIETY: A STUDY OF ORDER IN WORLD POLITICS 245–246 (1995) (1977).

[25] Jeremy Waldron makes a similar argument for jus gentium as a resource for the judicial resolution of common problems faced by distinct jurisdictions. *See* Jeremy Waldron, *Foreign Law and the Modern Ius Gentium*, 119 HARV. L. REV. 129–147 (2005).

[26] A. CLAIRE CUTLER, PRIVATE POWER AND GLOBAL AUTHORITY 108–140 (2003).

gave this system its resilience and vitality is that it stayed close to the mercantile practice of its origins: it remained a set of rules by merchants for merchants, about their needs, concerns, and objectives, governed by shared commercial understandings of fairness.

It is in this sense that I am suggesting that a network of consensual trade agreements can play a role in globalization similar to *lex mercatoria*: a global set of norms that arise from the nature of economic bargaining itself and the needs of its participants rather than from any prior normative consensus or single comprehensive legal system. Such rules do not presuppose any shared political or cultural values but instead the shared needs and objectives of economic actors.[27] By offering a set of rules that support and reinforce particular bargains and the possibility of bargains at all (as opposed to coercion or predation), such a system helps bring order and prosperity to its actors and the larger socioeconomic systems they are a part of.

What both *jus gentium* and *lex mercatoria* share in common is the evolution of systems of private ordering, one municipal and one mercantile, which have at their root a pragmatic need for some basic rule of law in the face of a necessary, perhaps even desirable, legal and normative

[27] Certain "values" may nevertheless operate at the core of such a system as a foundation for its rules, but in an internal sense (as discussed in Take Three) and not as shared external values. *See supra* Take Three.

pluralism.[28] In this, they share the root conditions that globalization is creating today, and the same need the global
economy is highlighting.[29] Such a set of rules would apply
despite, or more accurately regardless of, one's particular
political memberships, simply on the basis of shared interactions, shared goals, and shared needs.

In essence, I am arguing that trade agreements should
function more like *lex mercatoria*, in that they should begin
with the assumption of facilitating bargains and preserving
the conditions for future bargains, and be structured so as
to establish such conditions, and less like traditional international law with its focus on interstate power relations.
They should function more like the *jus gentium* in that they
should bring a minimum acceptable level of rule of law to
relationships that by definition occur without the benefit of
a comprehensive shared political and legal community.

It is trade's ubiquity, and the central role of consent
for anyone participating in trade whatever their politics or
community, which together could allow us to build such an

[28] *See* Ernst-Ulrich Petersmann, *Human Rights and International
Economic Law, in* RESEARCH HANDBOOK ON GLOBAL JUSTICE AND
INTERNATIONAL ECONOMIC LAW (John Linarelli, ed., 2013) ("as
instruments for enhancing legal security for international trade
and reducing transaction costs, private commercial law and public
trade regulation belong to the oldest fields of national and international law (*ubi commercium, ibi jus*).")

[29] *See, e.g.,* GUNTHER TEUBNER, GLOBAL LAW WITHOUT A STATE 3, 8
(1997) (lex mercatoria is the "most successful example" and the
"paradigmatic case" of "global law without a state.").

international economic system on a shared basis of consent and the need to safeguard consent through law. Call it a *jus mercatoria* – a framework of consensual trade agreements playing a role in globalization similar to the roles *jus gentium* and *lex mercatoria* played in their respective spheres of social interaction, as a pragmatic, self-interested set of rules ordering private behavior independent of one's membership in any normative political community.

b. Recasting Trade Agreements as Consensual Framework Agreements. If we adopt this perspective on trade agreements, what difference would it make? What elements of a trade agreement are consistent with consent and the need for future bargains? In other words, in what specific ways can safeguarding consent be a key element in promoting a more just trading system, and thereby a more just global economy, ensuring it is a *trading* system and not a disguised system for predation, coercion, or exploitation?

First, there is the matter of the proper object and purpose of a trade agreement. One of the principal effects of the global justice debate is to raise the question of the proper purpose of international trade law, as law. In order for law to be effective as regulation, it must begin with the clearest possible understanding of the phenomenon to be regulated. What is our objective? What are we trying to ensure? What are we trying to prevent? What are we hoping to safeguard? International trade law is no different in this respect.

Since the end of the Second World War the public, ostensible goal of international trade law has been to promote free trade. A considerable body of economic theory backs this up, and a remarkable policy apparatus, including the WTO, has emerged to implement this goal.[30] However, I would argue that in a fundamental way we have gotten it wrong. One way to understand the debate over economic globalization is as evidence that we are dissatisfied with the limits of our own ambitions with respect to international trade law and its effects in practice, given its increasing scope in a global economy and globalizing world.

The consent analysis in Take Three suggests that we have focused too much on the "free" part and not enough on the "trade" part. Most of us would not rally behind calls for open and unrestrained economic coercion, predation, or exploitation, but that is what "free trade" has become in many instances because we have misunderstood the nature of trade itself. When we ignore the role of consent in economic exchange, we risk facilitating coercion or exploitation instead of promoting open economic exchanges. The fact that in the process, our global deregulatory apparatus has reduced the domestic regulatory burden attendant on such transactions – the conventionally understood "free" part of trade – does not make the resulting transactions "trade," nor

[30] *See, e.g.,* Pascal Lamy, *About The WTO- A Statement by the Director-General (2010), available at* http://www.wto.org/english/thewto_e/whatis_e/wto_dg_stat_e.htm.

does it restore their intended social benefit or fulfill trade's larger social promise.

Instead, trade law should be about facilitating a thriving trading environment at all levels of this emerging global market. It is not simply about promoting economic exchanges of any kind, provided they are free of protectionist domestic regulation. That is not free *trade*. The problem arises when the methods we use to advance trade, so to speak, undercut trade itself because they undercut consent, both in the negotiations between nations about the rules and in the transactions that the rules facilitate. This is really a new form of mercantilism – the view that trade law should be about "my market trouncing your market," with law playing a dual role: supporting and regulating my market at home, and deregulating markets abroad in order to facilitate my exploitation of other markets internationally. This is a disservice both to the economic opportunities that trade offers and to law itself.

This makes it critically important that we understand what it is we are trying to regulate and protect. In this sense, the global economy has grown faster than our intelligent regulation of it. Some see in this the natural tendency for law to lag behind social facts; others see in it a deliberate attempt to create a particular vision of the global market: the under-regulated market of "robber baron" capitalism. It is probably a bit of both. But if we understand trade more accurately, we can create an environment that, over time, can make us all better off by truly promoting a market and not an open space for exploitation.

If we accept this premise, then it leads to a second basic implication for the nature of trade law today, and therefore for the possibility of a more fair global economic order: a change in how we negotiate trade agreements. A consent approach would alter the way we understand the bargaining process itself, as I outlined in Take Three regarding consent and its application to the CAFTA treaty. We can get some idea of the nature of this change by employing the metric that the consent approach generates, as identified earlier in this chapter: does a particular trade negotiation process respect or support the consent of its participants?

In order to more fully develop the nature of this shift in negotiation strategy, game theory can help us. As a set of tools to articulate rational behavior in the face of a variety of types of decision matrices, game theory offers a useful way to analyze trade negotiation strategies. The key insight from applying game theory literature to trade is that *trade is a repeated game*, in which partners must contemplate a series of ongoing exchanges with no clearly determined end point.[31] The self-interested calculation of what strategies

---

[31] This can alter the incentives of the players toward cooperation. *See* George Norman & Joel P. Trachtman, *The Customary International Law Game*, 99 AJIL 541, 559–560 (2005); Jeffrey Dunnoff and Joel P. Trachtman, *Economic Analysis of International Law*, 24 YALE J INT'L L 1 (1990); *see generally* GEORGE J. MALAITH & LARRY SAMUELSON, REPEATED GAMES AND REPUTATIONS (2007).

and tactics to employ changes when one contemplates a repeated game, as opposed to a finite game. Approaches that may seem attractive for their short-term gains in the latter scenario might seem less attractive if they depend on exploitation, coercion, or manipulation, which can all poison the well for future iterations of the game in the former scenario. Over time, the oppressive nature of such agreements becomes clearer. The result is that if we correctly understand trade as a repeated game, then we are led to favor pro-consensual strategies as rational self-interested strategies.

This brings me to the third basic implication of a consent approach for trade treaties: the question of their substantive provisions. The particular nature of pro-consensual rules will vary according to the subject of the agreement and the needs of the parties, and hence each trade agreement will be different. However, we can say with some assurance that truly consensual trade agreements will differ from contemporary "trade" agreements such as CAFTA in important respects with regard to key substantive areas such as the treaty's dispute resolution mechanism; the structure and timing of market access; the extent and nature of domestic law reform mandated by the treaty; and any provisions for special or differential treatment.

Moreover, I think it is possible to generalize about a few issues common to all trade agreements if they are to be pro-consensual agreements. My first point involves a concern for the sustainability of trade relationships when it comes to framing the objectives of the treaty. In terms of sustainability, it is important to reiterate the point that trade is not solely a series of one-off transactions but is a repeated game involving long-term relationships. This has implications for bargaining strategies, as was discussed earlier. In addition, through a long-term relationship of economic exchanges, one gains knowledge of one's partners, their economy, their strengths and weaknesses, their needs, and their aspirations. Such knowledge brings with it certain choices and certain responsibilities. Do we use that knowledge to increase our ability to manipulate, exploit, or coerce our partners? Or do we build in safeguards to maintain a trade environment between us, in which we preserve the possibility of consensual bargains, even in the face of insider knowledge that we could exploit?

Thus long-term economic relationships have the potential to deepen the links between societies through trade, or promote resentment, oppression, and violence through the misuse of knowledge. We tend to rely on conditions of fair bargaining and calculations of long-term self-interest to discipline the temptation to grossly exploit knowledge inequalities. When individual actors lose sight of the repeat nature of trade, the law must step in and regulate with that view in mind.

My second point has to do with the internalization of the costs of enforcement. One of the functions of law in economic matters is to restrain the human tendency to seek profit for one's self and to shift cost and risk onto other parties.

Economists describe this as the process of creating externalities. It is no surprise that human beings in economic relationships should seek to advance their own interests, trying to shift risk and costs to others. That is one reason we have law: to plan ahead for this tendency and build in certain safeguards. In corporate matters, we expect that corporate actors will seek to maximize profit, transfer risk, and externalize cost, and we legislate with that in mind. We consider economic law successful when it is effective in ensuring that parties who exercise control and derive profit bear an appropriate degree of risk and internalize their costs.

This is true in international trade as well. In designing instruments to create global markets through treaties, we must take care that we do not talk the rhetoric of trade while instead creating the reality of coercion. If trade agreements are negotiated under circumstances in which our trade partners have no real possibility of consent, and significant sectors of their domestic societies have no way of expressing their consent or lack of consent, such a treaty is not going to promote an effective trading environment. Instead, such a treaty promotes overreaching and instability to the degree to which it is coercive or exploitative, provoking resentment and unrest that often lead to violence by both citizens and governments.[32] This creates costs for the societies involved

---

[32] *See* Frank J. Garcia, *Trade, Justice and Security*, in TRADE AS GUARANTOR OF PEACE, LIBERTY & SECURITY? (Padideh Ala'I et al., eds.) (ASIL STUDIES IN TRANSNATIONAL LEGAL POLICY SPRING 2006).

and ultimately for all of us, as we are faced with the prospect of supporting oppressive regimes solely to maintain the economic opportunities we have created through predation or coercion.[33]

If the use of such force is not internalized as a cost of that production, then the goods coming from a factory in such countries might seem cheaper, since labor costs are lower. However, this would not be a true price, and consumers would not have an accurate reflection in the price of the costs they may also have to bear as taxpayers and citizens, resulting from the violence necessary to enforce that bargain. If, on the other hand, the costs of enforcement are internalized (through the possibility of imposing a social tariff, for example), then the full nature of the bargain will be clearer to consumers and to society as a whole, and it will be seen as the bad bargain it is. Such an approach in the trade area would be similar to the "political risk" calculations made in the foreign investment area and would be equivalent to adding a "social tax" to the cost of such goods.

Both points can be illustrated in a different, contemporary context, namely, the global financial crisis and the failures of domestic economic regulation.[34] Because of an

---

[33] One recent striking example has been the Unocal case alleging human rights violations by the oil giant in Burma. *See* Daphne Eviatar, *A Big Win for Human Rights*, THE NATION, May 9, 2005, *available at* http://www.thenation.com/doc/20050509/eviatar.

[34] *See generally* Brian Quinn, *The Failure of Private Ordering and the Financial Crisis of 2008*, 5 NYU J. LAW & BUS. (2009).

impoverished view of the free market, certain financial actors were allowed to pursue strategies that had tremendous short-term yields for them, but through a process that shifted the tremendous risks onto other parties and took advantage of their considerable insider knowledge of financial markets to the detriment of others (Wall Street versus Main Street). When this collapsed, all of global society was left shouldering the costs.[35] This illustrates the risks for us and for trade law when the conditions for a healthy market are misunderstood by the regulators, and parties are allowed to operate for the short term, while rampantly externalizing costs and risks.

Whatever the implications of such an analysis on the nature of future trade agreements, it must be admitted that the consequences of applying this framework to the evaluation of existing trade agreements are not pretty. Many trade agreements, particularly regional trade agreements between unequal partners, look more like CAFTA and less like the type of agreements outlined here. This yields a spectrum, if you will, of consensual agreements, from treaties we might say reflect consent as little as CAFTA does, in a Central American context where there was little functioning democracy and almost no freedom to walk away, to agreements reflecting a higher degree of consent, such as the U.S.-Canada FTA, where the parties had a higher

---

[35] Anup Shah, *Global Financial Crisis*, GLOBAL ISSUES, July 25, 2009, *available at* http://www.globalissues.org/article/768/global-financial-crisis#.

degree of functioning democracy and there was more freedom to walk away. It is not accidental that this spectrum of consent reflects the degree of inequality of bargaining power between parties. It is precisely this inequality in bargaining power that gives rise to the temptation, and opportunity, to overreach.

Does this mean that CAFTA and the many current agreements resembling CAFTA are fatally flawed and should be abrogated? Bringing Take One into play, are they so illegitimate as to make it hypocritical for liberal states to participate in them? Perhaps not. In *Perpetual Peace*, Kant argues that it is not necessary to destroy a legal, imperfect order in the name of justice.[36] In this, he says, prudence and justice agree. However, "we may properly demand that the necessity of such a change be intimately appreciated by those in power so that they may continue to approach the final end of a constitution which is best in accordance with right and law."[37]

I would argue that Kant's point about international relations in general holds equally true about treaties like CAFTA in particular: the flaws revealed by a consent analysis do not render such treaties irredeemably flawed, nor must they be abrogated in the name of justice. Nevertheless, current hemispheric trade agreements remain deeply inadequate

---

[36] IMMANUEL KANT, *Perpetual Peace: A Philosophical Sketch,* in KANT: POLITICAL WRITINGS 116, 93–130 (H.S. Reiss, ed., H.B. Nisbit, trans., 2nd ed., 1991) (1784).

[37] *Id.* at 118.

both in their consensual (or more accurately nonconsensual) character and in their wholesale failure to tackle distributive issues implicated by these economic relationships.[38]

What I am proposing here, however, are reasons *other* than moral ones why "those in power" (the United States in hemispheric trade negotiations, or any major developed country or system such as the European Union elsewhere) *should* "intimately appreciate" the need for such changes in negotiation and consent as Take Three suggests – both prudence and the nature of trade itself argue in favor of reinterpreting, amending, and otherwise reforming such treaties with all deliberate speed in favor of a more consensual kind of bargain (how many "Battles in Seattle" do we want? can we afford?). Moreover, prudence also dictates that future treaty negotiations (I am thinking here for example of a resurrected Free Trade Area of the Americas [FTAA]) be entered into with a clear understanding of the proper

---

[38] Andrew Hurrell is quite critical of NAFTA in this respect: "The [NAFTA] provides a particularly telling example. If arguments about ever denser integration leading to shifting understandings of moral community were to have force, then the U.S. – Mexico relationship should be a likely candidate. It is a relationship characterized by extremely high levels of economic and societal interdependence; by high levels of deprivation in Mexico, a good deal of which can be implicated in problems likely to have negative spillover effects on the United States; and by a rich and privileged partner well able to afford assistance. And yet the absence of any debate [over wealth transfers] is telling." *See* Andrew Hurrell, *Global Inequality and International Institutions*, 32 METAPHILOSOPHY 34, 39 (2001).

goal, and the type of bargaining process necessary to be consistent with that goal, and to achieve results consistent with that goal: a framework for truly consensual economic relations.

c. Consensual Agreements and the Global Justice Project. Let us assume that this analysis is correct and with time came to be incorporated into contemporary trade treaty practice. How would this move us from simply a set of better trade agreements (no small feat) to a basis for a more equitable global socioeconomic order?

Thomas Nagel asks a similar question in the concluding section of his essay on global justice, though not with this set of issues in mind. Nagel's insistence on sovereignty as that missing element in global institutions leads him to wonder whether there is an alternative form of legitimacy for global socioeconomic relationships that does not depend on sovereignty, "and yet can be embodied in institutions that are less cumbersome and feeble" than interstate trade agreements. "For the moment, I do not see such a possibility, though perhaps it can be invented."[39]

The alternative to the global sovereignty that Nagel seeks is not indeed global anarchy, as he fears. Instead, the clear and limited form of governance he calls for may not come from a political institution but from an economic one: a framework of reconstituted, consensual trade agreements

[39] Nagel, *supra* note 17, at 133.

that protect consensual bargains, not because liberalism demands it, but because that is the best way to safeguard a flourishing trading system – it is what trade needs, because that is what trade really is.

This is what the analogies to *lex mercatoria* and *jus gentium* are meant to suggest, and what a system of refocused, consensual trade agreements might be able to supply: a basis for legitimate transboundary socioeconomic relations that does not depend on global sovereign institutions, but instead depends on the protection and facilitation of consensual economic transactions among sovereign, yet integrated states and among their citizens. But in order to more fully understand the larger implications of this point, it is necessary for us to return again to Kant.

In *Perpetual Peace*, Kant posits a federation of independent republics as the optimum condition for safeguarding peace, or as he puts it, reconciling politics and the demands of justice.[40] This is so because only in such a system will consent (he means here political consent or the consent of the governed) be the foundation of both the domestic and the international orders, and a consensual system by its nature promotes rights and prevents certain pathologies (such as wars of aggression – this is the root of democratic peace theory).

If we return to Kant's vision of perpetual peace through a federation of liberal republics, we can see that a consent

---

[40] KANT, *supra* note 36, at 102.

approach to trade offers an alternative vision of, if not perpetual peace, then orderly and equitable economic relations
(certainly a worthwhile and valuable form of peace). This
vision operates through a "federation" or network of states
that have negotiated truly consensual economic treaties,
which themselves create and protect the basis for truly consensual economic interaction by private parties.

Kant himself acknowledges a key role for commerce
as a driver pushing states toward such a system of democratic federation, insofar as the conjunction of self-interest
and the rule of law is fortuitously strong in commercial
relations.[41] In this way, Kant thought, human nature (read
as self-interest) would argue for the same ends as practical
philosophy, namely, a peaceful federation of republics. The
remarkable development of the European Union would seem
to confirm this belief.[42]

In a similar way, both Kant's account of the role of commerce and the success of the European Union foreshadow
the opportunity that both globalization and its dominant
economic regulatory component offer us on a larger scale: the
establishment of an economic network of states that respect
and promote consensual economic relationships between
themselves and their citizens. Such a system may not rise to
the level of integration Kant proposes in a federal system of
liberal republics, but it bears important similarities.

[41] *Id.*at 114.
[42] *See, e.g.*, Christopher Layne, *Kant or Cant: The Myth of Democratic
Peace*, 19 Int'l Sec. 5–49 (1994).

First, by proposing that such a federation be built through commerce, Kant is presuming consent, in that he presumes trade between *liberal* republics under a rule of law. The kind of commerce he believes will drive states toward liberal federation is the kind of commerce we are talking about in Take Three: consensual bargains in a framework of consensual governance.

Second, and here we are pulling in Locke and his social contract as well as Kant, there is an explicit presumption of normatively equal parties (both normatively equal states and contracting individuals) that mutually respect each other's "sovereignty" (here read as the power of consent). Such an arrangement would be disturbed by undue concentrations of political power, just as markets are disturbed by monopolies and pathologies of economic inequality.

The establishment of an economic federation of states built around consent may or may not work the way Kant suggests, by driving us closer to an orderly political system on a global level (I suspect it will, though the end is unclear). But what it *can* do is offer a stable, and more legitimate, basis for global socioeconomic order along the lines Nagel is longing for. As Hurrell rightly points out, if "rich states" want to be effective in tackling global issues of mutual concern – both economic and noneconomic, they "cannot simply ... bully governments into signing treaties."[43] Moreover, such an approach to order and effectiveness does not presuppose

[43] Hurrell, *supra* note 38, at 55.

a prior normative consensus, but instead depends upon a clear analysis of long-term economic self-interest and the consensual nature of trade itself.

Such a framework has the possibility of uniting support across a broad range of positions and views with respect to global economic regulation and global justice, since it eschews explicit normative argument in favor of a more market-based approach to protecting trade as trade. Despite the many things we don't all hold in common across the globe, we do share an interest in being able to do business with each other in a mutually beneficial manner. What a consent analysis adds to the global justice debate is a way to understand and develop the implications of such an aspiration, harkening back to the work of Kant, Locke, Smith, and others regarding the tremendous potential inherent in self-interest as a force for good in a well-regulated system.

C. Conclusion

This discussion of Kantian federalism echoes my early point about moral federalism and the idea – inherent in a plural grounding approach as well – that different theories of justice can play an essential and mutually reinforcing role in the global justice project. I want in conclusion to bring several strands together – the Three Takes, plural grounding, and the modes of justice discourse – into as comprehensive a "take" as possible on what moral federalism might look like in the case of a truly global approach to justice.

The Liberal Internationalism approach of Take One –
and the Justice as Integrity mode it exemplifies – illustrate
the enduring, even foundational, importance of a continuing
process of self-examination and self-discipline with respect
every society's responsibility to shoulder the yoke of justice (and here I am echoing one rationale advanced for the
necessity among artists of working within specific literary
or artistic forms, as "that discipline in the service of which
one finds perfect freedom"). Each society is built around
specific, historically grounded conceptions of justice, embedded in (or flowing from) shared traditions, practices, and
understandings unique to that society. It may well be that
all such conceptions naturally express themselves in the
Universal Mode (that is a question to be answered by moral
philosophers, psychologists, and artists). However, what is
key to Justice as Integrity (versus its shadow mode, Justice
as Discipline) is the focus on what that society believes is
just in terms of its *own* behavior with respect to others, and
what it must therefore both consider in its foreign relations
and advocate in all relevant transnational fora. There is no
end, and never will be, to the need for this kind of conversation and inquiry within the larger search for global justice,
whatever the decisions and outcomes of other societies and
international institutions.

Nevertheless, such an approach has to be supple-
mented by the approach – and mode – identified in Take
Two: Justice as Relationship, here global relationships.
No individual or society acts in isolation, and their many

engagements and interactions with others form over time a wide range of kinds of associations, networks, partnerships, and social or communal bonds. This complex web of relationships creates new difficulties, but also immense possibilities. Thus Take Two exemplifies the importance of continual scrutiny of and reflection upon such relationships as they emerge and develop, since they themselves become a source of new and important obligations including obligations of justice. Which kinds of relationships and which kinds of obligations are the subject of specific theories and debates such as the contractarian and communitarian contributions to global justice. What is important, and is the essential contribution of a relational mode, is the understanding that such relationships – with their opportunities and obligations – are a distinct and essential element in the global justice project.

Irrespective of what we believe we owe others as a function of our own principles and of the kinds of obligations which our many relationships may or may not create, we also continually find ourselves engaged in specific transactions, exchanges, and encounters of various kinds that each have a distinct nature and integrity of their own, so to speak, and each require of us that we consider what behavior is best calculated to reap the benefits of the exchange itself. This is the kind of transitory yet recurring obligation that Take Three highlights for us, and is a third source of norms or principles that through a different mechanism may themselves contribute to what we would otherwise call a just global order. How we manage our exchanges, for example, in a global market will determine a great deal about what we reap from that market, and what we sow, regardless of disagreements over universal principles of justice and the emergence – or not – of global community. That is the immediate and not inconsequential opportunity that a consent approach to trade suggests may be ours, if we grasp it.

Taken together, this can seem a confusing and imperfect kind of process of moral inquiry, which may never yield the full range of political and social benefits that we have come to expect from domestic governance within liberal democracies, nor harvest what cosmopolitans hope to gain from a global liberalism. However, I would suggest, it is not that different from the rich and complex universe of beliefs, relationships, and actions that each of us lives in all the time. And, more important, did we ever think that global justice would be *easier* than this?

For liberals, the full flourishing of liberal democracy and a regulated market, and the widest possible respect for human dignity, are worthy goals to continue to strive for, within our own societies and in the global public discourse on justice and governance. But, in the eloquent words of Andrew Hurrell, "[a]fter all, what meaning can be attached to even the purist and most serene universalist voice (whether of the Kantian liberal or of the religious believer) echoing down from the mountain if those to whom it is addressed do not believe themselves to be even part of the thinnest and most fragile shared community?"[44] In this respect, it is critical that our rhetoric neither reinforce any sense of exclusion nor ignore any basis for shared interest or agreement. We should proceed in the spirit of plural grounding and seek the strongest possible arguments across all normative and ideological dimensions for every aspect of minimizing injustice and promoting justice on all fronts. Given the world as we find it, and the gravity of injustice and suffering the majority of the world contend with daily, surely this is a better way to spend our time than in contentious squabbles over rival Universalist claims while in the meantime millions continue to suffer, starve, and perish.

[44] Hurrell, *supra* note 38, at 47.

Index

adhesion contracts, 234
adhesion treaty, 260
Anghie, Anthony, 227

bargain, 239, 243, 250, 298, 305,
    316, 320
bargaining power, 331
Barry, Brian, 195, 216
Best Alternative to a Negotiated
    Agreement (BATNA), 242,
    250, 268
Berman, Paul Schiff, 183, 186
Beyleveld, Deryck, 218
Bretton Woods System, 6, 97, 176
    and distributive justice, 99
Brierly, J. L.
    The Law of Nations, 62
Brilmayer, Lea, 24, 70

vertical thesis, 70–72, 117
Brock, Gillian, 53, 55, 57
Brownsword, Roger, 218
Bull, Headley, 318

CAFTA, 31, 240, 243, 248–249,
    256–257, 261, 305, 330
    agriculture, 252
    arbitration, 259
    coercion, 252, 260
    dispute resolution, 260
    exploitation, 252
    legitimacy of, 331
    negotiations, 244, 251, 254, 259
    predation, 243, 262
    textiles, 255
Caney, Simon, 53, 57
    Justice Beyond Borders, 16

Index

Carmody, Chi, 212, 214
Cavell, Stanley, 225
Chimni, B. S., 197
circumstances of justice, 158–160, 174
  global, 160, 164, 166
coercion, 230, 233–234, 237–239, 250, 295, 304, 320, 322–323
  definition of, 243
  exploitation (differentiated from), 237
  and game theory, 326
  and trade, 220, 298, 328
Cohen, Joshua, 18
command economy, 239
communitarianism, 30, 32–33, 35, 37, 54, 57, 142–143, 146, 152, 154, 157, 162, 163, 176, 180, 187–188, 269, 277–278, 291, 297, 302, 311
  communitarian accounts of global justice, 146, 149–151, 153, 157, 187
  and justice, 149
  and social conflict, 150
community of risk, 165
consent, 10, 39, 41–44, 211, 215–217, 219, 221, 230–233, 237, 239–243, 245, 247–248, 253–254, 267, 271, 294, 304, 306, 314–315, 323, 325–326, 328
  and coercion, 257, 323
  and contract law, 256
  and exploitation, 247, 249, 323

  and international law, 220
  and Justice as Fairness, 46
  and lack of representation, 244
  and reform, 257
  and theft, 244
  and trade, 45, 294
contractarianism, 33, 143.
  See also social contract
cosmopolitanism, 8–9, 16, 37, 51–54, 57–58, 141, 157, 163, 276, 280, 297, 340
  cultural, 57
  and distributive justice, 78
Costa Rica, 257

Deacon, Robert, 196
distributive justice, 21, 74, 80, 147
  and the Bretton Woods System, 99
  and currency, 101
  and globalization, 176
  and international political theory, 80
  and international trade, 83–84, 87
  and liberal states, 81
Domingo, Rafael, 20, 185, 195
duress. *See* coercion
Dworkin, Ronald, 120

economic value, 229
exploitation, 235, 237, 250, 304, 322
  definition of, 243
  and game theory, 326
  and trade, 220, 298

external approaches to political
theory and trade law,
207–209, 263, 264

Forst, Rainer, 31
free trade, 323
Free Trade Area of the Americas
(FTAA), 332
Fuller, Lon, 210

Galeano, Eduardo, 226
game theory, 240, 325
Gathii, James, Thuo 227
Generalized System of
Preferences, 92–93,
Global Basic Package, 36,
195–196, 198, 203, 303,
314
global basic structure, 174
global community, 34, 142, 153,
156–158, 163–164, 170–171,
173, 175, 180–181, 183–187,
189–190, 193, 196, 198,
200–201, 203, 206, 267.
See also communitarianism
global economy, 38, 324
and distributive justice, 39
global financial crisis, 329
global justice, 2–4, 7–8, 10, 12–16,
19–20, 23–24, 26, 30, 50,
52, 56, 59, 61, 63, 65–67, 85,
137–138, 140, 142, 146, 160,
163, 179, 190, 200, 202, 207,
209, 221, 223, 261–262, 269,
271, 277, 291

and communitarianism, 54,
186, 188, 190
and cosmopolitanism, 52, 58, 69
and globalization, 35, 144, 161
and human rights, 313.
See also rights-based
approaches to global justice
and international organizations,
28–29,
and international political
theory, 68, 72
and pluralism, 19, 48, 49
and trade, 49–50
global minimal ethics approach,
38, 190, 200, 203.
See also Global Basic Package
global society, 158
globalization, 11, 13, 144, 156–157,
164, 168, 181, 183–184, 192,
277, 323
and circumstances of justice, 160
and international institutions,
177
Grey, John, 15

Hale, Robert, 234
Held, David, 21, 22
Hinsch, Wilfried
moral federalism, 307
Hobbes, Thomas, 270
Hurrell, Andrew, 176, 178–179,
185, 195, 201, 336, 340

injustice, 282, 288, 291, 295
global, 291–292, 294